# THE LOGICAL ACCESSORY

## Instructor's Manual to accompany

## Critical Thinking, 2e

by

Brooke Noel Moore & Richard Parker

Additional exercises contributed by

Dan Barnett and Daniel Turner

 Mayfield Publishing Company

International Standard Book Number: 0-87484-914-4

Manufactured in the United States of America


Mayfield Publishing Company
1240 Villa Street
Mountain View, California 94041

# Contents

# Introduction

Welcome to the second edition of *The Logical Accessory*. We hope the resources provided here will help make your elementary logic or critical thinking course easier and more pleasant to teach. This book includes answers for all the exercises in *Critical Thinking* that are not answered in the answer section of the text itself. It also includes substantial banks of additional exercises, with answers, for each chapter of the text (Chapters 6 and 7 are combined). Finally, it includes some tips and suggestions that have come from our own experience with this material and that of several correspondents who have used the first edition.

This time around we've enlarged the third category to include a few suggested lecture topics that we've found fit nicely with the material covered in several of the chapters. We realize that it may be presumptuous of us to recommend lecture topics to experienced teachers of critical thinking courses, but, as the number of such courses has grown, more and more new people find themselves standing in front of critical thinking classes. It is primarily to help these newcomers that we've added the additional material. If any of you old hands find it useful as well, so much the better.

We'd especially like to thank Dan Barnett of Cal State Chico and Daniel Turner of East Tennessee State for their contributions of exercises to this edition. We've credited them at the ends of chapters, correctly we hope.

It was our intention to produce a text that was extremely flexible, one that could be adapted to a variety of requirements, approaches, and emphases. We've been very pleased to see how flexible the book has turned out to be in actual practice. Our own experiences provide cases in point. They illustrate two very different approaches to teaching a logic/critical thinking course, and, since we've been asked by several colleagues just how we go about organizing our own courses around the text, we thought we'd tell you here.

Parker is the more old fashioned of the two. His format is standard lecture/discussion, with the course divided into four parts. Those four parts, and the chapters covered in them, are

    I.   Introduction: Claims & Arguments [Chapters 1-3]
    II.  Deductive arguments [Appendices 1 & 2]
    III. Persuasion and pseudoreasoning [Chapters 5-7]
    IV. Inductive arguments [Chapters 10-11]

Chapter 4 is sometimes included last in part I, sometimes first in part IV, and sometimes omitted, depending on how fast a class seems able to move through the material. The end of the term is often reached before Chapter 12 is, but exercises from that chapter are often used and an essay question from back there is always assigned. Each of the four parts of the course includes a written assignment and is followed by an examination—a machine-graded one if the class is large. The latter is based largely on questions from the banks in this manual.

Lately, Moore has taken a different approach. Although it isn't clear to what extent the skills and habits of a critical thinker can be self-taught, students do seem to be able to read and understand the text without a lot of external help in the form of lectures. So he assigns one chapter each week for students to master on their own; their attention is assured by a brief weekly quiz. Certain exercises from the chapter are assigned as homework. Prior to the quiz, he goes over the required exercises and discusses any questions that arise. The "objective" portion of the quiz, which is usually composed of unassigned exercise problems or questions from this manual, is graded in class; it sometimes produces lively discussion.

This approach allows for doing other things during the remaining class periods. Thus, if the class meets on Tuesdays and Thursdays, Thursdays are free to hear guest speakers, have student debates, watch video presentations, write in-class essays, or do other things. Some chapters (9, 10, 11) require more discussion than others, and even a bit of lecturing, but he's had good results with most of the material by just letting the book explain itself.

Incidentally, we've used this text in classes ranging in size from fewer than ten students to over two hundred, although most of them run about forty. We're not sure how successful we've been in the over-two-hundred classes, but that's probably no reflection on the book.

## A Commercial Message

We've heard from a number of people who have adopted the text. The fact that so many have found it so teachable is very gratifying to us. But we're sure we've not got it quite right yet, despite our attempt to take as many suggestions and criticisms into account as possible. There will surely never be a critical thinking book that suits every instructor, and we have no delusions about ours being such a one. But we are convinced of both the importance of this subject matter and the difficulty of teaching it effectively in the usual ten or fifteen weeks we have to do it. In the text, this *Accessory*, the CT Fleamarket newsletter, and the Test Maker computer program we and Mayfield Publishing hope to provide a package that helps you accomplish that chore as painlessly as possible. And sometimes, with luck, helps make it fun.

If you can think of a way to make it better, we'd be pleased to hear from you.

# Chapter 1
# Critical Thinking

Students like to know what they'll be doing in a course, so we tell them our objective straight off: to develop their ability to determine whether or not to accept the assorted assertions, sales pitches, proposals, ideas, theories, pleas, remarks, observations, comments, and other sorts of claims with which they will be confronted throughout their waking lives. We point out that some of these claims come with supporting reasons attached and some don't, but even those that don't, or that come with poor supporting reasons, may still be worth accepting. What's important, we stress, is whether there *are* good reasons for accepting a claim, regardless of whether those reasons are explicitly given.

Students often appear remarkably naive about language. We find it interesting that, if we ask the question, "True or false: Claims can serve many purposes, but only one purpose at a time," a substantial minority of them will answer "true." They'll do this despite their obvious ability to recognize irony, double meanings, and subtle digs in their own conversations as well as the frequent multipurposeful use of language in advertising. Part of the problem may be that they see an academic classroom as a different world from the one of their everyday lives, so they give the responses they think the former requires rather than the one they know from the latter to be correct. The section on the uses of claims can help reinforce the idea that it *is* their everyday world that this material is about.

The distinction between supported claims—i.e., arguments—and unsupported claims is easy enough for students to grasp; but in practice it is sometimes difficult for students to tell whether a passage is or contains an argument. A quick reference to the "premise indicator" and "conclusion indicator" boxes in Chapter 8 can be helpful, but so many arguments occur without these telltale signs that they can't be depended upon.

The section on identifying issues is new to this edition. We've added it because students sometimes have such trouble determining what a passage is about. They'll often pick up on the simplest or most concrete notion in a paragraph just because it's the easiest to understand and articulate. Presidential campaigns, and particularly the 1988 version, show us what happens to rhetoric and debate when speakers think they can get away with confusing, conflating, and evading issues.

Incidentally, the distinction between arguments and explanations has been exported to Chapter 4, where it will not bring up difficult problems right off the bat.

\* \* \* \* \*

Lecture/discussion suggestions

Most students come into a critical thinking course with an overly simple view of both factual and theoretical matters. Were they to learn nothing else, they're likely to learn that things are often more complicated than they previously thought. We think this is a good thing, since it can make them more cautious in the future, and, we hope, more thoughtful.

One way to convince students right off that there's more than meets the untutored eye is to bring up a clutch of distinctions and problems surrounding the nature of claims. Although claims are the building blocks for practically everything the text covers, the book does not examine the notion beyond stipulating that claims are the bearers of truth values. The following annotated list provides a skeleton for further discussion of the topic.

• *Types and tokens.* If you write, say, "I don't have any money" on the chalkboard twice and then ask a class how many sentences you've written, students will ordinarily divide about evenly into those who say you've written one and those who say you've written two. Aside from producing some instant controversy, this little exercise allows making the type/token distinction in a natural way: You've written two tokens of the same type; that is, you've produced two entities with physical sizes and shapes (or pitches and volumes, if spoken aloud, although spoken examples can be trickier) and locations in space and time—characteristics that physical objects in general have. The two arrangements of chalk on the board are sentence *tokens*. On the other hand, both sentence tokens have the same words and arrangements— they both fit a common description. What the two have in common is being of the same *type*. (We might characterize the type as something like: The word *I*, followed by the word *don't*, followed by the word *have*, etc.) Types are clearly abstract in a way that tokens are not.

Although things are already complicated enough, bright students sometimes ask if a printed sentence token is of the same type as one written cursively. Whether it is depends on the description of the tokens of that type. In the long run, we're forced to a hierarchy of types. This is seen nicely if we talk about half dollars: At the top of the hierarchy is the type *half dollar*. Then a layer of subtypes: *1989 half dollar, 1962 half dollar,* and so on. A given token, the half dollar in your pocket, is a token of one of these subtypes, and every token of one of these subtypes is a token of each type above it.

It would be nice if we could stop here and say that it is sentence types—or at least types of declarative independent clauses—that bear truth values. But we can't, because many such types are token-reflexive. That is, when I say I'm broke and you utter the same words, we're producing two tokens of the same type, yet what I say might be true while what you say is false. We have to look further to identify just what kind of thing carries truth values.

• *Propositions, sentences, and claims.* Another interesting reaction is nearly automatic if you say *"Je n'ai pas d'argent," "Ich habe kein Geld," "No tengo dinero,"* and "I don't have any money," then ask the class how many things you've said. They'll settle on something like "You've said the *same thing* in several different ways." Since our sentences are of different languages, they are clearly of different types, but noticing that they say the same thing allows pointing up the difference between a *sentence* (qua a particular group of words) and a *proposition,* which is an abstract and rather mysterious kind of thing invented by philosophers to do a certain job—namely, to bear truth values. If we solve one problem by stipulating that propositions are whatever it is that is true or false in what we say (or "underlying" our words, or "hiding behind" them, or whatever), we invent another problem in that we cannot produce a direct example of a proposition. When we attempt to give an example of one, we always produce a sentence instead.

Clearly, in order to avoid more confusion than the problems deserve—especially in a course where there's so much more to do—the text has to run roughshod over these distinctions or it would never get past them. You'll probably notice that we use the word *claim* sometimes in the way we might use *proposition* and sometimes in the way we might use *sentence* (either type or token). (For example, see Chapter 2, where we say that syntactical ambiguity is eliminated by rewriting the claim.)

• *Use/Mention.* Finally, we've had success in discussing the use/mention distinction at the beginning of a course. Most students think of quotation marks as being reserved for direct quotations and, occasionally, to express irony (He "borrowed" my car). The paradigmatic use of quotation marks, the one from which the direct quotation usage is derived, is to mark a word or group of words that is being *mentioned* rather than *used.* Consider:

Alexander is twelve years old.

is a sentence about a person. The name that occurs at the beginning of the sentence is *used* to mention that person. But in

"Alexander" is spelled with seven letters, two of which occur twice.

4

the sentence begins with a reference not to a person but to a name—to the word "Alexander." Hence it is the *word* that is being mentioned. (The sentence would make no sense if it was construed to be about a person.)  In short, we *use* words in combination with quotation marks (sometimes called "quotation names") to *mention* whatever it is that falls between the quotation marks.

If nothing else, learning about the distinction enables students to see remarks like

> Drink "coke"

as exhortations to do the impossible—in this case, to drink a word.

To see if students understand the use/mention distinction, they can be asked to put quotation marks in the proper places in a sentence like this:

> Richard's dog is named Cy, but Brooke calls him
> Sai, and sometimes Richard refers to Cy as Sigh.

Correct placement of quotation marks should produce:

> Richard's dog is named "Cy," but Brooke calls him
> "Sai," and sometimes Richard refers to Cy as "Sigh."

Technically, the commas and periods should be *outside* the quotation marks, since they are not part of the expressions being mentioned.  But we are overwhelmed by grammatical convention in this matter.  Maybe someday whoever dictates such rules will get it right.

(Because of constraints imposed by standard publishing practices, the text itself uses the convention of putting mentioned words and phrases in italics rather than between quotation marks.  There's more than one way to skin this particular cat.)

A concise treatment of the use/mention distinction is found, among other places, in Benson Mates' *Elementary Logic,* 2nd edition (Oxford:  1968).

✳   ✳   ✳   ✳   ✳

## Exercises Unanswered in the Text

### Exercise  1-1

2. Logic is concerned about whether a claim *would* have to be true *if* the reasons for it were true (whether they are actually true or not); critical thinking is concerned with whether the reasons for a claim and the claim itself are *in fact* true.

5. No, although *parts* of an argument can be left unstated.

6. Yes, but communication of information is just one of many purposes that claims can have. Oftentimes even claims that communicate information do not have such communication as their main purpose.

13. We don't agree.  You can be justified in accepting a claim on the basis of reasons that are

only *probably* true. For that matter, you can be justified in accepting a claim on the basis of reasons that in fact are false. There was a time when it was reasonable to believe that the earth was flat, and this false belief would in turn have justified the belief that someone sailing west from Europe could never return home without reversing direction. We treat this question (#13) lightly in critical thinking classes, using it as an icebreaker.

14. An argument is a claim taken together with others—reasons—that are offered in its support.

17. Yes

18. You might try smiling sweetly at him or her as you ask. You have not verbalized any reasons, so you have not produced an argument. (We can't guarantee any success for such a method, of course.)


## Exercise 1-2

4. To urge that the U.S. cut or eliminate its contributions to the United Nations; "We should stop contributing to the U.N."

6. To marry a couple (to each other); traditionally, not much else will do.

8. To motivate the potential buyer to make an offer (or a more generous offer) on the car. Notice that the claim ostensibly communicates facts (or alleged facts); the buyer is left to draw the obvious conclusion for himself. "If you want this car, you'd better make an offer now."

10. To get the teenager to wear seatbelts; "Wear your belt."

12. To communicate information; these claims are already straightforward.

14. To express admiration; "Gould may seem strange, but he's a genius."

16. To indicate that either team can win despite the odds; "No game is a sure win for any team."

18. To suggest that he is a moderate conservative; "I'm not an extreme conservative."

20. To keep his options open; "Maybe."

22. To create an unfavorable attitude toward Michael Jackson's music and film and toward the "American lifestyle which the U.S.A. is trying to foist on the world." The claims themselves express this purpose pretty directly.

24. It's a little hard to tell exactly what Bennett's purposes may be, but clearly he intends to express an attitude of disapproval toward teen sex.


## Exercise 1-3

Although this exercise is answered in the text, we recommend that you develop a few similar exercises of your own using fresh specimens from your daily newspaper. You needn't overwhelm students at this point, however; they'll be scrutinizing arguments much more closely in the second part of the book. (Incidentally, we find that juicy local issues generally capture students' interest at least as well as juicy national issues. The same holds true for Exercise 1-5.)

### Exercise 1-4

2. Whether North would be a good president, or whether North should become president

4. Whether turkeys are dumb birds

5. Whether Senator Baldwin is not as liberal as she seems

6. Whether the speaker should ask Brigitte out again

8. There are two issues present in the passage: (1) whether the story in question was accurate, and (2) whether Ronald Reagan's economic record was one of accomplishment.

9. Whether the speaker should cook his roast for 19 minutes per pound, or, more generally, how long a roast of a given size should be cooked

# Chapter 1 Test Question-Exercise Bank

### Bank 1-1

Try to determine the main purpose of each of the following claims insofar as it is possible to do so without a context to guide you.

1. "Michael Dukakis thinks a foreign market is a place to go for French bread."
   —Rich Bond, a member of George Bush's campaign staff during the 1988 election, speaking about Dukakis's inexperience in foreign policy

   *Purpose: to ridicule and to sway people from Dukakis to Bush*

2. "No, we have plenty."
   —San Francisco Forty-Niner Randy Cross, when asked if the Forty-Niners have a drug problem

   *To amuse*

3. "Henceforth, all patient rooms are to be designated as nonsmoking, except when ordered otherwise by a physician."
   —Directive from the chief administrator of a hospital

   *To order*

4. "I am talking to you now that I'm gone, and I'm telling you right now, without any question in my mind, that you must stop smoking. . . . It is suicide. It is taunting, taunting death."
   —Actor Yul Brynner, a heavy smoker, in a statement written to be released after his death from lung cancer

   *To warn*

5. "If everyone in this country were to buy American, our deficit would come down and America would prosper once again, with full employment."
   —Letter to the editor, Midfield *Sentinel*

   *To encourage people to "buy American"*

6. Mother to a daughter who is about to eat another piece of cake: "It's delicious, but it's fattening."

   *To discourage*

7. Daughter, in response to her mother: "It's fattening, but it's delicious."

   *To express her intent to ignore her mother's warning*

8. "You can't look at a sleeping cat and be tense."
   —Jane Pauley

   *To amuse*

9. Old saying: "What's finished is finished."

   *To encourage resolve not to dwell on past misfortune*

10. "Rather than fire personnel, [the president] either 'promotes' or accepts resignations— as in the case of Alexander Haig, whose resignation as Secretary of State was accepted even before it was offered."
    —Lloyd Shearer

    *The first part of the quotation, up to the dash, states a thesis; the remainder of the passage uses humor to gloss over a counterexample to that thesis.*

11. "When I hear Jane Fonda criticize the free enterprise system on which this country is based I wonder if it ever occurs to her that without this system her films and books and the money that comes with them would not be."
    —Letter to the editor, *Tri-Counties Observer*

    *To criticize and express displeasure*

12. "What a dog. What a dog. A stupid dog."
    —New York City Mayor Ed Koch, remarking on questioning by ABC News' Sam Donaldson

    *To complain*

13. "Greyhound reminds you that when you travel by car, you take chances, especially if you are travelling alone—anything can happen: dangerous thunderstorms, engine trouble, blowouts."
—Greyhound advertisement

*To instill fear of automobile travel and thus make taking the bus a more attractive alternative*

14. Not-so-newlywed to spouse: "I'd like to remind you that we do have a finite supply of money."

*To encourage thrift*

15. "You are about to enter a bizarre microculture so different from your life as a wealthy father, husband, lawyer and Wall Street titan that you will feel you have been dropped in a totally foreign society."
—John Erlichman, who served time in federal prison, to Ivan Boesky, who went to prison in 1988 for insider-trading in the stock market

*To advise*

16. I'm sure I'll do a good job for you if you will just give me a second chance. My husband has already been laid off and my child, my poor baby, is very sick. I don't know what we're going to do if I lose my job too.

*To elicit sympathy in order to keep her job*

17. She is the most conceited, self-centered, stuck-up person I have ever met! You should have heard her yesterday, going on about how *she* doesn't think *she* has time to go to the lake with us . . . and, oh! you just should have heard her!

*To express and arouse feelings of indignation*

18. What's a cistern? Well, I think it's just a tank they use for storing water.

*To inform*

19. I really wish I had not been late, and I'm very sorry about it.

*To express regret; to apologize*

20. Those tires are really bad. You should be very careful about driving on the highway with them.

*To inform and to warn*

21. If you got twenty-five points on the exam and I got fifty, I guess I just did *twice* as good a job as you did, didn't I?

*To boast*

**NOTE:** The following items are more subtle.

22. "Operating at an extremely high temperature [a cremation oven] reduces the body to a few pounds of bone fragments and ashes in less than two hours. . . . Most of the cremated remains are then placed in an urn or canister and carefully identified."
— From a pamphlet distributed by many funeral directors called "Considerations Concerning Cremation"

*According to author David Owen, who wrote "Rest in Pieces" in 1983, the funeral industry's pamphlet subtly discourages the use of cremation by using the word "most" in the sentence concerning where the beloved's remains eventually go. The essay appears in* The Man Who Invented Saturday Morning *(New York: Villard Books, 1988).*

23. "Every civilization gets the universe it deserves."

*An amusing introduction to modern cosmology and how explanations of the origin of the universe have changed; from* The Dark Side of the Universe, *by James Trefil (New York: Scribner's, 1988)*

## Bank 1-2

Determine whether or not each of the following passages is, or contains, an argument.

24. "Like short-term memory, long-term memory retains information that is encoded in terms of sense modality and in terms of links with information that was learned earlier (that is, *meaning*)."
—Neil R. Carlson, *Psychology, The Science of Behavior*

*Answer: no argument*

25. "Fears that chemicals in teething rings and soft plastic toys may be cancer causing may be justified. Last week the Consumer Product Safety Commission issued a report confirming that low amounts of DEHP, known to cause liver cancer in lab animals, may be absorbed from certain infant products."
—Associated Press

*Argument*

26. "Can it be established that genetic humanity is sufficient for moral humanity? I think that there are very good reasons for not defining the moral community in this way."
—Mary Anne Warren, "On the Moral and Legal Status of Abortion"

*No argument. This is a nice one, since Warren is claiming that there* is *an argument for her conclusion—she just doesn't give it.*

27. "The argument advanced at a recent government hearing—that because we will not be dependent on plutonium for more than a few hundred years it 'will not be an important problem indefinitely'—entirely misses the point. Though we may rely on plutonium for only a relatively brief period, the plutonium produced during that period may be with us indefinitely, and it may jeopardize the lives of many times the number of generations that profit from its use."
—Ronald M. Green, "International Justice and Environmental Responsibility"

*Argument*

28. You'd better not pet that dog. She looks friendly, but she's been known to bite.

    *Argument*

29. Computers will never be able to converse intelligently through speech. A simple example proves that this is so. The sentences, "How do you recognize speech?" and "How do you wreck a nice beach?" sound almost the same when they are spoken, but they mean something different. A computer could not distinguish between the two.

    *Argument*

30. It is obvious why some men have trouble understanding why women become upset over pornography. Pornography depicts women as servants or slaves, and men cannot conceive of themselves in this role.

    *Argument*

31. I don't care how well Thompson played last week. If he misses practice one more time he's not going to play in the tournament and that's that.

    *No argument*

32. Except maybe for finance and business law, schools of business really don't have very much of their own subject matter to teach to students. All the rest is really mathematics, psychology, English, speech, and other standard subjects that business schools call by other names.

    *Argument*

33. There are right now as many as half a million military-style assault guns in the hands of private citizens in the the United States. These small, light, easy to handle weapons are exemplified by the Israeli UZI, the American MAC-10 and AR-15, the KG-99. All of these are sophisticated weapons manufactured for the single purpose of killing human beings in large numbers very quickly.

    *No argument*

34. "It is clear that the right of punishing crimes against the law of nature, as murder and the like, is in a state of mere nature vested in every individual. For it must be vested in somebody; otherwise the laws of nature would be vain and fruitless, if none were empowered to put them in execution; and if that power is vested in any *one*, it must also be vested in *all* mankind, since all are by nature equal."
    —Sir William Blackstone, *Commentaries on the Laws of England*

    *Argument*

35. "Hayek argues that we cannot know enough about each person's situation to distribute to each according to his moral merit (but would justice demand we do so if we did have the knowledge?) . . . ."
    —Robert Nozick, *Anarchy, State, and Utopia*

    *No argument*

36. "Gene splicing is the most awesome and powerful skill acquired by man since the splitting of the atom. If pursued humanistically, its potential to serve humanity is enormous. We will use it to synthesize expensive natural products—interferon, substances such as insulin, and human endorphins that serve as natural painkillers. We will be able to create a second 'green revolution' in agriculture to produce new high-yield, disease-resistant, self-fertilizing crops. Gene splicing has the potential to synthesize new substances we can substitute for oil, coal, and other raw materials—keys to a self-sustaining society."
—John Naisbitt, *Megatrends*

*Argument*

37. "It is better to be a human being dissatisfied than a pig satisfied; better to be Socrates dissatisfied than a fool satisfied. And if the fool, or the pig, are of a different opinion, it is because they only know their own side of the question."
—John Stuart Mill, *Utilitarianism*

*No argument*

38. "Cinema rarely rises from a craft to an art. Usually it just manufactures sensory blizzards for persons too passive to manage the active engagement of mind that even light reading requires."
—George Will

*No argument*

39. "The personal computer revolution is marked by accidental discoveries. The entire market for these things was a big surprise to all the pioneers who put simple ads in hobbyist magazines and were stunned by an onslaught of eager customers."
—John C. Dvorak

*No argument*

40. "Recent reports coming out of central and east Africa confirm that approximately ten percent of the population there is now infected with the AIDS virus, and that in time fully one-half will have it. We can expect similar figures in the United States if no more is done than is currently planned. Given the calamitous potential of such an epidemic, the current administration's refusal to recognize the need for massive increases in AIDS research is incredible. That the administration insists on seeing the disease as a problem for small segments of the population—and as something like divine punishment for homosexuals—is an outrage."
—Editorial, the Manchester *Sentinel-Record*

*Argument*

41. "If American business is to regain an advantageous position in the international marketplace, it must recreate a climate of flexibility and entrepreneurship. Unfortunately, the trend is to seek personal success not through entrepreneurship but through professionalism, as a continued climb in the number of advanced degrees in business and law confirms. If this tendency to seek personal security and prestige by joining the ranks of the professionally comfortable continues, the real winners will be America's overseas competitors."
—Irving Greenberg

*Argument*

42. "Employers know that attitudes and habits cross the line between personal and job life. . . . It is when there are three or more failed marriages that the strong suspicion arises that the much-divorced individual has some judgment and attitude problems that call for hiring caution."
—LaVerne H. Ireland, *The Sacramento Bee*

*No argument*

43. "It may be true that people, not guns, kill people. But people with guns kill more people than people without guns. As long as the number of lethal weapons in the hands of the American people continues to grow, so will the murder rate."
—Susan K. Mish'alani, East Bay *Voice*

*Argument*

44. Some would prefer to say that every human being is both a body and a mind. Bodies are in space and subject to the mechanical laws which govern all other bodies in space. But minds are not in space, nor are their operations subject to mechanical laws. Bodily processes and states can be inspected by external observers, but the workings of one mind are not witnessable by other observers. And so a person lives through two collateral histories; but the actual transactions between the episodes of the private history and those of the public history remain mysterious, since by definition they can belong to neither series.
—Adapted from Gilbert Ryle, *The Concept of Mind*

*Argument*

45. "[Lionel L.] Lewis discovered that, in recommendations of merit written by administrators and faculty themselves, although they put much emphasis (two-thirds) upon student related activities—teaching, advising, course planning, and popularity—no one argues from any supporting evidence other than, 'Everyone knows.'"
—David A. Downes, "The Merit Muddle in the University"

*No argument*

46. "[Television evangelist Pat] Robertson made a plausible [presidential] candidate. The son of a former senator from Virginia, he graduated Phi Beta Kappa from Washington and Lee, has a law degree from Yale, is a Marine veteran, a former Golden Gloves boxer and a shrewd entrepreneur. His cable-TV network is second only to Ted Turner's, reaching more than 30 million homes."
—*Newsweek*

*Argument*

47. "The main danger of war, even of a war fought with conventional weapons, lies in its unpredictability."
—*Breakthrough* (New York: Walker, 1988) in the essay "Security for All in the Nuclear Age" by Anatoly Gromyko

*No argument*

48. "If the Bhagwan were guilty of any crimes, he would have left the country months or even years ago. But look, he didn't do that, he stayed here until just this fall. That ought to tell us something."
—follower of Bhagwan Shree Rajneesh

*Argument*

49. "The recent failure of a Drake University student to halt his former girlfriend's plan for an abortion focuses light on a seldom considered situation: While a woman's right to an abortion should not be weakened, the idea of 'fathers' rights' raised in this case should be discussed."
—The *Daily Iowan*

*No argument*

50. "Today, there is strong evidence—not only in theory but in practice—that families who try to protect dying children from knowing they're dying rarely serve the child's best interests. This conspiracy of silence, however well-meaning, often puts nurses, relatives, and others who spend the most time with the patient, especially in their lonely moments, on the spot."
—From *Playing God: The New World of Medical Choices,* by Thomas Scully and Celia Scully (New York: Simon and Schuster, 1987)

*Argument*

## Bank 1-3

State in your own words which claims, if any, support has been given for, and state in your own words the reasons that have been offered for these claims. (The same directions may be applied to the items in the preceding bank, if desired.)

51. "For about $200 a ticket you can take a breathtaking flight through the Grand Canyon by helicopter. Fine, unless you are one of the two million people who visit the canyon each year on the ground. For these millions, the pleasures of the canyon's solitude is destroyed by the almost uninterrupted noise from the air. That fact in itself demonstrates that air traffic in the canyon must now be banned—or at least heavily regulated. If the enjoyment of those on the canyon's floor is not enough reason for banning air traffic, then this is: the vibrations may destroy Indian ruins and the noise may drive the peregrine falcon and bighorn sheep out of their normal habitat in the canyon."
—Letter to the editor, *Tri-Counties Observer*

52. "So Rambo has stormed the country and now Coleco Industries, Inc., is trying to capitalize on the fact and has announced that it plans to market an 'action' figure modeled after Rambo in time for the Christmas season. This is an outrage. It glorifies neo-Neanderthal perspectives on war and is a flagrant disregard for the concerns of parents who wish to transmit to their children thoughtful and civilized approaches to conflict-resolution."
—Letter to the editor, *Gulf Coast Social Democrat*

53. "The arrogance of some State Department and U.S. Information Agency employees who took luxury cruises at government expense is shameful.

"Instead of flying by economy class to and from their overseas assignments, some traveled on the Queen Elizabeth or other cruise ships. Costs of the ocean voyages averaged $6,084, nearly four times the average airline cost of $1,665.

"One family of four billed the government $21,956 for a 26-day voyage along the eastern

14

coast of South America. A couple were paid $13,761 for a 24-day trip from Bangkok to Honolulu. One official sent in a bill for $12,270 for a Mississippi River cruise on the Delta Queen.

"That's not all. The time spent on the cruises was considered by the department to be duty—not vacation.

"General Accounting Office investigators said they were told by foreign service officers that ocean travel was considered 'a fringe benefit.'

"If that is the case, the fringes are due for a good trimming."
—*The Omaha World-Herald*

54. "The California State University trustees showed considerable foresight in their recent unanimous decision to strengthen the system's admission standards. . . .

"Public high school curricula deteriorated to such a degree throughout the state during the last two decades that English literature included courses in science-fiction and detective stories.

"That's not all. Social studies courses often were reduced to consciousness-raising sessions complete with rock music and feature films. Foreign-language requirements were abandoned, along with several advanced courses in science and math.

"And students could generally earn credits for working after school . . . ."

"[The new standards are] certain to raise the level of education among would-be college students. And that has to be a good thing."
—Chico (Calif.) *Enterprise-Record*

55. "I don't know whether to be amused or annoyed. the U.S. government spends millions of dollars rounding up herb farmers. Ridiculous! Deaths from alcohol abuse are overwhelming. Surely this is a bigger problem. I doubt even a single death from smoking pot and driving has been reported. And the idea that smoking pot leads to heroin is nonsense. Anyone who is going to become an addict will do so regardless of what they have around."
—Letter to the editor, *Glenn County Today*

56. Trout do feed on mosquito larvae, but they seldom feed on adult mosquitos. So it is not likely that fish take an imitation mosquito because they are fooled into thinking it is a real one. Most likely they take the mosquito fly for a midge or a gray caddis.
—Adapted from Jack Dennis, *Western Trout Fly Tying Manual*

57. "The breaking of secret codes (cryptanalysis) provides an example of inductive reasoning closely resembling the inductive reasoning scientists carry out. However, cryptanalysis can be carried out using pen and paper, needing no laboratories. In addition, even simple forms of cryptanalysis can be quite intriguing. Simple forms of cryptanalysis can therefore be very useful as classroom examples of inductive reasoning."
—*CT News*

58. "Flamenco and the *Fiesta* (spectacle of bullfighting) are deeply related. This connection is undeniable, and vital for an understanding of either. Both stem basically from the common people, and they stir the same basic emotions and passions. Both are given flashes of erratic genius by gypsies, and a sense of indomitable steadiness and responsibility by the Andalusians. And they have in common another important factor: they are the two most probable ways that the commoner can break out of his social and economic level."
—Donn Pohren, *The Art of Flamenco*

59. "What is the best move to begin a game [of chess]? At one time the masters began automatically with 1 P-K4; then they switched to 1 P-Q4. Paul Morphy, considered by many critics the greatest chess genius that ever lived, *never* played 1 P-Q4. In contrast,

Ernest Gruenfeld, one of the greatest living authorities on opening play, ventured on 1 P-K4 only once in his entire tournament career (against Capablanca at Karlsbad 1929). When asked why he avoided 1 P-K4, he answered, 'I never make a mistake in the opening.'"
—Irving Chernev and Fred Reinfeld, *The Fireside Book of Chess*

60. "A pine cut down, a dead pine, is no more a pine than a dead human carcass is a man. Can he who has discovered only some of the values of whalebone and whale oil be said to have discovered the true use of the whale? Can he who slays the elephant for his ivory be said to have 'seen the elephant'? These are petty and accidental uses; just as if a stronger race were to kill us in order to make buttons and flageolets of our bones; for everything may serve a lower as well as a higher use. Every creature is better alive than dead, men and moose and pinetrees, and he who understands it aright will rather preserve its life than destroy it."
—Henry David Thoreau, "Chesuncook"

**Bank 1-4**

Identify the passages that contain arguments; in those that do, identify the main issue.

61. "A witty experiment by Philip Goldberg proves what everyone knows, having internalized the disesteem in which they are held, women despise both themselves and each other. This simple test consisted of asking women undergraduates to respond to the scholarship in an essay signed alternately by one John McKay and one Joan McKay. In making their assessments, the students generally agreed that John was a remarkable thinker, Joan an unimpressive mind. Yet the articles were identical; the reaction was dependent on the sex of the supposed author."

*Issue: whether women "despise both themselves and each other"*

62. NBC's coverage of the '88 Olympics was not very exciting. The anchorman was cool and detached, and they never zeroed in on a single event, except for basketball, long enough for anyone to care. Plus, there was just too much coverage. Anytime you turned on NBC, there was the Olympics. It was like air—always there. And what's so exciting about air?

*Issue: whether NBC's coverage of the Olympics was exciting*

63. "When it comes to airborne pollution—chiefly from coal-fired and oil-fired power stations—Britain is again the dirty old man of Europe. In 1985, 21 nations approved of a European Community convention calling for a 30-percent reduction in sulfur emissions by 1993. Britain is the only major North Sea nation that has not signed."
—Brian Jackman, *Sunday Times Magazine*

*Issue: whether Britain is the major European contributor to air pollution*

64. "My folks, who were Russian immigrants, loved the chance to vote. That's probably why I decided that I was going to vote whenever I got the chance. I'm not sure if I'm going to vote for Dukakis or Bush, but I am going to vote. And I don't understand people who don't."
—Mike Wallace

*Answer: no argument*

65. It's wise to allow states to deny AFDC (Aid to Families with Dependent Children) benefits to unmarried kids under 18 who live away from their parents. This would discourage thousands of these kids from having children of their own in order to get state-subsidized apartments.

*Issue: whether states should be allowed to deny AFDC benefits to youths under 18*

66. A judge's finding that the FBI discriminated against its Hispanic agents is the second time in less than a year that the bureau has been embarrassed by its treatment of minority employees. Last November, black FBI agent Donald Rochon filed a lawsuit in U.S. District Court accusing the bureau of racial harassment when he was an agent in Omaha. The suit is pending.

   Increasing the hiring of minorities and treating them equally for promotions must become a matter of greater concern to the FBI. Currently, there are only 423 Hispanic agents and 412 black agents out of a total of about 9,400. The statistics speak for themselves.

*Issue: whether the FBI should be more concerned with hiring from minorities and with treating minority agents fairly with respect to promotion.*

67. "Those who accept evolution contend that creation is not scientific; but can it be fairly said that the theory of evolution itself is truly scientific?"
   —*Life—How did it get here? By evolution or by creation?*

*Answer: No argument*

78. "Because real estate is a local investment, I recommend investing within an hour's drive from your home. Personally, I invest within a half-hour drive because then I can properly manage the property and watch it to be sure it is not declining in market value."
   —Real estate columnist Bob Bruss

*Issue: whether you should invest in real estate located close to where you live*

79. "It is indeed said that the Japanese work more than 2,000 hours a year, but this is not so. At Sony — and at Sanyo or Matsushita — the total is somewhere between 1,800 and 1,900 hours."
   —Akio Morita, chairman of Sony

*Issue: whether the Japanese work more than 2,000 hours a year*

70. Obviously the commission should prepare regulations that are consistent with the law. We admit that isn't always easy. But there's no reason for the commission to substitute its judgment for that of the people.

*Answer: no argument*

71. Letter to the Editor: "Instead of criticizing Mike Dukakis for belonging to the American Civil Liberties Union, George Bush ought to give the ACLU a hearty thank-you. If it weren't for action by the ACLU, Bush campaigners would not have been permitted to distribute political literature in the malls in this county."

*Issue: whether Bush should criticize Dukakis for belonging to the ACLU*

72. "And he went from there, and entered their synagogue. And behold, there was a man with a withered hand. And they asked him, 'Is it lawful to heal on the sabbath?' so that they might accuse him. He said to them, 'What man of you, if he has one sheep, and it falls into a pit on the sabbath, will not lay hold of it and lift it out? Of how much more value is a man than a sheep! So it is lawful to do good on the sabbath.'"
— Matthew 12:9-12

*Issue: whether it is lawful (or right) to heal on the sabbath*

**Bank 1-5**

Identify the main issue in each of the following passages. If there is more than one issue present, indicate how they are related—e.g., does the settlement of one depend upon the settlement of another?

73. "We sometimes make the mistake of thinking that whatever qualifies someone as an expert in one field automatically qualifies that person in other areas. Even if the intelligence and skill required to become an expert in one field *could* enable someone to become an expert in any field—an assumption that is itself doubtful—it is one thing to possess the ability to become an expert and an entirely different thing actually to *be* an expert. Thus, informational claims put forth by experts about subjects outside their fields are not automatically more acceptable than claims put forth by nonexperts."
—From Chapter 3 of the text

*Issue: whether informational claims from experts about subjects outside their fields of expertise are automatically more acceptable than claims from nonexperts*

74. The results of a survey conducted by the Public Opinion Laboratory at Northern Illinois University in the fall of 1988 show that on very basic ideas, vast numbers of Americans are scientifically illiterate, Laboratory Director Jon Miller said. Only about five percent of American adults have a minimal knowledge of scientific vocabulary, methodology, and an understanding of the impact of science on the world. (Fifty-five percent did not know that the Earth goes around the sun once a year; twenty-eight percent didn't know that the Earth goes around the sun at all.) In an election year, when candidates are talking about the Strategic Defense Initiative, acid rain, and the greenhouse effect, this survey shows that many Americans have little idea of what the candidates are talking about.

*Issue: whether American adults know enough about basic science to understand discussion of current scientific issues*

75. It's clear, given the recent increases in hate groups and racist violence, that we still need the laws crafted originally to combat the racism of the 1860s. A federal court jury recently ruled that two white-supremacist groups must pay nearly a million dollars in damages to racism protesters. This welcome message tells bigots of all types that if you violate others' rights, you'll be hit where it hurts—in the pocketbook. Ironically, the current Supreme Court has voted to reconsider its 1976 Runyon vs. McCrary ruling, which permits individuals to seek punitive damages for private acts of discrimination. The irony is compounded by the fact that the current administration made such a strong case for the victims of crime in the last presidential election.

*Issue: The first issue is whether bigotry is sufficiently widespread to require repression by the law; the second, less clearly stated issue, is whether the current Supreme Court (and administration) really has a strong enough commitment to stamp out racism.*

**Bank 1-6**

True/False

76. If no reasons have been given for a claim's acceptance, it should always be rejected.

    *False*

77. If poor reasons have been given for a claim's acceptance, it should always be rejected.

    *False*

78. Sometimes arguments contain only unstated reasons.

    *False*

79. The reasons that appear in arguments may be either good or bad reasons—if they are bad reasons, we still have an argument; it's just a bad argument.

    *True*

80. Claims may serve any of several purposes, but never more than one purpose at a time.

    *False*

81. Even though it may not be an important issue that people are fussing over, there must still be an issue present wherever there is an argument present.

    *True*

NOTE: Items 22, 23, 47, and 50 were contributed by Dan Barnett; items 61 and 72 were contributed by Daniel Turner.

# Chapter 2
# Understanding Claims

Our experience is that, in general, students easily comprehend and enjoy working with the material in this chapter. If you're so inclined, you can have a class rolling in the aisles with a well-delivered stock of ambiguous claims (especially syntactically ambiguous ones). It's a good way to begin the first class meeting on this material. Produce a good example, and then ask the class "What's the matter with that claim?" (You'll find that some of your students are quite good at finding or making up new examples—augmenting your supply for the next term.) Not all ambiguous claims are innocent jokes, of course: They sometimes contribute to serious confusion, and advertising often turns them into misleading weaselers.

We're grateful to Professors Donald Henson and John Stevens for their contributions to the discussion of vagueness and ambiguity, especially for noting the distinction between proper and contextual vagueness. Professor Henson has pointed out that, aside from being fun, discussion of deceptive cases of ambiguity can produce a sense of satisfaction in students early on in a course, and this can help them to appreciate the value of critical thinking skills long long before they've learned to detect pseudoreasoning or analyze arguments.

A modest warning: Since grouping ambiguity is just a subspecies of semantical ambiguity, you have to be careful when you give a quiz where all three answers are available. Where "grouping" is correct, so is "semantical," unless the directions specify otherwise.

The attention that this chapter puts on vagueness seems to have been appreciated by students—we've had students tell us they hadn't realized how much of what they heard was vague to the point of being useless. But then, as this edition is being finished, we've just had a presidential campaign. . . . Incidentally, if students insist on a notion of vagueness that is precise, this works for *some* cases: Claim $A$ is more vague than claim $B$ if $B$ implies $A$ but $A$ does not imply $B$. Thus, "John worked in the garden" is more vague than "John pruned his rose bushes," because the latter implies the former but not vice versa. In short: If one claim has truth conditions that are a subset of the truth conditions of another claim, the latter is more vague than the former. This is of less help, or maybe not worth the trouble, when the claims' truth conditions are not one a subset of the other.

We've been pleased that students seem to like the simplifying technique described in the section on complexity (pp. 37ff.). They should be encouraged to develop a facility for applying the technique in their heads, without benefit of a pencil and paper, if they are to make the best use of it.

The section on understanding spoken claims (pp. 44ff.) can be useful in developing an important study skill; an unfortunately large portion of students are truly terrible at taking notes.

One source of potential difficulty with this chapter's material lies in the tendency of some students to try to correlate the three kinds of meaning—denotation, sense, and emotive force—with the three kinds of definition—definition by example, analytical definition, and definition by synonym; and to regard two important *uses* of definitions—to reduce vagueness ("precising definitions") and to convey or evoke attitudes ("persuasive definitions")—as two additional *kinds* of definition. However, students do seem to understand the distinctions between kinds of meaning, kinds of definition, and uses of definitions if you explicitly call their attention to these distinctions.

\* \* \* \* \*

Textbook material on definitions can be pretty boring for a lot of students—they tend to find it unexciting even if they know it's good for them. We've tried to keep our discussion in the text brief and to the point, but we thought we'd throw in a suggestion here that has enlivened our classroom more than once.

After the three types of definition in the text are described, we point out a dilemma: Ostensive definition (definition by example) seems necessary on one hand, but it can also be made to seem almost miraculous that it works at all. That it seems necessary can be shown by imagining people in a primitive language-learning situation, for example, children, early homo sapiens, two people thrown together neither of whom knows a word of the other's language, and so on. Since a language learner in any of those situations knows no words at all, or at least none that those around her knows, the first words have to be learned without reference to known words. This eliminates analytic definitions and definition by synonym, as well as other types not discussed in the text. We're stuck with ostensive definitions to learn those first words. When you question students about how someone in the circumstances described might begin learning, they come up with ostensive definitions pretty quickly.

Then, though, you point out the difficulty in drawing conclusions from *anything* a person might do to ostensively define any particular word. One way to do this is to imagine that it's you trying to begin linguistic communication with your students. You point across the room while uttering a nonsense word, say, *fargle*, which is a word you mean to teach them. Say that you point in the general direction of the door to your classroom. Students are likely to react: "*Fargle* might mean the same as *door*," or "Maybe *fargle* means brown." Indeed, it might. Or flat, or [color of door] or exit, or east, or who-knows-what. How can you help them? By pointing to something *else* that's a fargle and letting them figure out what the two have in common.

You point to a tabletop of a different color from that of the door. This allows them to rule out *some* of their earlier suggestions, but not all. *Fargle* does not mean vertical or exit, but hosts of candidates for synonyms remain: *flat*, *indoors*, *material object*, or, to make things interesting, maybe *fargle* refers to the act of pointing. (Thinking that pointing was going to be crucial in your shared enterprise, you decided to start by teaching them how you refer to this crucial notion.)

To further complicate matters, you might explain to them that they weren't even looking in the right direction: In your land, people extend an arm and finger and the observer traces from the finger to the elbow and on that direction—that is, your people have a pointing convention backward from ours.

Matters can continue to be made worse in all manner of ways. *Fargle* could have a disjunctive meaning—such as that of "either flat or brown"—or it could have a conjunctive meaning—"both flat and brown."

It could be that, as Eskimos have many more words for snow than most of us, your students don't have a single word or handy combination that is synonymous with *fargle*. In fact, the same may be true of *most* of the words in your language.

One way to finish off this little episode is to use Wittgenstein's cube trick. You can tell your students that, if words are such trouble, you'll try pictures. Tell them that you're going to draw a picture of a cube. Go to the chalkboard and draw the following figure.

When they look puzzled, tell them they probably expected something like this—and draw the usual view of a cube. After insisting that your picture is as good a cube as the one they expected, explain that, if they were to go down to the bank building on the corner and lie down on the sidewalk at the corner of the bank—there's room for remarks about lying in the gutter if you're so inclined—and look at the bank, it would look just exactly like your picture. And the bank building is most certainly cube-shaped. You may have to use a Savings & Loan, or an auditorium, or whatever's handy. Of course your students are probably more used to seeing ice cubes than cubes of this size and from this angle.

It may not be a good idea to go much further than this, unless you want to wind up giving a lecture on symbols, natural signs, nonlinguistic shared experiences, and, finally, a seminar on Wittgenstein. What you *can* accomplish with this little lecture is impressing on your students that the most obvious features of communication are not so simple as they probably thought. This may make it easier later to convince them that careful attention and critical thinking skills are truly important if they're to avoid the pitfalls that abound in all but the most superficial communication.

\* \* \* \* \*

## Exercises Unanswered in the Text

### Exercise 2-1

2. Semantical ambiguity
3. Syntactical ambiguity
4. Semantical ambiguity. This is an interesting one because the ambiguity is purely a matter of seeing a word as an adjective or a verb.
5. Syntactical ambiguity
6. Syntactical ambiguity
8. Grouping ambiguity
9. Semantical ambiguity
11. Semantical ambiguity
12. Syntactical ambiguity (We tend to discount a semantical ambiguity on "greatest.")
14. Semantical ambiguity
15. Syntactical ambiguity
17. Semantical ambiguity
18. Syntactical ambiguity. This one bears close scrutiny. If it is designed to be as misleading as it seems, it's a very clever—and a very misleading—piece of work.
20. Syntactical ambiguity ( Does *independent* modify *laboratory* or *tests*?)

### Exercise 2-2

2. As a group (If this is wrong, we're willing to travel.)
3. As a group
5. As individuals
6. As a group
8. As individuals
9. As a group
11. As individuals
14. As a group (although maybe they'd have a better chance as individuals)
15. As individuals

### Exercise 2-3

2. In order of decreasing vagueness: (c), (a), (e), (b), (d)
3. (d), (c), (b), (a), (e)  (Items (d) and (c) strike us as almost equally vague, although not equally important, of course.)
5. (b), (a), (c), (d), (e)

### Exercise 2-7

Just in case, here are some thumbnail definitions:

1. Gaudy
2. Upstart
3. Short-winded due to corpulence
4. Stupefied, muddled, as from drunkenness or infatuation
5. Incisive, penetrating
6. Courage
7. Foul-smelling
8. Bearlike
9. Very obstinate
10. An earnest appeal or a solemn oath

### Exercise 2-8

3. The World Trade Center
5. The square root of 2
6. Einstein
8. A Rolls-Royce
9. Can't do it; a drawing of a unicorn is an example of a drawing of a unicorn
11. "He wiped his moustache off."
12. We think this word is too vague to give a good definition by example.
14. We don't think you can get much closer than indicating someone who's having a toothache, although even at that it won't be clear that it is the toothache and not the person's behavior that you are exemplifying.  Like other sensations, pains are not the sorts of things we can point to, although we can point to the places where we're *having* them.
15. This is more difficult than it appears.  A drop of blood is an example of a red thing, but is it an example of *the color red?*
17. Sulphur dioxide
18. A proof in geometry; any of the examples or exercises in Chapter 8
20. Number 20 in Exercise 2-8

### Exercise 2-9

1. Denotation, although it's arguable that the inclusion of "places like. . ." actually specifies a rudimentary sense
2. Sense
3. Sense
5. Sense
6. Sense (Had a specific example of the laying down of a life been mentioned, the proper answer would have been denotation.)
8. Denotation

9.  Sense, if it's either

### Exercise 2-10

2.  Analytical
3.  Analytical
5.  Analytical
6.  Analytical
8.  Neither. Michener is simply praising perseverance.
9.  Example, although analytical is not unreasonable, because of the "anyone like"
11. Analytical
12. Analytical, although not purely so, since *land* is a synonym for part of the meaning
14. Analytical

### Exercise 2-11

2.  Not analytic
3.  Not analytic. What is said about hot climates is not part of the meaning of the phrase.
5.  Not analytic, at least by the definition in our our dictionary
6.  Analytic. It is part of the meaning of *eighteen* that it denotes a number smaller than twenty.
8.  Analytic, by a combination of categorical and truth-functional inferences (see Appendices in text)
9.  Analytic. Our notion of matter is of space-occupying stuff, so we think this one is analytic. A different concept of matter may give you a different answer.
11. In the usual sense of "seeing," you can't see what doesn't exist, even though you might *think* you see something that turns out not to exist. In this sense, the claim is analytic.
12. Analytic, by our dictionary's definitions of "love" and "hate." But notice that these two notions, as well as that of time, are quite vague. Very loose interpretations of all three may allow love and hate for a person to coexist in one (rather confused) individual.
14. Not analytic
15. We don't think this is analytic, but it's a controversial matter. Certainly, the claim's negation, "I don't exist," is paradoxical, if not self-contradictory. (The negations of analytically true claims are self-contradictory; this is generally taken as the mark of an analytic truth.) This item can stimulate a nice class discussion. For brushing up purposes, we recommend René Descartes' *Meditations,* or the article on Descartes in the *Encyclopedia of Philosophy,* Paul Edwards, ed.

### Exercise 2-12

What you wind up with in this exercise depends pretty much on how far you want to boil the passage down. We come up with something like this:

A bank or bank holding company may only sell life, disability, or (certain types of) unemployment insurance, though a commercial bank may sell insurance as provided in Section 1208 of the Financial Code. The restriction doesn't apply to a bank or bank holding company that had a subsidiary or affiliate insurance license prior to January 1, 1976 or to anyone authorized to make loans pursuant to Divisions 7, 9, or 11 of the Financial Code.

## Exercise 2-13

1. Yes, with the prior written consent of the owner
2. Yes, if such grounds are a part of the premises and are exclusively for the use of the tenant
3. The tenant, unless the breakdown is the unavoidable result of normal wear and tear
4. This is not clearly specified.

## Exercise 2-14

1. The owner may terminate the lease after giving three days written notice.
2. Since the tenant paid the rent ("cured the default") within the required three days of written notice, the owner must continue the lease.
3. The lease may be canceled if the owner chooses to do so.
4. Yes, at least a portion of it. The portion is determined by subtracting from that six months' rent any rent she collects from rerenting the property. If she does not rerent it, but the tenant proves that she could reasonably have done so, the amount she *would* have received from such rental is subtracted from the six months' total.
5. Yes, less the amount of lost rent which, as in #4, the tenant proves could reasonably have been avoided

## Exercise 2-15

1. U.S. service personnel
2. Commodore Carmichael, Commander of Naval Base San Diego
3. 8:00 p.m. to 5:00 a.m.
4. Three months
5. Reports of U.S. sailors and marines mistreated by Mexican police
6. That it may not be such a bad idea
7. At least some don't like it.
8. Eighteen months
9. No end to the curfew is mentioned in the article.
10. They arrived at no resolution of the problem.

## Exercise 2-18

2. Schoolfellow
3. To make the subject of a lawsuit
5. Buffoon
6. Thoughtful
8. Instructor
9. Aid
10. Tightwad

## Exercise 2-19

2. Frugal, tight
3. Self-respectful, haughty
5. Agriculturalist, hick
6. Government worker, bureaucrat
8. Docile, wimpy

9. Aged, rotted

### Exercise 2-20

2. One dedicated to public benefit through governmental service
3. A person devoted to the cause of righting the wrongs of economic and political inequality and social injustice for women
4. One who preserves and transmits knowledge and culture to succeeding generations

### Exercise 2-21

2. A person who murders animals
3. An ignorant youth between thirteen and twenty known for poor judgment, bad manners, and a short attention span
5. A person who teaches a subject because he can't make a living actually doing it

### Exercise 2-22

2. To reduce vagueness
3. (Probably) to reduce the vagueness of "better students"
5. To eliminate ambiguity
6. A humorous definition that casts a cynical light on our notion of conscience
8. To explain the term *tax shelter*
9. To explain the term
11. A persuasive definition of sorts, intended humorously to denigrate committees
12. To invoke an attitude about Cold Duck—but Ciardi does explain what cold duck is while he's at it
14. To invoke an attitude about interior decorators. Unlike #12, this one does nothing to explain what its subject actually is or does.
15. To distinguish *disinterested* from a word with which it is often confused and to define it by synonyms
17. A persuasive definition, designed to make one think that the use of logic is devious
19. A pun, but one designed to upgrade the listener's attitude toward teachers

### Exercise 2-23

We have found exercises of this sort quite useful. They not only exercise and measure skills in reading comprehension but also allow students to work on their writing skills in a format that is easily graded by the instructor. Such exercises are also easy to construct. In case you want to have the examples reproduced for students, here are numbers 2 and 3:

2. The *Journal of the American Medical Association* reports that Retin-A, a prescription cream used against severe acne, can diminish fine wrinkles and other defects caused by exposure to the sun. Retin-A contains retinoic acid, a chemical related to vitamin A. Tests by dermatologist John Voorhees at the University of Michigan Medical School on 30 subjects, aged 35 to 70, showed that Retin-A reduced fine wrinkles on subjects' forearms, and it reduced them on the faces of 14 out of 15. Microscopic analysis showed that the treated skin grew new tissue to replaced dead or sun-damaged cells.

3. Last Tuesday night Michael Dukakis spoke to an enthusiastic group of supporters at New York's Omni Park Central Hotel.

# Chapter 2 Test Question-Exercise Bank

## Bank 2-1

Determine which of these claims are semantically ambiguous, which are syntactically ambiguous, which contain grouping ambiguities, and which are free from ambiguity.

1. People who go shopping often go broke.

    *Semantically ambiguous: "go broke," and syntactically ambiguous: does "often" go with "shopping" or with "go broke"? (Because of a distant relationship with grammar, many students read "broke" as "broken" and thus get a second version of a semantical ambiguity.)*

2. All snakes are not poisonous.

    *Syntactically ambiguous*

3. The wizard made a pig of himself.

    *Semantically ambiguous (on both "made" and "pig")*

4. John plays with toys more than Linda.

    *Syntactically ambiguous*

5. He went to the store but was held up in the process.

    *Semantically ambiguous*

6. The team was upset.

    *Semantically ambiguous, both on "upset" and grouping on "team"*

7. He passed out and was later found by a group of stray sheep.

    *Semantically ambiguous*

8. She watched him dance with intensity.

    *Syntactically ambiguous*

9. Carlton harassed the man on the motorcycle.

    *Syntactically ambiguous*

10. When the head waiter asked whether she had reservations, she said, "Yes, but I'm going to eat here anyway."

    *Semantically ambiguous*

11. If properly frosted, a person shouldn't notice lumps in a cake.

    *Syntactically ambiguous*

12. San Francisco (AP) December 13, 1985—A group of citizens angry about the lack of public restrooms downtown is planning a sit-in at City Hall, leaving employees no place to go.

    *Semantically ambiguous*

13. She looks more like her mother than her father.

    *Syntactically ambiguous*

14. He dislikes her smoking.

    *Semantically ambiguous*

15. Residents of the continental U.S. have more pets than those of Alaska.

    *Grouping ambiguity; semantically ambiguous*

16. Susan got in trouble for messing up the house with her younger sister.

    *Syntactically ambiguous*

17. Sign in a hotel: "NO SMOKING ROOMS AVAILABLE"

    *Syntactical ambiguity*

18. Eighteen people have slept in the new hotel's most expensive suite.

    *Grouping ambiguity*

19. After finishing his term paper, he went out for a beer and left it in his instructor's mailbox.

    *Syntactically ambiguous*

20. There is a job for everyone.

    *Grouping ambiguity*

21. "Police said Sunday that a Lebanese woman arrested in Milan planned to deliver photographs of American hostages to an Italian man who has been linked to arms scandals .... The man ... was questioned by police after they found the photos and a letter from a hostage hidden in a false bottom of the woman's suitcase Thursday ...."
    —From an Associated Press dispatch, *Sacramento Bee,* October 24, 1988

*Syntactically ambiguous: Was the hostage hidden in the suitcase?*

22. "My husband got his project cut off two weeks ago, and I haven't had any relief since then."
—From a letter requesting public assistance, as quoted in Ann Landers, *Chicago Tribune*, May 22, 1988

*Semantical ambiguity*

23. "A lot of people are living to 100 who never used to. . . ."
—Herb Caen, *San Francisco Chronicle*, October 5, 1988

*Syntactical ambiguity, or something worse*

24. "I want Michael Dukakis to be the next president of the United States in the worst way."
—Senator Joseph Biden, D-Del., campaigning for Dukakis. *San Francisco Chronicle,* October 4, 1988

*Syntactically ambiguous*


## Bank 2-2

Our students generally have a good time with these.

25. Invent three examples of semantically ambiguous claims.
26. Invent three examples of syntactically ambiguous claims.
27. Invent three examples of claims containing grouping ambiguities.


## Bank 2-3

28. Find an example of an ambiguous claim in a paper you have written for another class.
29. Find an example of an ambiguous claim in a newspaper or magazine. (Hint: headlines are sometimes great sources of such claims.)


## Bank 2-4

The claims in these sets should be ranked from most vague to least vague.

30. Joanna
    (a) is left of center in her political views.
    (b) has voted for the socialist candidate for president in the last four elections.
    (c) usually doesn't vote for Republicans.
    (d) is a liberal.

*Decreasingly vague: (a) and (d) are about equal, (c) somewhat less vague, then (b)*

31. When Louis returned from his trip he told me
    (a) that the airline lost his bags twice.
    (b) that it had been a nightmare.
    (c) that all the clothes except those on his back spent the weekend in Miami and Cleveland while he was in New Orleans and Detroit.
    (d) that he had to wear the same clothes for three straight days because of airline foul-ups with his luggage.

*Decreasingly vague: (b), (a), (d), (c)*

32. (a) I hear a funny noise in my engine.
    (b) I have an engine problem.
    (c) When I give it gas, I hear this funny sound in my engine.
    (d) My engine makes a strange noise sometimes but not others.
    (e) There is an unusual ticking sound in my engine when I accelerate from zero to around thirty.

    *Decreasingly vague: (b), (a), (d), (c), (e)*

33. (a) The students with the most points at the end of the semester will get the best grades.
    (b) The top ten percent of the class will receive As.
    (c) Everybody whose average is ninety or above will get an A.
    (d) The class will be graded on a curve.
    (e) Grading will be relatively tough in this course.

    *Decreasingly vague: (a), (e), (d); (b) and (c) about equal*

34. The administration has indicated it would
    (a) not be satisfied until the problem was solved.
    (b) propose new legislation to combat the problem.
    (c) send a bill to the Congress during the next session.
    (d) take the problem under advisement.

    *Decreasingly vague: (d), (a), (b), (c)*

35. (a) Smoking is hazardous to your health.
    (b) Smoking is linked with lung disease.
    (c) Smoking has been demonstrated to cause lung cancer and emphysema.
    (d) Smoking is not good for you.
    (e) Smoking is linked with lung disease and emphysema.

    *Decreasingly vague: (d), (a), (b), (e), (c)*

36. (a) Dennis was a monster all evening.
    (b) Dennis was well behaved while the guests were here.
    (c) Dennis was ill mannered toward the guests.
    (d) Dennis threw a tantrum in front of everybody.

    *Decreasingly vague: (a) (and ambiguous, too), (d); (b) and (c) are about equal*

37. (a) Whitney was hungry so she helped herself to more potatoes.
    (b) "I'm drowning!" she screamed. "Someone help me!"
    (c) Morgan helped her mother at every opportunity.
    (d) Derrick discovered he could not lift the box unless someone helped him by lifting one end.
    (e) The word *help* has four letters in it.

    *These are all about equally precise with the exception of (c), which is more vague.*

38. (a) His were the most awful, despicable, outrageous crimes that have been committed in this county in the entire century.
    (b) He murdered seven innocent people.
    (c) He shocked the sensibilities of the whole region with his horrible crimes.
    (d) He was guilty of seven felonies and about nine misdemeanors, including murder and abuse of the mails.
    (e) He chopped up seven people and sent their parts to the governor's office.

    *Decreasingly vague: (c), (a) (a close second), (d), (b), (e)*

39. Are these claims properly vague or contextually vague?
    (a)    Mr. Miller carries a lot of cash in his wallet.
    (b)    You couldn't find Tony because he's staying with a relative.

40. Are these claims properly vague or contextually vague?
    (a)    If you're going to the newsstand, bring me a magazine.
    (b)    Karla wrote a long term paper.


**Bank 2-5**

These claims should be evaluated for excess vagueness given the contexts that are stated or implied.

41. During his first news conference of the year, the president said today that his administration was going to crack down even harder on international terrorism.

    *Too vague to be very informative; this speaks as much of an attitude as it does of plans to combat terrorism*

42. Said at a party: "What did I think of *Back to the Future*? I thought it was pretty good. You ought to go see it."

    *Too vague to be much of a recommendation unless the listener knows her taste in movies is similar to the speaker's*

43. My aunt lost most of her possessions when her house burned down last month.

    *Sufficiently precise for most contexts; too vague, of course, if the remark is directed to an insurance claims agent*

44. Well, let's see. To get to the Woodward Mall, go down this street a couple of blocks and turn right. Go through several stop lights, turn left and go just a short way. You can't miss it.

    *Hopelessly vague*

45. Your chances of winning the grand prize in the lottery by purchasing a single ticket are approximately one in sixteen million.

    *Precise enough*

46. I can't tell you how much I love you. You make me very happy.

    *Vagueness is not inappropriate here.*

47. The 50k of memory that remains in the computer after the program is loaded is enough to produce short documents but not long ones.

    *Too vague to be of much use—how short is short?*

48. How many miles to a gallon does it get? Oh, you'll be quite satisfied if you buy this little beauty. It gets really impressive mileage.

    *Too vague for a potential buyer. But the vagueness is supportive of the speaker's purpose, which is to evade the question.*

49. Advertisement: "The Aquaclear water filter—it really will improve the taste and odor of your water."

    *Too vague to be useful*

50. From the label of a can of spaghetti sauce: "Made with real meat."

    *Too vague, if you care what kind of meat goes into your spaghetti*

51. Teacher to student: "How long should your term paper be? As long as it takes to do justice to your subject."

    *Too vague (How does your standard answer to this question compare?)*

52. Instructions for a lawn mower: "For best service, crankcase oil should be replaced at least once each season."

    *Too vague—"best service" means what? "at least once"? each growing season?*

53. Renaissance music simply lulls me to sleep.

    *Precise enough. The remark is not designed to describe the music, just the speaker's reaction to it.*

54. Property owner, showing his property to guests: "The lot extends back to about where that large oak tree stands."

    *Precise enough*

55. Same property owner, showing his property to a potential buyer: "The lot extends back to about where that large oak tree stands."

    *Too vague*

56. One father, speaking to another: "I read recently that young children who are required to do chores around the house tend to grow up to be happier, more secure adults than children who have everything done for them."

    *While this remark is not too awfully vague for a casual conversation, the listener should be very careful not to take it as advice. It does not lend itself to implementation without much more detail being spelled out, never mind confirmation of the general claim itself.*

57. From a gardening book: "Horse manure is many times more beneficial to your garden than that from cows."

    *Sufficiently precise to count as good advice*

58. It seems clear that by the end of this decade they'll have produced a machine that can really think.

    *Too vague in any context*

59. From a Johnson's Vinegar rebate offer sticker: "Mail this form, along with a proof of purchase from a one-quart bottle of Johnson's Vinegar to the address below. You'll receive your $1.00 rebate check in about four weeks."

    *"Proof of purchase" is too vague (given that there's nothing identified as such on the bottle). A label might be considered proof of purchase by some people, though others would claim that at best it shows possession, not purchase.*

60. Advertisement: "If your house is properly insulated, the Agwar console humidifier should enhance your comfort when the weather turns cold."

    *Too vague to help determine whether to purchase a humidifier or whether to purchase this brand. The vagueness does help protect the manufacturer from charges of false advertising, however.*

61. Overheard at a wine tasting: "This chablis is just a bit too ambitious for my taste."

    *Too vague, unless "ambitious" is an addition to the enologist's vocabulary that the authors have not heard about*

62. Take two of these pills three times daily before meals.

    *The meaning of "before meals" is standard enough to say that this claim is precise.*

63. The president has determined that tax reform will be his first priority during his second term in office.

    *Vague enough that we wouldn't make any predictions about taxes based on it*

64. From a consumer advice publication: "Electric heaters cost more to run than kerosene heaters, but they are safer."

    *Unless the publication goes on to elaborate more specifically on the cost disadvantages and safety advantages of electric as opposed to kerosene heaters, vagueness prevents this claim from being much help to a consumer wishing to make a wise decision.*

65. Instructions for this set of exercises: "These claims should be evaluated for excess vagueness given the contexts that are stated or implied."

    *What it is to be too vague is sometimes, unfortunately, pretty vague itself. But, we trust, the claim is not too vague for a set of exercises intended to foster discussion and illustrate that the vagueness of claims is a matter of degree and not something that has to be avoided in every context.*

### Bank 2-6

Students should be asked to discuss the appropriateness of the vagueness of the following passages to the contexts that are stated or implied. Pay particular attention to any underlined expressions. (These are a bit more difficult than the previous ones.)

66. According to estimates from the New York Medical College in Valhalla that were reported in the November 21 *New England Journal of Medicine,* <u>more than two million</u> people in the United States have been infected by the AIDS virus. Steven L. Sivak and Gary P. Wormser concluded that for every living adult with AIDS (7,152 as of early November), there are 300 infected individuals.

    This figure is <u>much higher</u> than those published by the Centers for Disease Control in Atlanta, which estimates that for each of the 14,653 cases of adult AIDS that have been diagnosed in the United States, there are only <u>a few hundred</u> infected individuals.
    —Adapted from a report in a weekly science news magazine

    *"More than two million" is not vague in this context, since the exact estimate can be derived by multiplying 7,152 by 300. "Much higher" and "a few hundred" are much too vague for a report in a science news publication, since neither expression makes it at all clear just how different the CDC estimate was from the NYMC estimate.*

67. ... one demographer thinks that more than twenty percent of the women born in the mid-50s may never have a child, almost triple the childless rate of their mothers.

    You will hear this ascribed to a breakdown of <u>traditional values,</u> or <u>rampant selfishness</u>. But this glib explanation misses the deeper truth, which is more subtle and less personal. People haven't suddenly become more selfish. <u>Changing economic and social realities</u> have simply made children less <u>economically essential</u> and, therefore, more a matter of choice. When people urge a return to traditional values, they're talking about the impossible: reversing centuries of <u>economic and technological change</u> that have altered women's roles. Women's liberation is less an idea than the result of changes that, by reducing pressures for childbearing, inevitably led to more educational and job opportunities. ...
    —Adapted from a news magazine essay

    *The first occurrence of "traditional values" is quite vague. Does a simple interest in having children count as such a value, or do the values referred to produce the interest in having children? "Rampant selfishness" presumably includes not wanting to share one's time, treasure, or energy with children; beyond that it isn't clear what is intended. The underlined expressions in the claim beginning "changing economic and social realities . . ." are quite vague, but we can easily guess at what the author has in mind for them. The same goes for the last of the underlined expressions.*

    *The main point of this paragraph—that having children is no longer an economic necessity—is somewhat more difficult to find than it might have been had there not been so many very general (and vague) ideas present in the passage.*

68. "The right of the people to be <u>secure in their persons</u>, houses, papers, and effects, against <u>unreasonable</u> searches and seizures, shall not be violated, and no Warrants shall issue, but upon <u>probable cause</u>, supported by Oath or affirmation, and particularly describing the place to be searched, and the persons or things to be seized."
    —United States Constitution, Fourth Amendment

*A discussion of this passage should highlight the notorious vagueness of "unreasonable" and "probable," as well as the fact that such vagueness is inescapable and (probably) desirable in a "living" constitution—that is, one flexible enough to adapt to changing circumstances. "Secure" is another term that students seize upon as too vague. It should be noted that the first claim of the passage, through the word "violated," means simply that people shall not be subject to such searches and seizures.*

69. "Comprehensive Coverage. The insurer will <u>pay</u> for <u>direct and accidental damage</u> to the insured's automobile and its <u>equipment</u> not caused by <u>collision or upset</u>."
—From an automobile insurance policy

*In this context vagueness is inappropriate, from the standpoint of both the insured and the insurer, though even here it is probably impossible to eliminate it completely. "Pay"—in whole or in part? Who determines the expense of repairing the damage? "Direct and accidental damage"—what all is included by this phrase? Rust damage? Oxidation of the paint? Mechanical damage caused by accident? Using the wrong type of gasoline? "Equipment"—is equipment added by you since purchasing the car covered? "Collision or upset"—are collisions with animals covered? With falling objects? (Students seem to enjoy discussing this item.)*

70. "I believe the worth of any economic policy must be measured by the <u>strength of its commitment</u> to American families, <u>the bedrock of our society</u>. <u>There is no instrument of hard work, savings, and job creation as effective as the family</u>. There is no cultural institution <u>as enobling as family life</u>, and there is no superior—indeed, no equal—means to rear the young, protect the weak, or attend the elderly—none. Yet <u>past government policies</u> betrayed families and <u>family values</u>. They permitted inflation to push families relentlessly into higher and higher tax brackets. And not only did the personal exemption fail to keep pace with inflation, in real dollars its actual value <u>dropped dramatically</u> over the last thirty years."
—Radio address given by Ronald Reagan in December 1985

*The first portion of this passage strikes us as containing much that is vague, although it improves somewhat toward the end. "Strength of its commitment" must mean simply the fairness of the amount families are taxed, although it sounds as though it might mean more; "the bedrock of our society" is a powerfully emotive phrase, but its meaning is especially vague. Perhaps the following sentence is designed to spell out that meaning, but it is not at all clear what it means either. Families may save (e.g., for the childrens' education), but it is not clear how they contribute to hard work or job creation. These phrases and claims, like "as enobling as family life" in the next one, are principally homilies and emotively charged expressions designed to produce a positive attitude about Reagan's view of families.*

*"Past government policies" is spelled out more or less clearly in the following remarks— at least one such past policy is identified; "family values" is not too vague; we are probably safe in guessing that these are simply whatever values contribute to keeping families together. (Is Reagan saying that past government policies have contributed to breakups of families? If not, what would follow from this claim?)*

*The last portion of the passage is much more precise and understandable, although "dropped dramatically" could mean nearly any decrease—one politician's dramatic drop is not necessarily another's.*

*As part of a political speech, this passage is probably typical in its overall degree of vagueness. Politicians—Democrats, Republicans, and others alike—would probably have a lot less to say if we held them to any high standard of precision.*

**Bank 2-7**

Ask students to do the following. (It's their turn.)

71. Make up a claim and a couple of contexts for it so that the claim is too vague in one context but sufficiently precise in the other.

72. In a paper written for another class, find a sentence or passage that is too vague for its context.

73. Find an example in a newspaper or news magazine of a sentence or passage that is too vague for its context.

74. Write another version of the example you gave for #73 so that it is no longer too vague.

75. Find an example in a radio or television advertisement of a claim that is vague enough to add nothing new to a potential buyer's information. (These are *easy* to find—it's safe to require a handful of them.)

**Bank 2-8**

Have students determine what kind of meaning is probably intended for the following: denotation, sense, or neither. As listed below, the first ten are denotation, the second ten are sense, and the last couple are neither. We leave it to you to mix them up as you like.

Denotation:

76. A superstar is someone like Bruce Springsteen.
77. What do I mean by a liberal? I mean the Kennedys, the Mondales, the Cranstons, people like that.
78. The West Indies includes Barbados, Cuba, Haiti, all those islands out there in the Carribean.
79. The tournament winner is that guy standing over near the scorer's table with the big smile on his face.
80. *Flower* refers to pansies, peonies, daisies, etc.
81. Spirits? That's like brandy, whiskey, vodka, right?
82. The *ex officio* members of this committee are Forbes and Lopez.
83. All the words in the world—that's what the word *word* means.
84. See that guy over there? He's a perfect example of what I have in mind when I say the people around here are weird.
85. Lady, as applied to this orchestra, *musician* means just one person, and he's talking to you.

Sense:

86. A mob is any group of Democrats.
87. *Levee* is an embankment meant to prevent flooding.
88. *Levi's* is a trademark that used to apply only to heavy denim jeans made by Levi Strauss.
89. When they say, "terminate with extreme prejudice," I think they mean kill somebody.
90. A celebration is a sesquicentennial only if it happens on something's 150th anniversary.
91. For a while there, streaking was running through some public place without any clothes on.

92. The matador is the main bullfighter, the guy who kills the bull if all goes well; the picador is a guy on a horse with a bunch of spears with ribbons on them.
93.  Anything that resembles a human can be called a hominoid.
94. Budgerigars are the kinds of parakeets that people keep as pets.
95. No, a brahman is not a kind of bull; it's a Hindu of the highest caste.

Neither denotation nor sense:

96. *Obbligato* is a very difficult word to spell correctly.
97. Ninety percent means you will get an A for the course.


## Exercise 2-9

Students should determine which member of the following sets of claims has the most negative emotive force. These are easy to answer; the point is to impress on students how many positive and negative ways there are to say essentially the same thing. It's then hoped that they will learn to control the emotive force of their own remarks. (Besides, these can be fun.)

98. Mr. Gardner
    (a) is a social drinker.
    (b) is alcohol-dependent.
    (c) is a heavy imbiber.
    (d) enjoys tippling.
    (e) is a drunk.

99. Shirley always had trouble finding clothes that fit because she was
    (a) so petite
    (b) quite small
    (c) a runt
    (d) diminutive
    (e) tiny

100. (a) He did some unfortunate deeds in his day.
    (b) He had the moral sensibility of a reptile.

101. (a) She occasionally lapsed in her duty toward others.
    (b) She was vicious toward others.

102. (a) He was a cautious sort.
    (b) He was spineless.

103. She was
    (a) well traveled.
    (b) shopworn.

104. When he told others what he thought of them he was
    (a) honest.
    (b) blunt.
    (c) ruthless.
    (d) rude.

105. Luigi is
    (a) clumsy.
    (b) like a bull in a china shop.
    (c) a klutz.
    (d) not very well coordinated.

106. My new roommate
    (a) talks all the time.
    (b) loves to talk.
    (c) is loquacious.
    (d) hardly ever gives his larynx a rest.

107. (a) The Raiders gave the ball game away.
    (b) All the breaks went against the Raiders.
    (c) The Raiders couldn't buy a piece of good luck.

108. That novel you gave me to read
    (a) put me to sleep.
    (b) was dull.
    (c) wasn't as interesting as most of the rest of the things I've read lately.

109. (a) I've never been fond of bowling.
    (b) Bowling bores me to death.
    (c) I'd rather read the phone book than bowl.

*Students should be asked why (c) in #109 seems meaner than (a) and (b)—it's ironic that a touch of humor (ridicule, really) can make a remark more vicious.*

110. Professor Henderson's class
    (a) doesn't require much studying.
    (b) is a gut.
    (c) is easy.

111. He'll never make a good wide receiver because
    (a) he has trouble holding onto the ball.
    (b) he has bricks for hands.
    (c) he can't catch.

112. (a) Conversation is not Daryll's forte.
    (b) Daryll is not very clever.
    (c) Daryll would lose a duel of wits with a gum ball machine.

## Bank 2-10

The lettered items should be arranged in order of favorable emotive force. We suggest an increasingly favorable order after each set; you or your students may want to fuss about some of our rankings. (We've said, for example, (a)=(b) when (a) and (b) seem equally favorable to us.)

113. What a thing to wake up to each morning! All you hear are birds
    (a) chirping.
    (b) cheeping.
    (c) chattering.

(d) screeching.
(e) making a racket.
(f) singing.

*(d)=(e), (c), (a), (f)*

114. Karl's diet really took the pounds off; he looks really
    (a) slender.
    (b) thin.
    (c) svelte.
    (d) trim.

    *(b), (a), (c)=(d)*

115. (a) Danielle sings beautifully.
    (b) Danielle has an excellent ear for pitch, a wide range, perfect timbre, and fine phrasing.
    (c) Danielle sings like an angel.

    *(c), (a), (b) It might be worth pointing out that a flattering comparison or metaphor (or an unflattering one, for that matter) is often a stronger way of saying something than the simple use of adjectives.*

116. Personally, I find Harold very
    (a) agreeable.
    (b) congenial
    (c) manageable.
    (d) submissive.
    (e) flexible.
    (f) yielding.

    *(d), (c), (a)=(e), (b)*

117. In my view, Mrs. Tuttle might be described as
    (a) innocent.
    (b) childlike.
    (c) guileless.
    (d) simple.
    (e) artless.
    (f) naive.

    *(d), (e), (f), (b), (a), (c)*

118. The house the new architect designed for the Washingtons is
    (a) unique.
    (b) like nothing I've ever seen.
    (c) innovative.
    (d) different.

    *(d)=(b), (a), (c)*

119. Kim
    (a) reads all the time.
    (b) is a voracious reader.
    (c) is extremely well read.

(d) is a book worm.

*(d), (a), (b), (c)*

120. Lytton is quite rich, but then he is
    (a) frugal.
    (b) stingy.
    (c) thrifty.
    (d) miserly.
    (e) greedy.
    (f) a skinflint.

    *(f), (b)=(d)=(e), (a)=(c)*

121. I've known Hawthorne for twenty years, and you're right, he's
    (a) domineering.
    (b) masterful.
    (c) lordly.
    (d) overbearing.
    (e) dictatorial.
    (f) bossy.

    *(e), (d)=(f), (a), (c), (b)*

122. The paper you turned in last week was
    (a) mediocre.
    (b) fine.
    (c) competent.
    (d) adequate.
    (e) quite good.

    *(a), (d), (c), (e), (b) The last two are so close, one's tone of voice would make the difference.*

## Bank 2-11

123. Ask your students to write two letters of general recommendation, one positive and one not so positive, for the same individual. Both letters should describe the same facts—for example, that the individual graduated with a B average, played varsity tennis, seemed well liked by others, has a sense of humor.

124. Have students read a commentary or editorial in a newspaper and identify as many emotively charged words and phrases as they can. See if they can come up with neutral equivalents for the words on their lists.

## Bank 2-12

Below are descriptions of three characters from Anthony Trollope's *Barchester Towers*. Trollope's words produce some vivid images. It makes an interesting and useful exercise to ask students to write a brief (e.g., one-page) essay explaining what images are evoked and analyzing why and how Trollope's words succeed in creating these images. Alternatively, students may be asked simply to list the charged words in the descriptions.

(This is as close to literary analysis as we'll get—we promise.) The selections are from the 1963 Signet Classics edition.

125. "Mr. Slope is tall and not ill-made. . . . His countenance, however, is not especially prepossessing. His hair is lank and of a dull pale reddish hue. It is always formed into three straight, lumpy masses, each brushed with admirable precision and cemented with much grease. . . . His face is nearly of the same colour as his hair, though perhaps a little redder: it is not unlike beef—beef, however, one would say, of a bad quality . . . . His nose, however, is his redeeming feature: it is pronounced, straight and well-formed; though I myself should have liked it better did it not possess a somewhat spongy, porous appearance, as though it had been cleverly formed out of a red-coloured cork."

126. "In person Dr. Proudie is a good-looking man, spruce and dapper and very tidy. He is somewhat below middle height, being about five feet four, but he makes up for the inches which he wants by the dignity with which he carries those which he has. It is no fault of his own if he has not a commanding eye, for he studies hard to assume it. His features are well-formed, though perhaps the sharpness of his nose may give to his face in the eyes of some people an air of insignificance. If so, it is greatly redeemed by his mouth and chin, of which he is justly proud."

127. "Exteriorly, Mr. Arabin was not a remarkable person. He was above the middle height, well-made, and very active. His hair, which had been jet black, was now tinged with gray, but his face bore no sign of years. It would perhaps be wrong to say that he was handsome, but his face was nevertheless pleasant to look upon. The cheek-bones were rather too high for beauty, and the formation of the forehead too massive and heavy: but the eyes, nose, and mouth were perfect. There was a continual play of lambent fire about his eyes, which gave promise of either pathos or humor whenever he essayed to speak, and that promise was rarely broken. There was a gentle play about his mouth which declared that his wit never descended to sarcasm. . . ."

*Of course there is no one right set of remarks to make about these passages. At the very minimum, students should see (and, believe it or not, some don't) that Trollope describes Mr. Slope in a most unflattering way; that he is almost equally unflattering toward Dr. Proudie, but in a much more subtle way; and that, despite honestly detailing certain physical shortcomings on the part of Mr. Arabin, Trollope manages to convey a very positive impression of this individual. The TV generation seems to have a surprising amount of trouble with this exercise; all the more reason to take the time to do it.*

**Bank 2-13**

Some true or false items.

128. Definitions are used only to clarify the meaning of expressions that are not understood.

*False*

129. Definitions by synonym or definitions by example might serve to reduce the vagueness of an expression.

*False*

130. It is possible to explain the meaning of the word *thing* by using a definition by example.

    *False*

131. A definition by example could be used to differentiate the meanings of "creature with a heart" and "creature with a lung."

    *False*

132. The sense of an expression can be stated only in an analytical definition or in a definition by synonym.

    *True*

133. The word *centaur* could be defined by example.

    *False*

134. The denotation of at least some expressions can be stated in a definition by example.

    *True*

135. It is possible for two synonyms to have approximately the same emotive force.

    *True*

136. Definitions by example, definitions by synonym, and analytical definitions can all be used to evoke an attitude about the thing defined.

    *True*

137. A definition used to reduce the vagueness of an expression is called a precising definition.

    *True*

## Bank 2-14

With the help of a dictionary, students should explain the differences between the expressions paired below. (If critical thinking shades into improvement of vocabulary and word usage, so much the better.)

138. Childish, childlike
139. Continual, continuing
140. Oral, verbal
141. Flammable, inflammable
142. Famous, notorious
143. Imply, infer
144. Egoist, egotist
145. Valid, true
146. Agnostic, atheist
147. Uninterested, disinterested
148. Decayed, decadent
149. Precedent, precedence

150. Less, fewer
151. Original, aboriginal
152. Unnatural, supernatural


## Bank 2-15

Students should classify each of the following as either definition by example, definition by synonym, or analytical definition. Items 153-162 are by example; 163-172 are by synonym, and 173-182 are analytical. Mix them up as it pleases you.

By example:

153. My idea of a successful philosophy major is Steve Martin.
154. When I saw my old crowd at my high school reunion, I suddenly realized what the phrase "motley crew" really meant.
155. The *New York Times* is what I mean by a real newspaper.
156. What Lani just did from the high board is called a "full gainer."
157. The simple tools are the pulley, lever, inclined plane, wheel and axle, screw, and wedge.
158. The inscription over the door of the administration building is a sample of a gothic script called "fraktur."
159. *Tenor* applies to vocal ranges like Pavarotti's.
160. Four spades and a heart make a "four-flush."
161. I may not be able to explain what pornography is, but the magazines on that rack are cases in point.
162. "It was a dark and stormy night. . . ." is what I mean by "cliché."

By synonym

163. A foible is a weakness.
164. The public press is sometimes known as "the fourth estate."
165. Originally, the word *quarantine* meant forty days.
166. You can use *recreant* nearly anywhere you can use *cowardly*, but nobody does anymore.
167. To fledge an arrow is to fletch or feather it.
168. *Shirker* means the same as *slacker*.
169. Drywall and sheetrock are the same thing.
170. You can say either *oscillation* or *vibration*; they're both appropriate and they amount to the same thing.
171. I can never understand sports announcers' talk of "momentum". It seems to mean nothing more than "doing well."
172. *Pferd* is German for *horse*.

Analytical:

173. To philosophers, a realist is a person who believes in the existence of a world outside the mind.
174. The Ojibwa are a tribe of Algonquian Indians of the Lake Superior region.
175. "Bored person" is anyone over twenty-five who lives in Oklahoma, according to my cousin, who lives there.
176. An ogre is a monster who dines on humans.
177. "A miracle: an event described by those to whom it was told by men who did not see it."
   —Elbert Hubbard

178. "Fork, n.  An instrument used chiefly for the purpose of putting dead animals into the mouth."
—Ambrose Bierce
179. "Military intelligence.  A contradiction in terms."
—Groucho Marx
180. "Conservative, n.  A statesman who is enamored of existing evils, as distinguished from a liberal, who wishes to replace them with others."
—Ambrose Bierce
181. "Conversation—the enemy of good wine and food."
—Alfred Hitchcock
182. "A metaphysician is a man who goes into a dark alley at midnight without a light looking for a cat that isn't there."
—Charles Bowen

## Bank 2-16

The following definitions are for sorting into categories according to their use:  to reduce vagueness, to introduce or explain a new or unusual word, to evoke an attitude about something, or to accomplish some other purpose.

183. Energy-efficient house:  A house that, at a minimum, has no teenagers.

*To amuse*

184. When we use the word *argument* in this class, we'll mean a set of claims, one of which is supported by the others.

*To make precise; to reduce vagueness and ambiguity*

185. A *barrister* is a lawyer in Britain who actually argues the case in court.

*To define an unfamiliar word*

186. "'Best-seller' just means 'not written for anyone with an I.Q. of over a hundred and one.'"
—George L. Farris, author of several nonbest-sellers

*Persuasive definition; sour grapes in abundance*

187. The "HO" in "HO gauge" stands for "half-O," which refers to an older scale for model trains.  HO gauge is one-half the scale of O-gauge, or one-sixty-fourth of full size.

*To define an unfamiliar phrase*

188. No, as far as the bus company is concerned you count as a senior citizen only after you've reached sixty-five.  You won't be able to get the discount fare for three more years.

*Precising definition*

189. A floppy disk can come in 5-and-1/4 inch or 8-inch size or in 3-and-1/2 inch size, but in the case of the 3-and-1/2 inch size it's called a microdisk.

*To define an unfamiliar word ("microdisk")*

190. "Tombstone: an ugly reminder of one who has been forgotten."
—H. L. Mencken

*An analytical definition with a darkly humorous purpose, to underscore how short-lived will be others' memories of us after our demise*

191. Beard: a bettor who places bets for a friend with a bookie who has cut off the friend for not paying, for snitching to the police, or for having won too much.
—The Los Angeles Police Department

*To explain a word that may be unfamiliar to the listener*

192. "Conservatism is realism about mankind's limitations."
—George Will

*A persuasive definition favorable to conservatism*

193. "Marriage is not only a divine institution, but is the only one instituted in the Garden of Eden which has come down with its continuous line of blessings to the present time."
—Sylvanus Stall, *What Every Young Man Should Know* (1904)

*To produce an attitude about marriage*

194. "Now if we set about to find out what . . . [a] statement means and to determine whether to accept or reject it, we would be engaged in thinking which, for lack of a better term, we shall call critical thinking."
—B. Othanel Smith

*To reduce vagueness*

195. "The cliché is prefabricated language; it is packaged and ready for immediate delivery."
—William F. Irmscher and Harryette Stover, *The Holt Guide to English*

*Persuasive definition of a negative sort; of course a cliché is by definition trite and hackneyed.*

196. "In the category of *economically privileged*, we shall include families with total annual incomes of $75,000 or more."
—Sarah Hartford and Samuel Cohen, *Trends in College Admissions*

*Precising (stipulative) definition*

197. "All the perceptions of the human mind resolve themselves into two distinct kinds, which I shall call Impressions and Ideas."
—David Hume, *Treatise on Human Nature*

*To introduce two words*

198. "Subduction zone: In interpretations of plate tectonic theory, a belt along the under-margin of a continental plate, where the colliding oceanic plate descends toward or into the mantle."
—Robert M. Norris and Robert W. Webb, *Geology of California*

*To explain a new word*

199. "When we talk about formatting we are referring to the ways in which Multiplan [a microcomputer-based spreadsheet program] allows us to specify the appearance of our information on the screen and on the printer."
—Erwin Schneider, *Multiplan User's Guide*

*To introduce a new use for a word*

200. "In this book we use the word *universe* to denote a 'model of the Universe' and avoid making pretentious claims to a true knowledge of the Universe."
—Edward R. Harrison, *Cosmology*

*This definition seems to be some sort of vague statement of humility; the author is cautioning his reader not to expect the ultimate truth.*

201. "...what we call temperature is nothing else but a measurement of the degree of molecular agitation [in a substance]."
—George Gamow, *One, Two, Three . . . Infinity*

*This analytic definition is a precising one. If you and some bright students push on this one hard enough, some interesting discussions can happen.*

202. "Rock journalism is people who can't write interviewing people who can't talk for people who can't read."
—Frank Zappa

*A denigrating persuasive definition*


## Bank 2-17

The following terms should be easy to invent persuasive definitions—either positive or negative—for. It's a good idea to remind students that persuasive definitions can be analytical, by example, or by synonym; it will help them keep straight the difference between *kinds* of definitions and *uses* of definitions.

203. Attorney
204. Psychiatrist
205. Hippie
206. Republican
207. Poet
208. Banker
209. Education
210. Marxism
211. Ballet
212. Weight lifting


## Bank 2-18

213. Find an example of a persuasive definition.
214. Find an example of a precising definition.

**Bank 2-19**

The following should be sorted into analytic and nonanalytic truths. The first five are straightforward, six through ten require some thinking, and intelligent people can get into arguments about some of the final five. These sometimes make for good class discussions.

215. All baseball players are athletic.

*Nonanalytic*

216. The crocodile is a reptile.

*Analytic*

217. The juice of some aloe plants has therapeutic value for burns.

*Nonanalytic*

218. It's cold at the south pole.

*Nonanalytic*

219. Stalagmites are deposits that result from dripping water in caves; they stick up from the floors while stalactites hang down from the roofs.

*Analytic*

220. It's impossible to feel a color.

*Analytic*

221. Unicorns are mythical creatures.

*Nonanalytic*

222. In poker, a flush beats three-of-a-kind.

*Analytic*

223. A record that sells a million copies is a bigger financial success than one that sells fewer than a million copies.

*Nonanalytic*

224. "Made in Germany the way things are made in Germany."
—Slogan for Olympia typewriters

*Nonanalytic*

225. You can't steal what already belongs to you.

*The authors don't agree on this one; we're leaving it and the remainder (through #229) to you.*

226. Nothing is both red and orange all over.

227. If cats were as smart as people they wouldn't be cats.

228. You couldn't have been born before your parents were born.

229. "Analytic truths are intrinsically uninteresting to anyone who understands what they say."
—A claim from Chapter 2 of the text


**Bank 2-20**

Criticize the following claims based on the material from Chapter 2 of the text.

230. "A requirement for this course is a term paper on some topic."
—Statement on course syllabus

*Criticism: too vague*

231. CHILD'S STOOL GREAT FOR USE IN GARDEN
—Headline in Buffalo *Courier-Express*

*Criticism: semantically ambiguous*

232. LOUISIANA GOVERNOR DEFENDS HIS WIFE, GIFT FROM KOREAN
—Headline in *Milwaukee Journal*

*Criticism: syntactically ambiguous*

233. Cash customers this line only.

*Criticism: syntactically ambiguous*

234. "Who won?"
— ABC poll question, after the Bush-Dukakis presidential debate

*Criticism: ambiguous and exceedingly vague.*

235. "5 times 3 plus 2."

*Criticism: syntactically ambiguous*

236.     SLOW
CHILDREN AT PLAY
—An old joke.

*Criticism: the signs aren't really ambiguous.*

237. "Is evolution a fact?"

*Criticism: vague and semantically ambiguous*

238. Place the box next to the refrigerator before you open it.

   *Criticism: This type of ambiguity could be said to be semantically ambiguous ("it" has two referents) or syntactically ambiguous (the sentence is so structured that what it refers to is ambiguous).*

239. "The enormity of what's taken place is sinking in now."
   —George Bush, just after his election

   *Criticism: We don't think Bush knows what "enormity" means. Have students check their dictionary.*

240. "The instructor will not inform a student that he or she will be charged with cheating during an examination."
   —Statement on course syllabus

   *Criticism: syntactically ambiguous*

241. "Alcohol is present in about 50 percent of fatal traffic accidents among teenagers."

   *Criticism: "Alcohol is present" is pretty vague for almost any context; so is "about 50 percent," but in many contexts it would not be too vague.*

242. "All of you are not thinking."

   *Criticism: syntactically ambiguous*

243. Computer salesman to customer who does not know what kind of computer he needs: "You really need a model with a 100 meg hard disk and tape backup; those use 1-meg SIMMS for a total of 4 megs of RAM."

   *Criticism: Use of unfamiliar words, obviously intended more to impress the customer than to inform*

   **Bank 2-21**

   True/False items.

244. It is rarely if ever appropriate to insist that a claim be totally free from vagueness.

   *True*

245. Vague claims are more difficult to prove false than precise claims.

   *True*

246. Any definition by example of the phrase *traditional wife* would also qualify as a definition by example of the word *woman*.

   *True*

247. If you want to make a word's meaning more precise, a definition by synonym will work better than an analytical definition.

*False*

## Suggestions for exercises on complexity and spoken claims

There is perhaps no greater service we as instructors of critical thinking courses can do than help our students maximize their skills in reading comprehension and in understanding spoken discourse. Unfortunately, this is as difficult to do as it is easy to say, but one strategy we think may help (and certainly won't hurt) is to ask students to read or listen to an assortment of preselected passages of reasonable complexity and modest length—the length of exercise 2-14 in the text is about right, we think—and then answer questions about them. (An alternative is to ask them to distill the hard news from articles that appear in places like *Time* and *Newsweek* )

In most courses students are sent out to learn something in particular, as it were, and it's rare that they have a chance to develop the general skills—like reading, listening, and, yes, thinking—that are more fundamental than any particular subject matter. We find that doing exercises like those described at least brings the development of such general skills to students' attention, and without that step, nothing else can be accomplished.

Note: Exercises 21-24 were contributed by Dan Barnett.

# Chapter 3
# Evaluating Informative Claims

This chapter occupies an important niche in the overall scheme of the text. Since our position is that critical thinking includes determining whether a claim is worth accepting even when only bad reasons or no reasons (including pseudoreasons) have been given for it, something must be said about how to determine when such unsupported claims can reasonably be accepted. This chapter carries much of that burden.

Students find most of the material in this chapter familiar, except possibly the contrary-contradictory distinction, but not many of them have had occasion to contemplate its importance. Background knowledge, for example, is vitally important to each of them, but an appreciation of its importance runs contrary to the standard "is it going to be on the exam?" attitude. Similarly, they are vaguely aware that everything they know that they haven't observed themselves is the result of taking somebody else's word for it. But something so crucial as knowing when somebody else's word is worth taking is a matter they are unlikely to have contemplated very carefully, even though you will find that students often have strong opinions about the credibility of sources. Typically, they will distrust the sources of claims they find disagreeable and blindly trust the authors of the remainder. Sometimes, students (like the rest of us) would like to believe in a source just because he or she is charming, unusual, or what-have-you. The remark from Harry Truman in the box on page 69 is like that—we'd like to think that such a colorful curmudgeon knew what he was talking about. Harry would have been better off if he'd read the chapter.

You can expect a number of the exercises in the chapter to stimulate some discussion. So, even though there are fewer exercises in this chapter than in some of the others, you can expect at least some of them to eat up a good bit of class time.

In some of the exercises, we ask the reader to rank various sources in terms of their credibility about some subject. We predicate the task on the assumption that nothing is known about the sources beyond what is given in the exercise. Thus, if the request is to rank, say, a professor of sociology against a state senator with regard to some sociological question, we would expect the professor to be ranked above the senator even though in fact a given senator may be more of an expert about the issue than some particular sociologist. Your students—and quite likely you, too—may disagree with some of the rankings we give in the answers. But we've found that the discussion that results from the disagreement is useful to our objectives in trying to give guidance in the difficult task of ascertaining credibility.

The "Sensational" tabloid headlines are amusing (but the realization that millions of people buy those tabloids is less amusing); and students get a kick out of the "Presidential Expertise" and "Experts Disagree" boxes. The latter should not undercut our trust in the general reliability of expert opinion, however.

## Exercises Unanswered in the Text

### Exercise 3-1

2. Contradictories
3. Not in conflict
5. Contradictories
8. Contradictories
9. Contradictories

## Exercise 3-2

2. Contraries, on the assumption that Helgren could withdraw, get sick and not complete the term, be hit by a truck, or such.
3. Contraries. Both are false if George passed and Frank, also in Helgren's class, did not pass the exam.
5. Not in conflict, on the assumption that (a) is not intended as a universal general claim (see Ch. 10); i.e., that it is intended to apply to every single investor. Note too that these are vague claims, and it's harder to pin down conflicts with vague claims.
6. Contraries
8 Not in conflict
9. Not in conflict

## Exercise 3-9

We find the items connected by "=" approximately equal in credibility. Your judgments about the answers here may be different from ours—the important thing, we think, is whether your students can manage relevant grounds for their rankings.

1. (b), (c)=(d) (probably), (e), (a)
3. (g), (e), (b)=(c)=(f), (a), (d). *We think the magician is likely to be the best at spotting trickery and the least gullible; the psychologist, detective, and customs agent could vary in credibility but more likely due to personalities than job types.*
5. (b)=(f), (e), (a)=(c)=(d)

## Exercise 3-10

4. We think that the *New England Journal of Medicine* and the National Institutes of Health are the most credible sources for this and most matters relating to health. Your physician, *Runner's World,* and *Time* magazine are about equally credible, but all three of them must rely on other sources for their information about the subject, and all three have access to about the same sources (of which the *New England Journal of Medicine* is a prime example).
5. A physician would be a credible source of information about the physiological and biological processes involved in the development of a human being from conception to birth. A lawyer would be credible on the various legal issues surrounding abortion. A minister would be a credible spokesperson for a particular religion's position on the question asked. Because philosophers receive special training in detecting tacit assumptions, recognizing subtle distinctions, and evaluating reasoning, it would be reasonable to expect a philosopher to offer the most careful and comprehensive treatment of the question. If you thought that *you* are the most credible source, then you probably assume that the question is purely subjective. Such is not necessarily the case; it is another assumption that bears some examination, and for guidance in that examination it would again be reasonable to turn to a philosopher.

## Exercise 3-11

2. (a) Since he spent two years in the Peace Corps in Venezuela, Calhoun would be a credible source of information on this question. Note, however, that his experience in Latin America may have been limited to Venezuela and it may be somewhat out of date, though the fact that he is a consultant in "numerous developing countries" leaves open the

possibility of more recent and more widespread experience.

(b) The assessment of Calhoun's credibility on this subject parallels the previous answer for the most part. Calhoun was in Latin America very soon after the Cuban revolution, and so his views on its *immediate* effects, at least in Venezuela, should be very credible indeed. It is not clear how much this part of his experience would translate into credibility on the Revolution's long-range effects, however.

(c) We would expect Calhoun to be a real expert on the physical principles involved in water pumping and transportation (which would ultimately account for a faucet's leaking), and we would expect him to have had extensive "hands on" experience with pipes, tools, washers, etc. But he is not a plumber, and so he should not be assumed to be as much of an expert on leaky faucets as someone who spends each day dealing with these items and who knows the tricks of the trade.

(d) We would expect Calhoun to be a well-qualified expert on *some* aspects of technology in Third World countries, but whether he would be similarly qualified about *every* aspect— for example, the use of computers, is something the biography does not tell us. We would put his credibility ahead of that of most people on such subjects as computers in developing countries, but not ahead of someone whose expertise is in that very field.

(e) We would expect Calhoun to have some knowledge concerning this matter, but his company's involvement in the pipeline is likely to produce some bias in his opinions. Unless we had reason to think Calhoun was unbiased, we would prefer a neutral party's opinion, all things considered.

(f) Calhoun doubtless has some considerable expertise in matters like this, since he has had such substantial success in them. We would make him a very credible source.

(g) There is no reason to think Calhoun especially qualified in this matter.

## Exercise 3-13

5. Even in 1963, the year before the U.S. Surgeon General's report on smoking and health, this claim should have been a bit startling. Now, of course, we know that this claim is false—and dangerous.

6. No doubt cats that live indoors do tend to live longer than cats that are subject to the perils of outdoor life. (It's hard to get run over by an automobile inside the house.) If there were statistics available on how much longer indoor cats live on the average, we'd expect the cat-litter people to know them. But we suspect that such statistics would be difficult to establish (and probably not worth the effort), and we therefore have little confidence in the statistic cited here.

7. We find this incredible—that is, we don't believe it. That is, what we understand of it we don't believe. The "Foundation" referred to is, we expect, something short of a reputable scientific institution, and the fact that the manuscript (which one of the authors received in the mail) is not published by a known publisher hardly lends any credibility. Mainly, however, the observations expressed in this passage conflict directly with our background knowledge.

9. This claim is probably true, given that it is found in a respected garden book.

10. We would withhold judgment about this one pending further documentation of the charges. There may be some truth in the claim, but, given the political nature of the book from which the claim comes, we'd be cautious in accepting it without more evidence than the author's word.

12. We'd accept this claim as probably true; the source is a credible one on such subjects.

13. This is almost certainly false. It conflicts with our background knowledge and with standard physical theory, and it comes from a source known for sensationalism. To reject this claim as given, notice, is not to believe that *nothing* happened. There may have been a phenomenon that needed explaining, but we don't think the account given should be believed.

15. This comes from a credible source. Without hearing conflicting claims from other equally credible sources, we'd accept it as a reliable assessment of the evidence as of that date.

# Chapter 3 Test Question-Exercise Bank

## Bank 3-1

The following pairs of claims should be classified as contraries, contradictories, or not conflicting.

1. (a) The class began at 8:00 a.m.
   (b) The class began by 8:30 a.m.

   *Not conflicting*

2. (a) Maurie's dog is a purebred schnauzer.
   (b) Maurie's dog is not a purebred at all.

   *Contraries*

3. (a) There are an infinite number of prime numbers.
   (b) There are only 2,497,622,991 prime numbers.

   *Contraries*

4. (a) That cheap pet food you bought contains ash.
   (b) That cheap pet food you bought contains no ash.

   *Contradictories*

5. (a) Alekhine was better than Capablanca at simultaneous chess matches.
   (b) No, Capablanca was better than Alekhine.

   *Contraries  (They could have been equally good.)*

6. (a) Alekhine was better than Capablanca at simultaneous chess matches.
   (b) No, he wasn't.

   *Contradictories*

7. (a) You can never get something from nothing.
   (b) Sometimes you can get something from nothing.

   *Contradictories*

8. (a) The least expensive lunch at Le Bistro is eight dollars.
   (b) You can get lunch at Le Bistro for five and a half dollars.

   *Contraries*

9. (a) There was over three inches of rain in Caddo Gap last week.
   (b) Caddo Gap had at least two inches of rain last week.

   *Not conflicting*

10. (a) Babe Ruth's sixty home runs in a season that was much shorter than today's baseball seasons stands as the all-time greatest achievement in hitting home runs.
    (b) I don't care how sentimental you are about Babe Ruth, Roger Maris is the home run champion because he hit more than anybody else ever has in one season.

    *Not conflicting*

11. (a) You can't get Cuban cigars in the United States.
    (b) You can if you smuggle them in through Canada.

    *Contraries*

12. (a) Isaac's violin was made by Antonio Stradivari.
    (b) Isaac's violin is not an expensive instrument.

    *These do not conflict as they stand, but given the reasonable assumption, "All violins made by Stradivari are expensive instruments," the claims are contradictories.*

13. (a) No company makes it into the Kopp 500 unless it has annual sales of over $700 million.
    (b) Stanton Corporation has sales of over $700 million and it is not one of the Kopp 500.

    *Not conflicting*

14. (a) No company with less than $700 million in annual sales is in the Kopp 500.
    (b) Stanton Corporation has over $700 million in annual sales and it is not in the Kopp 500.

    *Not conflicting*

15. (a) Every company that has annual sales of over $700 million is in the Kopp 500.
    (b) Stanton Corporation has sales of over $700 million and it is not one of the Kopp 500.

    *Contradictories*

16. (a) An eye for an eye and a tooth for a tooth.
    (b) Turn the other cheek, do not return injury for injury.

    *Contraries (if both are taken universally—that is, as applying to every case)*

17. (a) To forgive is divine, a perfect being will always forgive.
    (b) Some sins are unforgivable.

    *Not in conflict, except on one or another assumption about a perfect being*

18. (a) Love is wonderful and anything that is wonderful won't hurt.
    (b) Love hurts.

    *Contraries, unless one exploits the vagueness of the notion of love, in which case they can be said not to conflict*

19. (a)  You shouldn't work so hard; don't try to do so much.
    (b)  Besides everything else you're doing you should iron my clothes!

*Contraries*

20. (a)  "Growing and decaying vegetation in this land are responsible for 93% of the oxides of nitrogen." —Ronald Reagan
    (b)  "Industrial sources are responsible for at least 65% and possibly as much as 90% of the oxides of nitrogen in the U. S." —Dr. Michael Oppenheimer of the Environmental Defense Fund

*Contraries*

21. (a)  Anything over 200 micrograms of selenium per day is considered unsafe for a human adult, according to the government standards.
    (b)  Nobody knows how much selenium it takes to be unsafe for a human adult.

*Contraries*

22. (a)  Steve Jobs's new computer will be the biggest seller on university campuses.
    (b)  I don't think so; it won't sell over a hundred thousand items because it costs more than most universities can afford.

*It may be that a hundred thousand items is all it would take to make it the biggest seller on university campuses, in which case these are not in conflict.*

23. (a)  Nicotine makes the body metabolize caffeine faster.
    (b)  Caffeine makes the body metabolize nicotine faster.

*Not in conflict; both could be true. (a) is in fact true, but we don't know about (b).*

24. (a)  Books are more efficient learning tools than computers, no matter what software is being used with the latter.
    (b)  Some of the new computer and software combinations are at least as efficient as books as learning tools.

*Aside from obvious vagueness, the difficulty with this one is that such claims as (a) are usually asserted "in general" or "on average," or some such. And, does (b) mean as any book, or as most books? If we take each one to be universal, the claims are contradictories. Otherwise they may not conflict at all.*

25. (a)  Most of the Savings and Loans in this country are in financial trouble.
    (b)  Most of the Savings and Loans in this country are in good shape.

*These could both be false, making them contraries, but only in the unlikely event that exactly half the S & Ls are in trouble and the other half in good shape. (We're taking "in financial trouble" and "in good shape" as complementary terms—that every S & L is either one or the other.)*

(a)  The United States should support covert actions in Angola.
(b)  The United States should not support covert actions in Angola.

*Contradictories*

56

26. (a) Julian Bream is the best contemporary classical guitarist.
    (b) No, John Williams is the best contemporary classical guitarist.

    *Contraries*

27. (a) Either Carlos or Julia will pass this course.
    (b) Neither Carlos nor Julia will pass this course.

    *Contradictories*

28. (a) Charles is taller than Daniel.
    (b) Daniel is at least as tall as Charles.

    *Contradictories*

29. (a) Soccer is the fastest growing sport in the country.
    (b) Field hockey is growing faster than soccer in this country.

    *Contraries*

## Bank 3-2

Each of the following claims should be assessed as probably true, probably false, as requiring further documentation before judgment, or as a claim that cannot properly be evaluated. Consider both the nature of the claim and the source.

30. "A few years ago AT&T did two surveys showing that technically trained persons did not achieve as many top managerial jobs in the company as liberal arts graduates did."
    —*New York Times*

    *It is often risky to accept what second-hand reports say about what surveys "show," but the* New York Times *is a very credible source. This claim is probably true. Note, however, the vagueness of "did not achieve" and "top managerial jobs."*

31. According to Funk & Wagnalls *Hammond World Atlas*, the three longest rivers in the world are the Nile, the Amazon, and the Yangtze.

    *Probably true; if you can't trust your Funk & Wagnalls in a matter like this, whom can you trust?*

32. Letter to the Editor: "Your editorial page of October 15 contained a cartoon that was highly offensive. . . ."
    —*Midfield Sentinel*

    *Probably true; an individual is the best authority on what he or she finds offensive*

33. "Driven by the Gramm-Rudman mandate to cut $46 billion from the budget for fiscal 1987, OMB director James Miller is proposing to sell off whole programs and agencies from the federal establishment. Miller's hit list is mostly secret for the time being, but administration sources say it includes some large, costly and much-venerated legacies of the Democratic past. One example: the Bonneville Power Administration, which provides low-cost electricity to the Pacific Northwest from a far-flung system of hydroelectric dams and

substations, including the Grand Coulee Dam."
—*Newsweek*

*This is probably true, since we would expect* Newsweek *to have good Washington sources in such matters. But notice: what is it that's probably true? The claim itself is quite vague. What does "proposing" mean, for example?*

34. "Q: Did Marilyn Monroe keep a diary about her relationships with John and Robert Kennedy?"
"A: No."
—Walter Scott's Personality Parade, *Parade*

*Scott's question-and-answer column is probably a reasonably reliable source of information about the questions asked. Secret diaries are always a possibility, of course.*

35. Remark heard in a coffee shop: "There is a disproportionate percentage of left-handed people in politics."

*This claim would take much more authority before we'd believe it. Much of this sort of casual conversation is based on anecdotal evidence (see Chapter 10). The claim is also vague: what does the speaker mean by "politics"?*

36. Comment from an acquaintance: "I saw Bigfoot with my own eyes! It was huge!"

*Probably false; an observational error is more likely than that our background knowledge is wrong*

37. "Every day 5,000 Americans try cocaine for the first time—a total of 22 million so far—according to estimates by the National Institute on Drug Abuse. About five million people are believed to be using the drug at least once a month, and they are administering it to themselves in increasingly destructive ways."
—James Lieber, *Atlantic Monthly*

*We don't know much about the National Institute on Drug Abuse, but we have found the* Atlantic Monthly *to be pretty reliable in factual matters. Notice that no exact figures are claimed; the first is explicitly said to be an estimate, and the phrases "about" and "believed to be" qualify the second. We would expect these claims to be close to the truth.*

38. "General Motors is on a journey to a far-off place just around the corner, the 21st Century. With the help of its thousands of scientists, designers, and engineers, GM is embarking on an odyssey into the unknown. Roads paved with scientific and technological wonders that might seem like science fictions. But at GM, they're reality. . . ."
—From a General Motors magazine advertisement

*We find this too vague to make a judgment about. (In fairness to the ad, we might note that a couple of later passages in it were less vague. But not much.)*

39. You've taken your car in to the local branch of a nationwide chain of brake and muffler shops for an advertised "free brake inspection." After the inspection, the service manager tells you: "I'm afraid your linings are almost completely gone and the drums need turning. You need a complete brake overhaul."

*Probably true. The fact that the brake shop is part of a nationwide chain gives a measure of credibility to the service report, even if the shop is independently owned, since there would be someone beyond the service manager to complain to in the event you discovered the service report was dishonest. However, unless you've been having problems with your brakes or have verified the service report by your own visual inspection, you should get a second opinion in a case like this. Brake inspections are widely offered free or for a small charge.*

40. From a short glossary at the end of an article on hard disk storage systems in a computer magazine: *"Transfer rate:* The rate at which stored data travels from the hard disk to the Macintosh bus. Mac serial ports clock at 920 kbits/sec, unless the hard disk is configured to run AppleTalk Transfer Protocols."

*Probably true. Most reputable specialty magazines get their facts right most of the time. There are many such areas, however, from automobiles to computers to fitness, in which magazines devoted to the subject print controversial opinions. A person familiar with the field usually knows which areas are controversial; if you're a neophyte, ask the opinion of a more knowledgeable friend.*

41. "Do you feel insecure? Or are you confident about your position in life? According to Dr. Ian Cameron, how and where you stand in an elevator will reveal the answers to these questions."
   —Reported in the *National Examiner.* Dr. Cameron is described in the article as "a noted scientist and researcher."

*Is this remark the conclusion of a study? A speculation on the part of Dr. Cameron? Who is Dr. Cameron, anyway? We are suspicious since so little information is given about him. More important, the claim runs counter to our background knowledge. Our experience indicates that when we are free to choose where we stand in an elevator, our choice is affected by whether we must push the elevator buttons, how many other people are in the elevator, how close our destination floor is, and so on. We don't think very much can be determined about one's personality by observing how and where he or she stands in an elevator.*

42. "[Atmospheric nuclear] tests do not seriously endanger either present or future generations."
   —Edward Teller, physicist, one of the "fathers" of the atomic bomb, 1958

*This is the kind of remark we'd expect to be able to trust, coming from such a source. That it turned out to be false probably shows either that Teller was biased or that there was not enough information on the effects of atmospheric tests in 1958.*

43. From a letter to the editor by a person we've never heard of: "Eighty-five percent of the jail population smokes."

*What's meant by "jail population" is a bit vague; we presume the letter is talking about inmates. We find the claim plausible—at least we would not be surprised if it were true. This plausibility is inherent in the claim; it is not due to the fact that any particular person made it, especially since no source information is provided.*

44. "Warning: St. John [in the Virgin Islands] is very much a 'cash only' island. Most restaurants and car rental agencies accept cash or travelers checks only."
   —Janet Fullwood, travel writer for the *Dallas Times Herald*

*Probably true*

45. "In the history books, the personal-computer slump of 1985 will be a footnote compared to the Japanese assault on the American semiconductor industry."
—*Newsweek*

*Probably true, but with reservations: this claim is phrased vaguely (what does it mean to be a footnote?)*

46. "The West German Cabinet has conditionally agreed to let private companies enroll in the research [on the Strategic Defense Initiative]."
—From an editorial in *The Los Angeles Times*

*Probably true*

47. "The yearly cancer rate for men in Glasgow, Scotland, is 130 cases per 100,000."
—"Atlas of Cancer in Scotland," World Health Organization (an agency of the United Nations)

*Probably true*

48. "My cat has fewer brains than a hubcap!"
—Spoken by one of the authors of the text after his cat had spent three days on his housetop

*Probably false*

49. "The American word 'yup' means 'sex' in Russia."
—Comedian Yakov Smirnoff (who was born and lived in Russia for sixteen years before emigrating to America in 1977). Smirnoff uses the claim in question as a basis for "yuppie" jokes.

*Probably true*

50. According to a Baron Gottfried von Swieten, King Frederick of Prussia claimed that he had once given a chromatic theme to Johann Sebastian Bach, who had immediately made of it a fugue in four parts, then in five parts, and finally in eight parts.
—From H. T. David and A. Mendel, *The Bach Reader*, reported in *Gödel, Escher, and Bach*, by Douglas R. Hofstadter

*One needs to know something of music to realize how incredible this remark is. To improvise a six-part fugue is nearly beyond imagination (Hofstadter likens it to playing sixty games of chess simultaneously while blindfolded and winning them all). Even Bach, whose genius strains credibility on many counts, is unlikely to have been able to improvise an eight-part fugue. Presumably either King Frederick or the good Baron was doing some exaggerating.*

51. Hudie Ledbetter ("Leadbelly") was not only a writer and performer of songs, but an unusually powerful man. Alan Lomax, the historian of American folk music, wrote that "In the Texas Penitentiary he was the number one man in the number one gang on the number one farm in the state—the man who could carry the lead row in the field for 12 or 14 hours a day under the broiling July and August sun." He could pick a bale of cotton in a day— that's 500 pounds!
—Adapted from liner notes to the record *Leadbelly* (Everest recording FS-202)

*We find this more likely to be true than the previous item, but one should be warned that claims like this are subject to exaggeration, especially over time. (Legends tend to grow after their subjects are gone.) No source is given for the last claim in the passage, but Lomax knew Ledbetter and probably had at least some first-hand information about his physical prowess.*

52. "1985 was a turbulent year. It was a year that began with record profits and sales. It was also a year in which we reported the first quarterly loss in Apple's history. We had to take swift action. We did. And it's working."
—Apple Computer, Inc., *1985 Annual Report*

*The remarks about profits, sales, and a quarterly loss are probably true; they are easily investigated. The remarks about taking swift action and that the actions taken are "working" are vague enough to be difficult to evaluate.*

53. "Of all species, only pigs and humans like liquor."
—Charles Halsted, Professor of Internal Medicine, University of California, Davis

*We'd ordinarily accept this claim as probably true except for the fact that one of us once had a dog that loved to lick wine jugs.*

54. "Lottery director Mark Michalko said Thursday that allegations that Californians are squandering money they once used for food to buy lottery tickets 'are just not correct.' . . . California Grocers Association president Don Beaver raised the issue earlier in the week, saying five supermarket chains had complained that grocery sales dropped about 5 percent after lottery tickets went on sale October 3."
—*Sacramento Bee*

*Based just on information contained in this news item, we'd suspend judgment on the question of whether lottery sales have diminished food sales.*

55. "Contrary to popular belief, 'The Star-Spangled Banner' has been the nation's official song only since 1931."
—James Kilpatrick, syndicated columnist

*We'd be very surprised if Kilpatrick were mistaken about a fact like this.*

56. "[A sixth century B.C. Greek named 'Bybon'] threw a 315-pound block of red sandstone over his head. The feat was reported after archeologists found a description of Bybon's act inscribed on the rock itself."
—*The Book of Lists*

*We think this may be true; there are people around now who could perform this feat. (It isn't said how far Bybon threw the rock.) Notice, however, that the documentation of Bybon's act would be a little difficult to corroborate at this point.*

## Bank 3-3

With the sources given in mind, discuss the credibility of the claims made in the passages.

57. "The UFOnauts are usually clothed in shiny, tight fitting, one piece suits, and in most reports seem able to breathe our air without difficulty. Telepathy seems involved in most contacts. . . . If you are tired of the same old pseudo-explanations, official debunkings, and lame duck logic from quacks suffering megalomania, then you are invited to join the concerted efforts of the UFO Contact Center. . . ."
—From a pamphlet, undated, issued in the 1980s by Aileen E. Edwards, director of UFO Contact Center International in Seattle, Washington

*The "Center" is a clearinghouse for those who have alien contact experiences to share their fears and insights without condemnation. Edwards herself has had an alien experience, says the pamphlet, and now is reaching out to help people with similar stories. The language is typical us/them, with those who would offer a more coherent explanation labeled as "quacks"; the assumption is that those who have certain experiences are best able to determine "what really happened."*

58.  "'You hear in the folklore about miracles happening, but I have never seen one thing yet that could be called an actual medical cure,' says Douglas Sharon, a University of California, Los Angeles, anthropologist who has studied curandrismo [Peruvian folk medicine] on the north coast of Peru for 18 years."
—From a *National Geographic Magazine* news feature, October 5, 1988

*This seems a clear-cut case of good credibility; yet the geographic magazine news feature goes on to point out that several other anthropologists, conducting a study for the National Institute of Mental Health, have found that in 38 cases of nervousness, faintness or dizziness, poor appetite, nausea, and the like, the curanderos, the folk healers, were effective in 35 of the cases in alleviating all symptoms. Researchers tentatively suggest the curanderos use psychotherapeutic methods to eliminate psychosomatic symptoms in their patients. So part of the credibility rests on what one calls "an actual medical cure."*

59.  "Based on a survey of more than 100,000 people, Toshitaka Nomi and Alexander Besher have drawn up some startling conclusions about blood type and personality. If you are type O, you are probably aggressive and realistic. Type A? You are naturally industrious, detail-oriented, and peace-loving. Type B's are creative and individualistic. AB's tend to be rational, but moody. YOU ARE YOUR BLOOD TYPE presents detailed analysis of the different blood types and explores the compatibility between the different types."
—From a news release from Pocket Books about the first Western account "of the Japanese pop-phenomenon of blood-type analysis. . . ." (May 1988)

*The principal author T. Nomi, is said in the release to be carrying on his father's work in blood-typing theory; Nomi's qualifications are that he has written many articles on the theory, has made many TV appearances, and has sold five million copies of twenty-two different books. Besher publishes translations of modern Japanese literature and contributes to the personal computer newsweekly* InfoWorld. *Given these qualifications of the authors and the nature of the reported results, we remain skeptical.*

60.  The mail order company Hammacher Schlemmer & Co. says in its consumer catalogs it sells nothing but the best. The company supports its claims by what it calls independent testing. But a book called *The Mis-Fortune 500* by Bruce Nash and Allan Zullo (New York: Pocket Books, 1988) says that while a 1986 letter to potential customers claimed that a "completely separate" "consumer" organization tested and compared the products offered by Hammacher Schlemmer, in reality:
"The testing organization is called the Hammacher Schlemmer Institute.
"The institute is funded by Hammacher Schlemmer & Co.
"The institute's board of directors is composed of Hammacher Schlemmer officials.
"The institute is located at Hammacher Schlemmer company headquarters in Chicago."

*The company maintains that the institute is separate from its other divisions; yet it strains credibility when the implied comparison is between the institute and say, Consumers Union. Presumably the authors of* The Mis-Fortune 500 *have presented the whole story in their book, but their claim to fame is to have been the coauthors of several baseball "hall of shame" books and to have appeared on "Late Night with David Letterman." The point is that the examples culled from press reports are intended to show business at its worst—*

*without including mitigating circumstances. We tend to swallow negative claims more easily, especially if they are embarrassing to Big Business or Big Government.*

## Bank 3-4

Each of these items consists of a brief biography of a real or imagined person followed by a list of topics. Discussion of the credibility and authority of the person described on each listed topic should be based just on the information given in the biography.

61. Robert A. Weinberg is a professor of biology at the Center for Cancer Research of the Massachusetts Institute of Technology and a member of the Whitehead Institute for Biomedical Research. His B.A. (1964) and Ph.D. (1969) are both from M.I.T. He did postdoctoral research at the Weizmann Institute of Science in Israel and at the Salk Institute for Biological Studies. In 1962 he returned to M.I.T. and the following year he was made a member of the faculty at the Center for Cancer Research. He joined the Whitehead Institute in 1982.

    (a) Whether your sore throat is "strep throat"
    (b) Whether there should be a constitutional amendment prohibiting abortion
    (c) Current investigative techniques in biology
    (d) The effectiveness of laetrile as a cancer therapy
    (e) The composition of red blood cells
    (f) The rate of heart disease among Eskimos
    (g) The effect of calcium supplements to the diet on high blood pressure

    *We'd expect Dr. Weinberg to be an expert in topics (c) and (e), and we'd expect him to be well informed about (d) as well. He'd be slightly less an authority on (f) and (g), but anything he might say about these subjects would carry more weight than those of a lay person. We would not expect him to be an authority on (a), and his views on (b) would have to speak for themselves—that is, his scientific background would not lend any special credibility to his views on (b).*

62. Robert Kuttner is the economics correspondent of *The New Republic*, a columnist for *Business Week* and *The Boston Globe*, and a contributor to *The Atlantic Monthly*. After graduating from Oberlin College in 1965, he studied at the London School of Economics and took a master's degree in political science at the University of California, Berkeley. In addition to his writing, Kuttner served in Washington from 1975 to 1978 as the chief investigator for the Senate Banking Committee. In 1979 he was a fellow at Harvard's John F. Kennedy School of Government. He subsequently edited the journal *Working Papers*. Kuttner is the author of *Revolt of the Haves* (1980) and, most recently, *The Economic Illusion* (1984), which was nominated for a National Book Critics Circle Award.

    (a) The effects of inflation on the stock market
    (b) The Federal Deposit Insurance Corporation (FDIC), which insures deposits at banks and savings and loan institutions
    (c) Restaurants in London
    (d) Politics and upper income groups in America
    (e) Poverty among American Indians

    *We would expect substantial expertise from Mr. Kuttner on topics (b) and (d)—the latter because of his 1980 book—and more than lay knowledge about (a). We'd sooner trust him than someone who hasn't lived in London on (c), and we would expect no more expertise about (e) than we'd expect from other well-informed nonspecialists.*

63. James A. Van Allen received a Ph.D. in physics from the University of Iowa in 1939. During World War II he was a gunnery officer with the Pacific Fleet. After the war he returned to the University of Iowa, where he became professor of physics and chairman of the Department of Physics and Astronomy. In 1958, during the mission of Explorer 1, the first successful U.S. earth satellite, he discovered the radiation belts surrounding the earth which are given his name. He was the principal investigator for the space probe of Jupiter's radiation belts and one of the discoverers of the radiation belts of Saturn. He was chairman of the group that developed the Voyager and Galileo space missions and is currently principal investigator for the Pioneer 10 and Pioneer 11 projects.

   (a) The number of women employed by the National Aeronautics and Space Administration
   (b) The uses of satellites for national security purposes
   (c) The biological effects of ultraviolet radiation
   (d) The structure of comet tails
   (e) Recent geological activity along faults in southern California
   (f) The impact of a manned space station on science and technology

   *We assume Van Allen's opinions on (f) would be very informed. He would also have great credibility on (d) and only slightly less on (c). His remarks on (b) would carry more weight than those of a lay person, but we would need further information about him before regarding him as an authority on (a) or (e).*

64. James W. Myers taught himself to program in three different computer languages by the time he was sixteen. At seventeen, he was a member of a loose-knit Southern California group of computer "hackers" that specialized in tapping the data-bases of large corporations, including the telephone company and several banks. In 1984 Myers was charged with using his home computer and a telephone communication device to manipulate data in the Pacific Bell Telephone data-base in such a way as to have avoided telephone bills for his household and those of several friends for almost two years. He was also discovered to have savings accounts at two Bank of America branches, with balances totaling over seventy thousand dollars, despite never having made a deposit or even "officially" opening the account. Myers was found guilty on several counts of defrauding the two companies and was put on three years' probation. During his probation, Bank of America hired him as a consultant to assess the security of its computer files, a job at which he worked for nearly a year. Now twenty years old, he works for a legitimate software house in the Silicon Valley. (Asked which side of the law he preferred working on, Myers claimed that, "Everything considered, being an outlaw was more fun.")

   (a) The morality of software piracy
   (b) Corporate data banks
   (c) Telecommunications
   (d) Purchasing a computer for a small business
   (e) Electronic games
   (f) Computer programming

   *We'd listen to Myers with attention on topics (b), (c), and (f), and we'd give his opinions more weight than our own on (d) and (e). We think we could get better authority on (a).*

65. Dave Vink Quigg is a scientist at the U.S. Department of Agriculture Forest Service's Northeastern Forest Experimental Station in Durham, New Hampshire. He graduated from Humboldt State University in California with a degree in biology (1958) and earned a Ph.D. in plant pathology from the University of West Virginia (1965). After serving for seven years as a consultant to the Pennsylvania State Park system, he was employed by the

U.S. Forest Service as a specialist in tree diseases. His major area of research has been in the resistance mechanisms of trees to injury and infection.

(a) The effects of improper pruning techniques on fruit trees
(b) The kind of fertilizer to use on ornamental shrubs
(c) Resistance mechanisms of mammals to disease and infection
(d) The characteristics of various types of softwoods relative to their use in the building industry
(e) How to transplant a small tree
(f) Use rates of campground facilities in Pennsylvania state parks
(g) Methods of controlling garden pests

*Quigg would have more credibility on each of these subjects than a lay person, though we would regard him as most qualified on (a) and (e) and least qualified on (b), (c), and (g).*

**Bank 3-5**

The credibility and authority of each individual or group listed should be discussed with regard to the questions or issues posed. Whom would you trust as most reliable on each subject?

66. You are thinking of insulating your attic and need advice relative to how much insulation you should install.

(a) A company that sells insulation, but does not install it
(b) A company that sells and installs insulation
(c) An energy consultant from your local gas and electric company
(d) *Consumer Reports*
(e) A friend who has recently had his attic insulated

*We think you are most likely to get the best information from (d), with (c) a close second. (a) and (b) are about equal in credibility, and (e)'s ranking really depends on where he got his information.*

67. You've purchased a wood-burning stove. You are uncertain, however, what kind of wood to burn in it. You've heard that some produce more smoke, some are more likely to contribute to chimney fires, some burn hotter than others, and so forth.

(a) The dealer from whom you purchased the stove
(b) A friend of yours who has used a wood-burning stove for years
(c) Another friend who sells firewood
(d) A U.S. Department of Agriculture publication, "Comparative Properties of Fuelwood"
(e) A professor of environmental horticulture at a state university

*All these sources are credible, but (d) should rank first and, most likely, (a) should rank last.*

68. You have saved up for a vacation and are considering taking a cruise on a cruise ship. You are unsure whether this would be the right kind of vacation for you and, if it is, what kind of cruise would be best for you and your budget.

(a) A travel agent
(b) A cruise line representative

(c)  A friend who has been on a cruise
(d)  A newspaper travel writer

*Notice that there are two issues at stake, not just one: whether to take a cruise and which cruise. We'd trust (d) first on both issues if you are fortunate enough to talk with him or her personally (and not just by letter to the paper). After that, we'd trust (c) and (a) more or less equally on the first question (one knows you and one knows cruises), and (a) on the second question. (b) could be expected to be biased in favor of a particular line, we'd think.*

69.  A number of your friends have taken up jogging, and you wonder whether your taking it up might have genuine health benefits for you.

(a)  Your family physician
(b)  A magazine for runners
(c)  A friend who teaches physical education in high school
(d)  The author of a best-selling book on sports medicine
(e)  A friend who is president of a local runners club

*(b), (c), and (e) might tend to be promoters of jogging, so we'd be mildly skeptical of any pro-jogging claims they might make (but less so of any liabilities of jogging that they might mention). We'd find (a) a more credible source, although many general practitioners may not have the time to keep up on such specialized areas. The best potential source is probably (d), although we'd be cautious unless we knew something about the author; he or she might also tend to exaggerate either the benefits—or the opposite—of jogging.*

70.  Spring has come, and it's about time to plant some tomatoes.  Or is there still a danger of frost?

(a)  Your local nurseryman or -woman
(b)  Aunt Maude, whose garden has kept her friends and family in tomatoes for years
(c)  A friend who grows tomatoes commercially
(d)  A friend who gives the weather report on Channel 8 News each evening
(e)  "Outdoor Planting Table" in *The Old Farmer's Almanac*

*Notice that this question is about weather, not tomatoes. We'd trust (c), though (a), (b), and (d) are also credible sources on this subject. As amazing as (e) sometimes is in the accuracy of its predictions, it may not be sufficiently fine-tuned to your locality.*

71.  You are looking at a sailboat that you're considering buying, but you've never owned one before and don't know whether you should buy this one.

(a)  The boat salesman at the marina that owns the boat
(b)  A boat salesman from another marina
(c)  A friend who has owned several similar boats
(d)  A buyer's guide published by a sailing magazine
(e)  Your own appraisal

*Of course you must consider (e), since if you have doubts from the beginning you're likely to be unhappy with the purchase. We think (c) can be either the best source on the list or the worst, depending on his or her judgment and experience. (What do you know about the friend's sailing experience?) Source (d) can be good with regard to the boat, but remember that the writers of the guide don't know you or your situation. (a) can be depended on to be more upbeat about the boat than a neutral party; (b) may want to sell you one of his boats.*

72. Even though your wisdom teeth are not bothering you, your dentist tells you they should be extracted because they may give you trouble later. Should you have them pulled or wait until they cause problems?

    (a) Your dentist
    (b) Your physician
    (c) A friend who is studying to become an orthodontist
    (d) Your sister, who is a dental hygienist
    (e) Your brother, who is six years older than you, who still has his wisdom teeth, and who has had no problems with them

    *Assuming your dentist specifies more clearly the risks you take by not having the teeth extracted now, we'd go with his or her opinion rather than any of the outside sources.*

73. Jones wants to quit smoking. He has heard of a kind of chewing gum that contains nicotine and is said to relieve some of the physiological symptoms of withdrawal. But the gum requires a prescription, is quite expensive, and he knows nothing of how well it works or any side effects it may have. Should he consider using it?

    (a) Jones's physician
    (b) An advertisement published by the manufacturer of the gum
    (c) A report in a newsmagazine of a study done on the use of the gum
    (d) A friend of Jones who has used the gum in an attempt to quit smoking

    *Clearly, opinion (a) is worth having, and required anyway for the prescription. We think that (c) is likely to be the next best source of information, since (b) may be one-sided and Jones may not have the same experience as (d)*

74. It's quite important that you travel to another town about four hours away by car, but you are concerned about whether you should drive because of adverse weather conditions.

    (a) The local television news
    (b) The local newspaper
    (c) A friend who has made the trip in all kinds of weather
    (d) The state police telephone service
    (e) The local police department

    *In descending order, we'd trust (d), (a), (e), (b), and (c). The local police probably know more about local conditions but less about conditions some distance away; the local newspaper's information may be too old to be useful; and we don't trust a friend who will drive in just any weather conditions.*

    For the following, discuss which source you'd trust more and give at least one reason why.

75. In the 1988 presidential campaign several Republican leaders expressed concern about the qualifications of Indiana Republican Senator Dan Quayle to become vice-president. Discuss whether such concerns should carry more weight with voters when expressed by Republican leaders than when stated by Democrat leaders.

76. Discuss whose opinion on the foreign policy of the current administration is more credible.
    (a) A former U.S. president of the same political party as the current president
    (b) A former U.S. president not of the same political party as the current president

77. Discuss whose opinion on the foreign policy of the current administration is more credible.
    (a) A Ph.D. in political science whose speciality is U.S. foreign policy.
    (b) The chairman of the U.S. Senate Foreign Relations Committee

78. Discuss whose opinion on the condition of the tires on your car is more credible.
    (a) A salesperson at Goodyear
    (b) A mechanic at a garage certified by the American Automobile Association

79. Issue:  A proposal for legislation regarding automobile insurance rates is on the ballot. Discuss whose opinion on the benefits of the legislation for consumers is more credible.
    (a) A spokesperson for the insurance industry
    (b) Ralph Nader

80. Is the pitcher tiring?  Discuss whose opinion is the more credible.
    (a) A minor league pitching coach
    (b) Reggie Jackson

81. Did life evolve or was it created? Discuss whose opinion is the most credible.
    (a) A biologist
    (b) A minister
    *Courage, fellow CT teachers!*

**Bank 3-6**

These are similar to the previous group, but the issues are somewhat more general.  You may want to add to or otherwise modify our lists of sources.  And do keep in mind that we are glad our livelihoods do not depend on a general consensus on *our* rankings.

82. Issue:  Should lawyers allow their clients to lie?

    (a)  The U.S. Supreme Court
    (b)  A law school professor
    (c)  A political science professor
    (d)  The American Bar Association
    (e)  A practicing defense attorney

    *This question is not so straightforward and simple as it might seem.  For instance, has a client who is forced to tell the truth in effect been denied an effective defense?  Can one even know that one's client has lied?  In forming our opinion on the subject, we'd be most influenced by the reasoning of the person who seemed to have the best grasp of the various subsidiary issues involved.  In other words, in this case it's the reasoning rather than the credentials of the reasoner that will carry the most weight.  (We would not anticipate that any of the sources listed would be deficient in powers of reasoning.)*

83. Issue:  Can Soviet compliance with a comprehensive nuclear test ban treaty be verified?

    (a)  Richard Viguerie (a right-of-center political columnist)
    (b)  A seismologist at the Seismic Monitoring Research Program at Lawrence Livermore National Laboratory

(c) The Deputy Assistant Director, Verification and Intelligence Division of the Arms Control and Disarmament Agency

(d) Mary McGrory (a left-of-center political columnist, maybe not quite so left of center as Viguerie is right of it)

(e) A spokesperson for the United States State Department who is visiting your campus

*We rank (b) first, then (c), (e), and (a)=(d)*

84. Issue: Whether the United States and the Soviet Union are approximately equal in strategic nuclear arms.

(a) The chairman of the U.S. Joint Chiefs of Staff
(b) The Soviet newspaper *Pravda*
(c) The U.S. Secretary of State
(d) Janes Publications (a respected British publisher on military weaponry)
(e) Jack Anderson (a syndicated columnist, well connected in Washington)

*We put (d) first and everybody else sufficiently biased to tie for last, except (e)—where we put Anderson depends on what source he quotes.*

85. Issue: Do mountain bicycles cause ecological damage when ridden on hiking trails?

(a) An environmental scientist at the Harvard School of Public Health
(b) The chair of the Sierra Club task force for determining club policy on the wilderness use of mountain bicycles
(c) A spokesperson for a bicycle manufacturer
(d) A park ranger from a state park where mountain bicycles have been permitted on hiking trains
(e) A representative of the Washington Mountain Bike Riders' Association

*Our ranking: (d)=(b) first, then (e)=(c)=(a)*

86. Issue: How have the economic policies of the Sandanista government affected the standard of living of most Nicaraguans?

(a) The editor of a daily newspaper in a small town
(b) A friend who just returned from a trip to Nicaragua "to see what was going on"
(c) A professor of Latin American Studies at Ohio State University
(d) A Republican state senator in Arizona
(e) A politically radical councilwoman on the city council of a middle-sized New York city

*Our ranking: (c), (a), (b)=(d)=(e). You might point out that it is difficult to use standard measurements of the effects of economic policies in places where a war is taking place.*

87. Issue: Whether graduate schools of business are turning out too many ill-prepared MBAs.

(a) The dean of the school of business at the University of Chicago
(b) The president of the Hewlett-Packard Corporation
(c) An editorial in *The Wall Street Journal*
(d) A recent graduate with a masters in business administration

*Our ranking: (c), (b), (a), (d)*

88. Issue: What levels of mercury and other metals in fish is high enough to make their consumption hazardous to humans?

   (a) An article in a journal called *Diet and Health*, published for vegetarians
   (b) A commercial fisherman
   (c) A family medical doctor
   (d) A spokeswoman for the National Institutes of Health
   (e) A toxicologist who works for the Los Angeles coroner's office

   *Our ranking: (d), then a substantial gap, then (e) and (c), another gap, then (a), (b)*

89. Issue: Whether a recently completed nuclear power plant is safe.

   (a) The power company that owns the plant
   (b) The contractor in charge of the plant's construction
   (c) A spokesman for the Nuclear Regulatory Agency
   (d) The president of the Sierra Club
   (e) A contractor hired by a nearby city who has seen the blueprints of the plant but has not made an on-site inspection
   (f) The author of a statistical study on safety, malfunctions, and accidents at power plants of the same type

   *Our ranking: (f), a gap, then (c), (e), then (a)=(b)=(d). We would not put too much confidence in any of the sources listed, as a matter of fact. (The last alternative, (f), is hypothetical; there are very few nuclear power plants of any one type; their construction has so far been "custom"—that is, idiosyncratic.)*

90. Issue: Whether it's possible for a person to have an "out of body" experience.

   (a) A psychic
   (b) A physicist
   (c) A person who claims to have had such an experience
   (d) A physician
   (e) A philosopher
   (f) A magician
   (g) A psychologist

   *Our ranking: (e), then everybody else. None of the other sources' experience or training is in what is possible. Were we evaluating the question of whether a given individual had actually had such an experience, we'd have required a different ranking.*

91. Issue: Whether Viking explorers actually landed in the New World before Columbus.

   (a) A historian
   (b) The publisher of a Norwegian-language newspaper in Willmar, Minnesota
   (c) A Norwegian archaeologist
   (d) An Italian archaeologist
   (e) An archaeologist of French ancestry who grew up in Texas

   *We take this one, including our ranking, lightly (although some Italians and some Norwegians don't): (e), (a), (c)=(d), (b).*

92. Issue: Were there unjustifiable cost overruns in the construction of ships made for the U.S. Navy by Lytton Industries?

(a) The chair of the Senate Armed Services Committee
(b) The accounting director for Lytton
(c) The Navy Chief of Staff
(d) The OMB (Office of Management and Budget)
(e) An article in *The Progressive* (a left-of-center political journal)

*Our ranking: (d), (a), depending on the individual's politics, then (c)=(e), (b)*


## Bank 3-7

Topics for brief essays

93. What factors help establish someone as an expert?
94. Discuss three ways a person can increase his or her background knowledge.
95. Are there conditions in which your own observations may not be totally reliable? Explain.
96. List several topics on which you may not trust yourself to give a totally unbiased judgment.
97. Discuss the conditions under which it is reasonable to regard an eyewitness account as credible.
98. Discuss the news media as a source of information about current events.
99. If the claims of an expert turn out to be in error, were you unreasonable in having accepted them in the first place? Why or why not?
100. How do you handle a conflict between the opinions of experts who do not agree?
101. Why do you suppose sensationalism (as found in supermarket tabloids, for example) has such a wide audience despite its frequent conflicts with our background knowledge?
102. Make up an issue and a list of sources like those in Bank 3-5 and give your own ranking of the credibility of the sources you listed.


## Bank 3-8

103. Repeat exercise 3-7 in the text, but this time list fifteen items that you believe to be true about current popular music.

104. To the instructor: Have a colleague come to your class and speak for four or five minutes about an unannounced topic. Afterward, ask the class some pointed questions about the speaker's appearance, presentation, and topic.

105. If there is a palm reader (or someone similar) nearby, send a couple of members of the class for a reading, then have them come back and make a report. Other members of the class should press for a full accounting.


## Bank 3-9

True/False

106. You should assume that the claims made by others are false unless you have some specific reason to believe otherwise.

*False*

107. For any two statements that conflict, one must be false and the other true.

    *False*

108. If you have reason to believe that an expert is biased, you should reject that expert's claim as false.

    *False (The possibility of bias is occasion to question his or her claims, to suspend judgment on them, to give more weight to alternative claims from unbiased experts, and so on— this is different from rejecting the original expert's claims as false.)*

109. Except when we have the means to record our observations immediately, they are no better than our memories happen to be.

    *True*

110. Fallible or not, our first-hand observations are still the best source of information we have.

    *True*

111. Reference works like dictionaries are utterly reliable sources of information—otherwise they wouldn't be reference works.

    *False*

112. Factual claims that conflict with what we think we know ought to be rejected, but only if we can disprove them through direct observation.

    *False*

113. A surprising claim, one that seems to conflict with our background knowledge, requires a more credible source than one that is not surprising in this way.

    *True*

114. Factual claims put forth by experts about subjects outside their fields are not automatically more acceptable than claims put forth by nonexperts.

    *True*

115. You are rationally justified in accepting the view of the majority of experts in a given subject even if this view turns out later to have been incorrect.

    *True*

NOTE: Items 57-60 were contributed by Dan Barnett; items 16-20 and 42 were contributed by Daniel Turner.

# Chapter 4
# Explanations

In the second edition of the text, we've imported the argument/explanation distinction into this chapter from Chapter 1, so exercises on distinguishing arguments and explanations are now found here rather than there. Experience with the text has shown that many students have real problems determining whether something is an argument or an explanation. This is sometimes true, of course, because it's sometimes very difficult or even impossible to tell whether a passage contains an argument, an explanation, or some combination. Unfortunately, it's often true because the student simply doesn't realize the different objectives of arguments and explanations. The latter is important. Hence there are a few pretty obvious exercises as well as some real tough ones.

The two categories do overlap: There are arguments that explain and explanations that attempt to convince. (There are also arguments the conclusion of which is that one explanation is better than another, which is a different matter, of course.) We've accommodated this overlap in the exercises, and we've added the further complication of distinguishing explanations from justifications, which are a species of argument.

Our idea is to foster in students some sense of what explanations are and how they operate, including an ability to evaluate them, without making them experts in explanation theory, action theory, or metaphysics (or requiring such expertise of the instructor). This turns out not to be as easy as it sounds; certainly not as easy as we'd like. We've identified a couple of problems that are apt to come up.

In the text we've limited causal explanations to physical explanations, segregating psychological explanations into their own category. Since psychological explanations, in our scheme, are those given in terms of one or more persons' reasons or motives, it appears that we have begged the question against the claim that reasons and motives can be causes. And so we have, but in a good cause and at no great expense. The benefit of our scheme is that it allows a relatively streamlined treatment of most explanations. The costs are twofold. The first is simply dogmatism in that we cannot give a convincing argument for why a reason is not a causal factor. (The question remains a controversial one among writers on the subject.) The second is that certain examples fall into a crack between physical and psychological explanations. ("He was unable to sleep because of his worry about her safety," illustrates the troublemaking group.) We expect that an accounting of explanations of this sort will blur the line between our categories. We are willing to live with that result. (We should restate here a point made in the text: Our three categories do not exhaust the varieties of explanations.)

The main point we wish to emphasize in our account of psychological explanations, whether or not they are viewed as causal, is that they make either explicit or implicit reference to psychological generalities, which allow for more in the way of exceptions than do the laws of physics or chemistry.

One other note on a similar subject: If you take a strictly reductionist view of the relationship between mental and physical acts (i.e., a hard interpretation of the identity thesis), you'd want to say that *all* psychological explanations reduce to physical explanations in the final analysis anyhow. Whether or not a person holds this view, very little is gained by it when it comes to a *practical* consideration of explanations. Even if we could give a purely physical account of, say, "She ran to the station because she thought the train was about to leave," by the time we were done talking about neurons and synapses we'd likely have forgotten about why we were considering the claim in the first place. The place for this issue, in our opinion, is in another course.

You may have students who think that the criteria for evaluating explanations provided in the text are a set of precise conditions that together are sufficient for determining the correctness of an explanation. They should understand that this is not the case; that is, the rules are not the analogue of, say, the rules for syllogisms. They are a set of considerations that, if kept in mind when encountering explanations, help one to distinguish those explanatory claims that merit further consideration from those that don't. Acquiring the ability to make this distinction is an important step toward becoming a critical thinker.

# Exercises Unanswered in the Text

## Exercise 4-1

2. Explanation
3. Argument; no justification
5. Explanation
6. Argument; justification
8. Explanation
9. Argument; no justification
11. Explanation. Could be an argument in some contexts.
12. Explanation
14. Argument; justification
15. Argument

## Exercise 4-2

1. Functional, psychological, physical
3. Yes
4. Our knowledge and interests
5. Pushing a line of questioning beyond the point of reasonableness (i.e., asking "Why" about every link in the causal chain, no matter how far it takes us back); requiring a reason or motive behind a causal chain; giving an explanation at the wrong level—either too simple or too technical for the audience
7. A physical theory
8. The explanation will make reference to (a) antecedent events or situations (b) a dependable psychological generality.
10. Yes
11. No
12. Is the explanation testable, relevant to the phenomenon, reliable? Is it circular or too vague? Does it require unnecessary assumptions, stand in conflict with well-established theory, or ignore a common cause? Does it explain as much as alternative explanations?
14. A literal comparison must be based on definite, identifiable similarities between the terms compared; a metaphorical comparison may not involve such similarities. (The line between the two may sometimes be difficult to draw.)

## Exercise 4-3

2. The phenomenon explained: why the grass in Southern California turns brown in the summer. The explanation given is causal.
3. The phenomenon explained: why refrigerators with bottom freezers cost more to run than those with top freezers. The explanation is causal.
5. The phenomenon explained: the decline in the ratings of "Hill Street Blues" during its sixth year. The explanation is psychological.
6. The phenomenon explained: why Montague dyed his hair black. The explanation is psychological.
8. The phenomenon explained: why spring came late this year. The explanation is psychological.
9. The explanation of why Thomas lost the gold medal is physical. The explanation of why she stumbled is psychological.
11. The phenomenon explained: the ban on two-way radios near blasting sites. The explanation is a combination of psychological (safety is the reason for the ban) and physical (radios transmitting on the wrong frequency can cause accidental detonations).
12. The phenomenon explained: why Pictionary placed second among hot-selling toys. The explanation is psychological.
14. The phenomena explained: (a) a coming famine crisis in Mali, and (b) doubled food prices and relief efforts in the other African nations mentioned. Both physical and psychological explanations are employed, the latter implicitly. The crises in Mali and elsewhere are accounted for primarily by a causal explanation (acute drought, decline in livestock and grain supplies are listed as links in the causal chain), while food prices and relief efforts require the addition of a psychological explanation (reasons for the decisions of those who set food prices and initiate relief efforts).
15. The phenomenon explained: the flaring of gas at petroleum refineries. The explanation is psychological (the reason for flaring is that the gas is unsalvageable) even though the physical impossibility of saving all the gas is mentioned.

## Exercise 4-5

2. This is a circular explanation. It also is untestable.
3. Uh huh, right. This explanation is too vague. It is also circular, if the sole criterion of biological "strength" is longevity.
5. Circular explanation
6. Vague, untestable, unnecessary assumptions, and, with some reflection, circular
8. Vague, untestable, unnecessary assumptions, and lacking in explanatory power
9. Ignoring a common cause — could be it was a good movie
11. Circular explanation
12. This requires unnecessary assumptions; and is unreliable.
14. This is vague, untestable, unreliable, and requires unnecessary assumptions.
15. A better explanation of Blackmore's negative results is the nonexistence of ESP. The given explanation requires the unnecessary assumption that psychic phenomena (a vague concept, of course) exist, and it is weaker in explanatory power as compared with the other explanation.

## Exercise 4-6

The explanations, call them R and D, compete with one another and are incompatible, since both are set forth as the primary cause of the drop in the inflation rate. The inflation rate's remaining low despite a reversal in or elimination of those factors cited in R would favor D. The rate's remaining low despite a repetition of the factors mentioned in D would favor R. Alternatively, a rise in the inflation rate despite a continuation of the factors mentioned in R would favor D, while a rise in inflation despite a repetition of the factors mentioned in D would favor R. One might look to history or to other economies for situations analogous to these.

### Exercise 4-8

3. The most credible, in our view, is Professor Shore and his associate James Randi because they can be expected to have the most experience in detecting trickery in similar cases. Roll also has some credibility, and could be expected to have experience in spotting trickery, but you would expect a professional magician (Randi) to be especially qualified to sniff out chicanery. On the other hand, the CSICOP team was not allowed to observe Tina (though it does not follow from this fact that we must accept a paranormal explanation of the phenomena).
5. The RSPK explanation comes up a distant second when compared with the natural explanation. The former is vague (what kind of "power" or "energy" are we talking about here?), which contributes to a serious lack of testability. It may be circular, depending on how it is described—is the "power" in question manifested in situations other than those that seem inexplicable? The existence of strange powers requires a suspicious assumption, and their existence conflicts with well-established theory, which does not support forces of the sort the explanation requires.
6. We don't think so. We find the second explanation easier to accept. In fact, we expect that cases of "average teenagers" hoodwinking adults are rather common.

## Chapter 4 Test Question-Exercise Banks

### Bank 4-1

Consider the following: Chris says to Lynn, "The car won't go because the battery was stolen."

1. If Chris was giving an argument what was the conclusion?

*The car won't go.*

2. If Chris was giving an explanation what was the fact taken for granted that was being explained?

*The car won't go.*

3. Suppose Chris and Lynn had just got in the car to go to the store, had tried to start it, and noticed that when Chris turned the key nothing happened. Chris got out, looked under the hood, came back and made her statement to Lynn. If this was the context of the statement was it an argument or an explanation?

*Explanation*

4. Suppose Chris and Lynn live together and share the car. They were talking about going to a movie and whether they should ride their bikes or take the car. Lynn doesn't know the car won't go, but Chris does and has found out why. If this was the context of the statement was it an argument or an explanation?

*Argument*

5. Could Chris have made this statement to argue that the battery was stolen?

*No*

## Bank 4-2

Determine which of the following passages contain arguments, which contain explanations, and which contain neither.

6. I did well in medical school in part because I was a philosophy major as an undergraduate.

*Explanation*

7. There must have been fire because there was smoke.

*Explanation*

8. Marijuana should be legalized because it is much less dangerous than alcohol or nicotine.

*Argument*

9. ". . . women are not creating culture because they are preoccupied with love."
—Shulamith Firestone, *The Dialectic of Sex*

*Explanation*

10. "A witty experiment by Philip Goldberg proves what everyone knows, having internalized the disesteem in which they are held, women despise both themselves and each other. This simple test consisted of asking women undergraduates to respond to the scholarship in an essay signed alternately by one John McKay and one Joan McKay. In making their assessments, the students generally agreed that John was a remarkable thinker, Joan an unimpressive mind. Yet the articles were identical; the reaction was dependent on the sex of the supposed author."
—Kate Millett, *Sexual Politics*

*Argument*

11. The reason he looks so awful is that he was up all night.

*Explanation*

12. He must have been up the entire night, since his eyes are red and swollen and his clothes are all wrinkled.

*Argument*

13. It is a very good idea to buy term life insurance rather than whole life insurance, because when you buy the latter you are in effect investing in a savings account that doesn't give you a very good return on your money.

    *Argument*

14. Your staff is having trouble learning to use your new computer system because the commands they have to type in are numerous, complicated, and not related to the machine's operations in any obvious way.

    *Explanation*

15. You really ought to relax a bit more with a good novel or something else you like doing.

    *Neither argument nor explanation*

16. Kim is really a terrifically talented photographer. Incidentally, did you know that he's just gotten a brand new 35 millimeter camera?

    *Neither argument nor explanation*

17. Even if the weather is clear tonight, you won't be able to see Halley's comet. The reason is that we're too close to the lights of the city to see anything that faint in the sky.

    *Combination argument/explanation*

18. Nevadans have traditionally opposed zoning ordinances because of their fierce individualism.

    *Explanation*

19. "But despite its enormous popularity, the Falcon did not bring in as much money as we had hoped. As an economical small car, its profit margin was limited. Nor did it offer many options, which would have greatly increased our revenues."
    —Lee Iacocca, *An Autobiography*

    *Explanation*

20. Possibly the reason you have trouble sleeping is all that coffee you drink.

    *Explanation*

21. "On the morning of his great 'peace' speech, Hitler had promulgated in the greatest secrecy the Reich Defense Law, which completely reorganized the armed forces and introduced a spartan war economy. While talking peace to lull the outside world, he was going to make ready for war as rapidly as he could."
    --William L. Shirer, *The Nightmare Years*

    *Neither*

22. Steve never calls Elisa. But she forgives him; she knows how busy he is.

    *Explanation*

23. Of *course* the real estate industry depends on tax benefits. Just look at how hard the real estate lobby fought to preserve those benefits.

    *Argument*

24. A recent study shows that you are three times as likely to suffer a heart attack just after you wake up in the morning than at any other time. It is theorized that this may be due to the blood's having more of a tendency to clot when you first wake up.

    *Explanation*

25. "As a matter of logical necessity, if someone is certain of something then there never is anything of which he or anyone else is more certain. . . . Thus, if it is logically possible that there be something of which any person might be more certrain than he now is of a given thing, then he is not actually certain of that given thing."
    —Peter Unger, *Ignorance: A Case for Scepticism*

    *Argument*

26. If you are seventy-five years old, the light you see when you look at the Big Dipper originated the year you were born.

    *Neither*

27. Directed by the solar wind, a comet's tail always extends away from the sun. Hence, when the comet itself is heading away from the sun, its tail precedes it.

    *Argument, although in certain circumstances this could be put forth as an explanation*

28. "Eskimos have a lower incidence of heart disease than do other populations, even though their high-fat, high-cholesterol diet ought to make them a high-risk group for heart disease. How do the Eskimos get away with it?
    "The answer lies in the kind of fat they eat. The Eskimo diet consists mostly of fish, seal, and whale. Fat from these animals contains 'omega-3 fatty acids,' which are structurally distinct from the 'omega-6 fatty acids' that most Westerners get from domestic meats."
    —Jennie Dusheck, *Science News*

    *Explanation*

29. "'Crash' is not a word pilots ever use. I don't really know why the word is avoided in describing what happens when several tons of metal plows itself and its pilot into the ground. Instead, we might say, 'He augured in.' Or, 'He bought the farm.'"
    --Chuck Yeager, *Yeager, An Autobiography*

    *Neither*

30. ". . .nothing in the universe occurs haphazardly; there is a cause-and-effect pattern to all phenomena, including weather. It follows, therefore, that . . . weather is predictable."
    --*The Old Farmer's Almanac*

    *Argument*

31. Even though fifty million American adults still smoke, the rate of cigarette smoking has declined over the past twenty years. Experts believe this is responsible at least in part for the decline in cardiovascular mortality.

*Explanation*

32. Although the case of the computer is double-insulated, as are the casings on the interface cables, the pins in the cable connections are not insulated. In fact, they are connected directly with the motherboard inside the machine. So, if you are carrying a charge of static electricity and you touch those connector pins, you risk frying the logic circuits of your computer.

*Argument*

33. The dietary laws of Moses forbid eating pork because pigs do not chew a cud and are therefore deemed unclean. But the babirusa, a pig native to Indonesia, was thought for a while to be kosher--it has a pinched stomach that biologists believed enable it to chew cud like cows, sheep, and other multiple-stomached animals.

*Explanation*

34. Unfortunately for those who wish both to eat pork and to follow Jewish dietary laws, the babirusa turns out not to be a cud-chewing kosher pig. This was determined after long observation of the animals produced not one sighting of a babirusa chewing its cud.

*Argument*

35. "All the major Modern movements except for De Stijl, Dada, Constructivism, and Surrealism began before the First World War, and yet they all seem to come out of the 1920s. Why? Because it was in the 1920s that Modern Art achieved social chic in Paris, London, Berlin, and New York. Smart people talked about it, wrote about it, enthused over it, and borrowed from it."
--Tom Wolfe, *The Painted Word*

*Explanation*

36. "More than half of all mothers with children under age six have jobs, and the number is increasing. Whatever its problems, day care is indispensable. . . ."
--Dorothy Wickenden, in *The New Republic*

*Argument*

37. Ralph Nader practically invented the issue of automobile safety when he published *Unsafe at Any Speed* a little over twenty years ago. It's true beyond doubt that hundreds, maybe thousands, of today's yuppies would not have survived to pursue their individual interests had Nader not put the interests of the public above his own.

*Neither*

38. The history of metaphysics in Western philosophy began with speculations by the Ionian cosmologists in the sixth century B.C. about the origin of the physical universe, the matter or stuff from which it is made, and the laws or uniformities everywhere present in nature.

    *Neither*

39. "This year's election scares me. It was conducted with a brutality and lack of attention to basic issues which appalled, and the success of its ugly strategies flashed signals that this was the kind of electioneering we should expect during the next two national campaigns of this century."
    —James A. Michener, on the 1988 presidential campaign

    *May plausibly be viewed as either an explanation or an argument*

40. "In California, without necessarily very much effort, almost everyone changes his life."
    —Herbert Gold

    *Neither*

    We find that students tend especially to see arguments in passages about current, controversial topics whether they're really there or not. Fresh ones from your daily newspaper make for good practice in class. If they can get those right, they can probably get the others.

## Bank 4-3

Identify any phenomena explained in the following passages and determine for each what kind or kinds of explanation are employed.

41. The class decided on four quizzes instead of two because two quizzes would have required that each one be quite long.

    *Psychological explanation*

42. The skin of some people is darker than that of others because of a greater amount of melanin present in the former.

    *Physical explanation*

43. Flowers have bright colors so that bees and insects can see them.

    *Functional explanation*

44. Owls have large eyes so that they can hunt at night.

    *Functional explanation*

45. Flying in an airplane with a head cold can be painful because changes in air pressure produce internal pressure in the sinus cavities.

    *Physical explanation*

46. The plane's departure has been delayed because of fog.

    *Physical explanation, although implicit is a psychological explanation: Presumably someone decided that the fog provided a sufficient reason for delaying the departure.*

47. "The United States plans to renounce its security obligations to New Zealand because of that nation's intention to ban visits by U.S. ships carrying nuclear weapons."
    —*Washington Post*

    *Psychological explanation*

48. The Washington Redskins didn't make it to the playoffs in 1985 because they had too many injuries.

    *Physical explanation*

49. "'The ranch lies in the swamps,' he warned me as we set forth, and this seemed an unlikely statement, since one visualizes a bull ranch as occupying hard, rough soil which strengthens the bull's legs, 'a common misunderstanding,' the matador assured me. 'It's the nature of the grass, the minerals in the water … something in the essence of the land and not its hardness. That's what makes a good bull.'"
    —James Michener, *Iberia*

    *Physical explanation*

50. The large roller with spikes on it that the tractor is dragging around the campus is a soil aerator. It pokes holes in the soil so that air and water can penetrate the surface.

    *Functional explanation*

51. Halley's comet was producing water vapor at the rate of four tons a second on November 5, 1985, when the comet was 170 million miles from the sun. This explains why it was unusually bright.

    *Physical explanation*

52. Sam gave up running because, in his words, "I'm bored with the park, and I'm bored with my neighborhood, and there's no other safe place to run in this city."

    *Psychological explanation*

53. "Nairobi, Kenya (UPI)—The killer famine has ended in most of Africa but long-term recovery has been jeopardized by the reluctance of Western nations to supply cash and farm equipment instead of food aid, the U.N. Food and Agricultural Organization reports."

    *Psychological explanation*

54. There's too much yellow in the photograph because you didn't take the filter off the lens before you snapped the picture.

    *Physical explanation*

55. "It is noteworthy that the negative reaction to the Soviet peace initiative came at the time when major experiments are to be performed within the framework of the U.S. 'Star Wars' program."
—Yuri Romantsov, Deputy Director of Tass, the Soviet news agency

*Implied psychological explanation*

56. That little hole is there at the front of the disk drive so that, if all else fails, you can eject a disk by poking a paper clip into it.

*Functional explanation*

57. The reason Edward Kennedy withdrew from the 1988 presidential race is that his own privately commissioned polls indicated that he would have a difficult time winning the election.

*Psychological explanation*

58. Highlighters don't really make a marked bit of text any easier to read; they simply call one's attention to the marked passage.

*Physical explanation*

59. In a report prepared at the request of the New Zealand AIDS foundation, Dr. John Seale, British expert on sexual diseases, said that the AIDS virus might have been man-made and released either deliberately or by mistake from a biological warfare research laboratory. There are serious flaws in theories that AIDS developed from spontaneous mutations of a human virus or was transferred to humans from animals, he said.

*Physical explanation. Had reasons been given for a deliberate release of the virus, we would add psychological explanation.*

60. The *cejilla*, or capotraste, both raises the tone of the guitar, producing a more brilliant sound, and it makes rapid playing somewhat easier by lowering the action of the strings.

*This complex little passage is primarily a functional explanation, although a physical explanation of ease of rapid play is also given. Would you say that the raising of tone is a physical explanation of the more brilliant sound and that a desire to produce a more brilliant tone is a psychological explanation of raising the tone, or neither?*

61. According to a letter to the editor of the *Athens Courier*, the last three winters in the United States have been unusually harsh "to test our faith in a power beyond ourselves."

*Functional explanation*

62. Question: Why doesn't the moon rotate? Answer: The moon does rotate, but in synchronicity with its revolution around the Earth, once every 27.32 days, so that the same face of the moon always faces us.
—adapted from the *New York Times*

*Physical explanation*

63. The reason behind the "spite fence" ordinance against fences more than six feet tall is the prevention of one person's effectively "walling up" a neighbor by obstructing the latter's view.

*Functional explanation*

64. "Here is what made Francine think he was becoming happier:  Dwayne began to sing songs which had been popular in his youth, such as 'The Old Lamp Lighter,' and 'Tippy-Tippy-Tin,' and 'Hold Tight,' and 'Blue Moon,' and so on.  Dwayne had never sung before."
    —Kurt Vonnegut, Jr., *Breakfast of Champions*

*Psychological explanation*

65. Dense fog can sometimes be dissipated by seeding the fog with dry ice pellets from airplanes.  If the fog is cold enough, the pellets freeze the droplets of water in the fog, which then form together as ice crystals that drop from the sky.

*Physical explanation*

66. The round thing is a thermostat.  It's a switch that turns current on when the temperature falls below a set level and off when it rises above another set level; it does that so that the coffee in the pot stays hot but never reaches the boiling point.

*Functional explanation*

67. The reason chronic abusers of cocaine suffer sleeplessness is that sustained use of the drug inhibits the body's production of serotonin, a substance known to be important in inducing sleep.

*Physical explanation*

68. I don't think Louise is losing her voice at all; I think she sang that song badly so they wouldn't ask her to sing another one.

*Psychological explanation*

69. The main reason ragtime music was frowned upon during the early twentieth century—the American Federation of Musicians passed a resolution condemning it in 1901—was simply that it was the music of black people and that it was first heard in sporting-houses, saloons, and honky-tonks.
    —Adapted from Max Morath, *Music Journal Magazine*

*Psychological explanation*

70. ". . . the cause of the Challenger accident was the failure of the pressure seal in the aft field joint of the right solid rocket motor."
    —From the report of the Presidential Commission on the Space Shuttle Challenger Accident

*Physical explanation*

71. "Synthetic rubber 'O-rings' . . . were emplaced around the circumference of the joints where the booster segments were mated to seal the joints against hot gas leakage. . . ."
—Richard S. Lewis, *Challenger: The Final Voyage*

*Functional explanation*

72. The Presidential Commission on the Space Shuttle Challenger Accident investigated pressure put upon NASA officials at the Kennedy Space Center as a contributing factor in the disaster. "Satellite customers requested changes in scheduled launch dates because of development problems, financial difficulties, or changing market conditions," the report said. As Kennedy processing people complained, this was no way to run a trucking business.
—Richard S. Lewis, *Challenger: The Final Voyage*

*Physical and psychological explanation*

73. "The sight of a single bloody, mangled body horrifies us. But if we see such bodies all around us every day, day after day, the horrible becomes normal and we lose our sense of horror. We simply tune it out. Our capacity for horror becomes blunted. We no longer truly see the blood or smell the stench or feel its agony. Unconsciously we have become anesthetized."
—M. Scott Peck, *People of the Lie*

*This is one of those explanations, noted above, that fit into the cracks between physical and psychological.*

74. "Employees gossip to explain a situation that they don't understand, one that might have a direct and personal impact on their own lives. They spread news where none exists. . . . Having some understanding gives everybody a sense of control over her or his life."
—Jack Levin and Arnold Arluke, *Gossip, The Inside Scoop*

*Psychological explanation*

75. Athletes take anabolic steroids to help build muscle and stamina during training.

*Psychological explanation, though many students will say that it's a functional explanation.*


**Bank 4-4**

The explanations in the following passages should be evaluated against the criteria listed in the text.

76. According to *Shape* magazine, "research shows that regular exercisers have far fewer diseases than their inactive counterparts." Dr. Joseph Cannon, a University of Michigan researcher, believes that the explanation may be that exercise raises body temperature, *Shape* reports. According to the magazine, Cannon maintains that the high temperature may benefit the body in the same way that fevers do, namely, by making protective white blood cells work faster, by increasing the number of antibodies in the blood, and by decreasing blood levels of iron, which microorganisms need to grow.

*Measured against the criteria in the text, Cannon's conjecture is reasonable (which does not necessarily mean that it is correct, of course).*

77. Alcoholics find it so difficult to give up drinking because they have become physiologically and psychologically addicted to it.

    *Circular*

78. Maria drove up from Austin today because I dreamed about her a few nights ago.

    *Irrelevant*

79. "Question: I have two healthy, vigorous Gravensten apple trees with trunks about 8 inches in diameter. . . . [E]very year they drop their fruit before it ripens."
    "Answer: Gravensten apples are a short-stemmed variety, and the falling of fruit before and during harvest sometimes results from the apples actually pushing themselves from the spurs as they increase in size."
    —Dick Tracy, University of California Master Gardener

    *A reasonable explanation. Note that this is not a case of "they fall off because they fall off."*

80. According to some psychologists, we catch colds because we want to. Most of the time we are not aware of this desire, which may, therefore, be said to be subconscious. Viruses are present when we have a cold, but unless we desire to catch cold, the viruses do not affect us.

    *Untestable; requires unnecessary assumptions*

81. Despite being arguably the best living writer of detective fiction, Elmore Leonard's books weren't selling more than 20,000 copies each. But his latest, *Glitz*, had 200,000 copies in stores in a very short time, the result of hard promotional work aimed primarily at chain stores by Leonard's publisher, Arbor House.
    —Adapted from a story in *Newsweek*

    *Reasonable explanation*

82. "People suffering from rheumatism often complain that their aches increase as bad weather approaches and barometric pressure falls. Some scientists believe that the decreased pressure of the air causes the air in the cells of the body to exert an increased outward pressure. This pressure may cause pain in the sensitive tissues of rheumatic persons."
    —*New York Times*

    *Reasonable explanation*

83. After a record-breaking rise over the course of several months, the stock market took a substantial nose dive during the first couple of weeks in January. Wall Street analysts noted that this was an expected technical adjustment.

    *If indeed this is intended to be an explanation, and commentators on the stock market seem to think they have explained something by such remarks, it isn't a very good one. It's marked by vagueness, a possible lack of testability, and possible circularity.*

84. According to projections by the American Cancer Society both the chance of developing cancer and the chance of dying of cancer have gone up over the past decade. Investigators have offered as an explanation of these discouraging statistics that, as infectious diseases and heart disease are better controlled, people are surviving longer. They are then more vulnerable to cancer, because their immune systems may be weakened by age.

*In terms of the text's criteria, the explanation is reasonable. But it does create a minor (but not unsolvable) puzzle: If people are more vulnerable to cancer because of a weakened immune system, then they should also be more vulnerable to infectious disease. We presume that these other diseases are to some extent controllable even for persons with weakened immune systems.*

85. The current crisis among American farmers is not all bad news. One reason our farmers are having a difficult time selling their crops is the fact that many countries that were incapable of feeding themselves only a decade ago are now self-sufficient and so no longer require American imports. China is exporting both cotton and corn and Bangladesh is now self-sufficient in food grains.

*Reasonable explanation*

86. One reads almost nothing good about the Soviet Union in the American press and hears nothing good about it from our politicians. This contrasts sharply with what I've seen on my five trips to Russia. Why the contradictions between what I've read about Russia and its people, and what I've seen? The answer can be traced to nationalism, compounded by 40 years of Cold War. Nationalism—patriotism carried a little too far—tells us we're the "best." It makes it awkward to publicly admit that foreign nations can do some things as well or better.
—Adapted from Brian Kahn, "What We Don't Know About the Russian People," *Sacramento Bee*

*Reasonable, but vague*

87. The reason you should continue to use unleaded gasoline in your late-model car is that leaded gasolines, even though they now contain less lead than they used to, still have enough in them to seriously damage your car's emission system.

*Reasonable explanation by our criteria*

88. They beat us as bad as one team could beat another in this league. We had some momentum at the beginning of the game, but we just lost it and never got it back.

*Vague, circular*

89. The reason we like some people and dislike others is because of our experiences with similar personalities in an earlier life.

*Untestable; involves unnecessary assumptions; reincarnation may conflict with well-established principles of biology*

90. Why have some people claimed to have seen UFOs or reported being kidnapped by aliens? According to Sebastian von Herner, Ph.D., of the National Radio Astronomy Observatory in Green Bank, West Virginia, " . . . only a few hundred years ago, many people, the well educated included, reported seeing the devil. . . . People tend to see things which 100 or 200 years later are believed to be nonsense." And Alvin Lawson, a professor of English at California State University, Long Beach, has speculated that people who claim to have

been aboard a UFO are in fact recalling their own births.

*The first "explanation" is not an explanation at all but a way of saying that UFO sightings are nonsense. The second remark is an explanation but a defective one in lots of ways: "Recalling" is vague and ambiguous, depending on what it means the explanation may be untestable and unreliable, and it may conflict with what we have reason to believe about our powers of remembering.*

91. —Prices keep going up and up.
    —Yeah, that's the result of inflation.

    *Circular*

92. I heard a feature on *All Things Considered,* the Public Radio show, on Donna Reed. I hadn't thought about her for years and years, although I used to be a big fan of her television show. That was on January 13th, 1986. The next day, January 14th, she was dead from pancreatic cancer. I'm telling you that's scary.

    *No it isn't. If there is an explanation intended here, it's most certainly an irrelevant one.*

93. "One study that showed an unexpectedly high prevalence of AIDS antibodies in Zairian patients sick with malaria led researchers to speculate that screening tests for AIDS antibodies may be less accurate in Africans or that malaria does something to the blood that produces positive AIDS tests results."
    —Paul Raeburn, Associated Press Science Editor

    *The correlation between malaria and positive AIDS tests may both be the result of a common cause: transmission of AIDS and malaria by mosquitos. Instructor please note: Research after the date of this writing may rule out this possibility (or it may confirm it).*

94. Janice has never done well in mathematics and she never will. She just doesn't have the head for it.

    *This is either circular or no explanation at all.*

95. The area along this part of the coast is especially subject to mudslides because of the type of soil that's found on the slopes and because there is not enough mature vegetation to provide stability with root systems.

    *Reasonable explanation*

96. Women usually have little solidarity because they've accepted the idea that their life is a failure without a man, and thus that they have to compete with each other for the scarce resource, men.

    *Vague; untestable*

97. Americans have the reputation of being the worst lovers in the world because they are the worst lovers in the world.

    *Vague; untestable*

98. Human beings have noses so that they look more like God.

   *Lacking in explanatory power and reliability; requires unnecessary assumptions, and is untestable*

99. Robin got what she worked so hard for, money; but she died unhappy. That's because of Karma, an undetectable force permeating the universe that affects people's lives.

   *Vague, untestable, lacks reliability and explanatory power, requires unnecessary assumptions, and may be circular*

100. Why is Tracy a Buddhist? Because she couldn't stand Baptists.

   *Lacks explanatory power*

101. Lots of people go to that restaurant because the local newspaper reviewed it and was very positive toward it.

   *May be reasonable but may ignore a common cause*

102. White males control most of the world's wealth because of the way things have worked out in history.

   *Circular, lacks explanatory power*

103. The reason physics, astronomy, and geology all have evidence that the earth and universe are more than 4 billion years old is that God wants to test our faith in the Bible.

   *Untestable, lacks explanatory power*

104. "A certain Canon Bourne and his two daughters were out hunting, and the daughters decided to return home with the coachman while their father went on. 'As we were turning to go home,' say the two Misses Bourne in a joint account, 'we distinctly saw my father waving his hat to us and signing us to follow him. He was on the side of a small hill, and there was a dip between him and us. My sister, the coachman and myself all recognized my father and also the horse. The horse looked so dirty and shaken that the coachman remarked he thought there had been a nasty accident. As my father waved his hat I clearly saw the Lincoln and Bennett mark inside, though from the distance we were apart it ought to have been utterly impossible for me to have seen it . . . it took us very few seconds to reach the place where we had seen him. When we got there, there was no sign of him anywhere. . . . We all reached home within a quarter of an hour of each other. My father then told us he had never been in the field, nor near the field in which we thought we saw him, the whole of that day . . . '"
—G. N. M. Tyrrell, *The Personality of Man*, originally published in the *Journal of the Society for Psychical Research* in 1893

   Tyrrell's explanation is that the two girls and the coachman had a telepathic vision: "The cause which set the telepathic machinery in motion in this case is obscure. No accident had happened to Canon Bourne. It more often happens that the vision coincides with some accident or peculiar event happening to the agent. . . . [Apparently] Canon Bourne unconsciously imposed the pattern or theme of his presence in that particular field, with details of horse, and so on, on the minds of his two daughters and the coachman."

   A different explanation is that of C. E. M. Hansel, who views the incident as probably a case of simple mistaken identity: "It would appear likely that the witnesses saw something they thought was Canon Bourne although, in fact, it was not Canon Bourne—that is, if his statements about where he had been that day were truthful or if he had had no lapse of memory. They reported that the horse looked dirty, but at a distance they would not recognize dirt as such; they would only infer its presence from the appearance of the horse. They apparently saw a horse that was similar, but not identical, in appearance to Canon Bourne's; they assumed it to be the Canon's and that its changed appearance was due to dirt."

—C. E. M. Hansel, *ESP and Parapsychology: A Critical Re-evaluation*

Hansel goes on to explain psychological experiments in which a drawing is exposed briefly to a subject who is then asked to draw exactly what he has viewed. Most subjects introduce changes and add details that were not present in the original drawing, Hansel says. The same phenomenon would account for one of the party "seeing" the Lincoln and Bennet label inside the hat, he hypothesizes. In addition, he believes that the members of the party would have conversed with one another and thus would have influenced the others by suggestion.

*Lack of space prevents detailed analysis. The most glaring defects of Tyrrell's telepathic explanation are that it requires us to make unnecessary (and implausible) assumptions and that it conflicts with well-established psycho-physical theory (e.g., that telepathy presumably is a transference of information that does not involve physical media and does not utilize any known sense organ). Incidentally, it can be pointed out in connection with this item that a shorter explanation that conflicts with well-established theory, like Tyrrell's, should* not *be favored over a more complex theory, like Hansel's, that does not make for such conflicts.*

105. From some angles a quarter will be seen as elliptical; while looked at from straight on it will be seen as round. The explanation is that the quarter changes its shape as the viewer changes vantage point.

*For those instructors so inclined, here is an opportunity to do a little epistemology.*

## Bank 4-5

Students may be asked to propose an explanation for each of the following phenomena. Their products can be given to other students for identification and evaluation.

106. The death rate from coronary artery disease (mainly heart attacks and sudden coronary death) has fallen abruptly since 1968.

107. Sometimes when you call a friend you discover that he or she was thinking about you just before you called.

108. Despite strong evidence that cigarette smoking is a major health threat, one-third of American adults are smokers.

109. Prenatal and birth complications are more frequent for babies who are born between January and April.

110. A road seems shorter the second time you travel on it.

111. During the 1970s nearly one out of every two marriages broke apart.

112. There were 9,100 fewer highway traffic fatalities in 1975 than in 1974.

113. If your fireplace smokes for a while when a fire is lit, you can stop it by burning a couple of sheets of newspaper on *top* of the wood when you light the fire.

114. The presence of oil pressure gauges and warning lights on the dashboards of automobiles

115. People with back trouble tend to find that sleeping on hard mattresses results in less pain than sleeping on soft mattresses.

## Bank 4-6

Here are some explanations for identification, analysis, appraisal, or what-have-you. We've also included a couple of items that look like explanations, but really are arguments, in case you want to construct another "Argument or Explanation?" exercise.

116. "What makes our marriage work is that we talk so much. That and the fact that he's so funny."
—Barbara Bush

117. "The Nixon administration authorized the Watergate break-in and coverup because it screwed up."

118. SHE: "Why on earth would that guy get up at 4 a.m. to deliver newspapers, do you suppose?"
HE: "He probably just likes getting up early."

119. Six years after running unsuccessfully for the U.S. Senate, former California governor Jerry Brown decided to plot a return to politics by seeking the chairmanship of the state Democratic party. When asked why, Brown replied, "The party needs some thrust. It needs rapprochement between the grass roots and the elected people. It needs to really become effective."

*Note that this explanation is really a justification offered by Brown for seeking the Democratic party chair.*

120. "As we have seen, the evidence for creation is enormous. Why, then, do many people reject creation and accept evolution instead? One reason is what they were taught in school. Science textbooks nearly always promote the evolutionary viewpoint. The student is rarely, if ever, exposed to opposing arguments. In fact, arguments against evolution are usually prevented from appearing in school textbooks."
—*Life -- How did it get here? By evolution or by creation?*

121. "Does California really need 3700 new laws? Only the most passionate advocate of big government would answer 'yes.' In fact, I vetoed hundreds of those bills because I don't believe it is wise or necessary for government to extend its reach into every aspect of our lives. Nor do I believe that government should spend money it can't afford to spend."
—California Governor George Deukmejian

*Comment: This could be viewed as an argument or as an explanation. Either way it's not very good.*

122. On October 19, 1987, the New York stock market crashed, sending markets around the world plunging the next day. A rally beginning at the beginning of the year had inflated stock prices and lowered their values. Meanwhile, the yield on bonds was rising as prices weakened. The yields gap became too great and people sold stocks and bought bonds, thus producing the crash.

*Comment: This doesn't seem defective according to our criteria. (It's pretty plausible on any criteria, as a matter of fact.)*

123. "Yes, there are unemployed people who steal to live -- because of taxes, government regulations, and labor laws that keep businesses from creating jobs."
—Rebuttal to Argument in Favor of Proposition 80, 1988, California Ballot Pamphlet

124. The reason there is a housing shortage is the massive influx of illegal immigrants into Texas, New Mexico, Arizona, and California.

125. The Red Cross first abandoned its legendary discretion in 1983 and publicly denounced Iran and Iraq for violating humanitarian accords. As a rule, based on very strict criteria of impartiality, the Red Cross never criticized anyone (a practice harshly condemned in the Nazi era). But faced with an Iranian declaration that prisoners who do not convert to Iran's brand of Islam offend God and do not deserve to live, there was little choice.
—Mauro Suttora, *Europeo*

*Note that this is an explanatory justification.*

## Bank 4-7

True-False

126. Explanations are designed to provide reasons for believing that a claim is true.

*False*

127. A bad explanation is usually more helpful to someone than no explanation at all.

*False*

128. There are only three kinds of explanations, physical, psychological, and functional.

*False*

129. Physical explanations of specific events always refer to events that happen or happened earlier than the one being explained.

*True*

130. It is often incorrect to evaluate an explanatory comparison in terms of its correctness.

*True*

## Bank 4-8

Short answer

131. The two parts to a psychological explanation of a specific event are:

    *Reference to an antecedent psychological event and to a dependable psychological generality*

132. One type of physical explanation explains specific events. What does the second type explain?

    *Regular occurrences*

133. What have we produced when we give a series of physical causes of the following sort: $w$ caused $x$, $x$ caused $y$, and $y$ caused $z$?

    *A causal chain*

134. Aside from the causal role it plays in the production of an event, what factors determine what we identify as the *direct* cause of the event?

    *Our own knowledge and interests*

135. Why do we generally have somewhat less confidence in a good psychological explanation than we do in a good physical explanation?

    *The generalities referred to in psychological explanations are somewhat less reliable.*

## Bank 4-9

Evaluate the following explanation in a brief essay.

136. The correlation between heavy smoking and lung cancer is not be be explained by saying that smoking causes lung cancer. There is a chemical substance, known as phenomenthasorbitol, that is secreted in the brain of some individuals, disposing them to take up smoking. This same substance triggers the growth of cancer cells, usually (though not always) in the lungs. However, phenomenthasorbitol cannot be detected in a person who has lung cancer, because the human immune system, in reaction to the unwanted cancer cells, destroys all traces of the substance.

    *We would especially want student's answers to refer to unnecessary assumptions and to testability.*

137. An interesting phenomenon has occurred in a number of American cities. A large portion of the employees in a new, modern office building will begin to exhibit a set of symptoms ranging from sneezing, itchy eyes, and sore throats to dizziness and fainting. There will be no simultaneous outbreak of these symptoms in neighboring buildings.

    One explanation for these occurrences is that a large variety of chemicals are used in the manufacture of new buildings (insulation, paint, adhesives, etc.) and the furniture that is placed in them. While the building and interior fixtures are new, they go through a period of "off-gassing," that is, throwing off gases from the chemicals in the building environment. Then, since modern buildings are built to be energy-efficient and hence are sealed from outside air, the ventilation system recirculates the gases over and over through the building before they are vented to the outside. Hence people working in the building are exposed to the gases, some of which can be low-level toxic, for a considerable period of time.

*We'd expect this explanation to get high marks from students. A really good answer might mention that there are other ways in which pollutants can get into a ventilation system besides off-gassing from new materials. (Many products, like copy machines, use chemicals that can also release gases into the environment, and a source of pollution near the system's outside intake can produce the same effects.)*

Note: Items 67-71 were contributed by Dan Barnett; items 1-10 and 96-103 were contributed by Dan Turner.

# Chapter 5
# Nonargumentative Persuasion

There isn't a lot to say about the material in the first part of Chapter 5, except that we and our students run across it more than any other kind of material found in the book. We note in the text that our list of nonargumentative persuasive devices is not exhaustive. Since many attempts to win acceptance for claims by means of the techniques of slanting will not fall under our list of those techniques (although we have expanded that list just a bit, by adding dysphemisms), we encourage our students to *explain* how and in what way a given passage is slanted, rather than to try simply to classify.

Maybe we're insinuating something ourselves by putting the section on the news media in this chapter, but this is where it seems to us to fit best. We have no such second thoughts about the section on advertising.

## Exercises Unanswered in the Text

### Exercise 5-1

2. "Negative cash-flow" is a euphemism. Harvey can't afford the trip.

3. "Resettled" is hardly the right word; this word is compatible with the desires of the "resettlers," while in fact these people were moved against their will. "Internment camps" is also euphemistic; and the use of the phrase "many people . . ." weasels; many thousands of West Coast Japanese were included.

5. "Slithered" is innuendo, insinuating that Thompson's book made it onto the best-seller list in some less than honorable way, or at least that it has no place there. The hint of snakes brings what for many people is a repugnant association to the book. It also downplays the fact that the book is a best seller. "If any more were required" implies that there was already plenty of evidence for the poor taste of the American people. "Insatiable" is hyperbole; it represents a mere taste for something as an obsessive craving. In this context, "the American people" is also something of a stereotype.

6. "Japan, Inc." is innuendo of a sort. It indicates that Japan acts in single-minded pursuit of business and industrial interests.

8. "Even though" is a downplayer. The definition of "capitalism" is a flattering persuasive definition.

9. The use of "preside" is a mild slanter (by comparison with the rest of the remark); the simile of the sixteenth century monarchs is a persuasive comparison.

## Exercise 5-2

2. The word "gooey" tells us right off what the *Newsweek* writer thinks of the story. "Choice nuggets" is obvious irony. In the last sentence, "but" downplays what's just been quoted, in favor of the claim coming up. "Fawning" hardly needs pointing out.

3. Unfortunately, the perfectly good word "rhetoric" seems to have been permanently relegated to the ranks of slanters. The use of ironical quotation marks and the phrase "dead hand" completes the list in this passage.

5. "Open season on blacks" is obvious enough as hyperbole to be taken back in the next sentence, or taken most of the way back. Given the nature of the subject, we are not sure whether to count the strong phrases that occur later on, for example, "morally bankrupt," as hyperbole or not. "19th century racist thinking" is probably not hyperbole, although the "19th century" part is exaggeration—the thinking referred to has been all too much a feature of the twentieth century as well. "Boiling cauldron" is emotively powerful language.

## Exercise 5-3

1. Delwood is not very intelligent.

3. Postal rates will be raised.

5. Uninteresting assemblyline work will eventually be done by robots rather than by people.

7. Fords and Mercurys are for sale at Owens Motors in Clifton Heights.

9. The PRS claimed responsibility for the killing of six government officials and three bystanders in El Salvador. In a letter to a newspaper, the PRS regretted the deaths of the bystanders but continued to threaten members of the government.

10. New two- and three-bedroom homes are for sale at Forest Hills.

## Exercise 5-11

2. The passage portrays Moynihan as full of hot air. "Huffer and puffer," "posturing," and "baloney" all have obvious negative emotive meanings. "Ignore Moynihan," Kilpatrick is telling us.

3. "The better to prevent AIDS, my dear," is a patronizing introduction. We'll get to horse laugh in Chapter 6, but the remark about the Puritans certainly is a case of it. For now, we'll call it ridicule. The use of irony quotation marks around "crisis" seems strange even just a few months after this remark was published—"crisis" is beginning to sound too weak to describe the situation. In short, the message is, "We'd do a better job of fighting AIDS if we'd forget the safe sex education and teach traditional morals in the public schools."

4. The "built-in ideological bias of the major media" is an unargued-for assumption. (Note that the section of the text on news media offers an alternative explanation: There are biasing factors other than ideology.) According to the passage, abuses in one place are "alleged," but repression in another is not. Other slanters include "America's Free World empire," including the capital letters. The message, put simply, is, "American news media

report more on human rights abuses in countries friendly to the Soviet Union than they do on such abuses in countries friendly to the United States."

## Exercise 5-14

What we'll do here is tell you what *The Conservative Digest* said about these questions. You can then convert its remarks into another exercise by asking the class to evaluate them. You may find other uses for them as well.

1. *CD* finds the term "badly deformed" highly subjective and faults the question for asserting that the baby could have lived only a few years. "Similarly afflicted babies have lived well into adulthood," *CD* says.

2. *CD* says the question is loaded; it implies that there has been a continuation of the nuclear arms buildup. The U.S. has in fact decreased its nuclear arsenal since 1972, according to the magazine.

3. This question "insinuates that the U.S. is the aggressor," writes *CD*.

4. "This question asserts Reagan's program 'results in hardship for many blacks.'" *CD* thinks a fairer question would be to ask whether his program does result in hardship for many blacks.

5. According to the magazine, the problem with the poll question is that it presents a biased statement in advance. The *CD* asks, given this biased statement, "is it any wonder they [the respondents] answered 'no' by a 66-21 percent margin?"

## Chapter 5 Test Question-Exercise Bank

### Bank 5-1

Slanting devices that appear in these passages should be isolated and discussed.

1. "Not everyone thinks that Senator Jesse Helms is the least admired American public figure (as opinion polls show). Even now one or two southern Republicans lust after a Helms endorsement."

   *"Not everyone" implies that most do—innuendo. The parenthetical remark is a proof surrogate. "Even now" insinuates (innuendo) that by this time hardly anyone has regard for Helms or for a Helms endorsement. "One or two" is a weasler. "Lust after" belittles the desire for a Helms endorsement: It cheapens both Helms and those who want his support.*

2. From a letter to the editor: "In Sacramento, money talks, which is why our politicians kowtow to the local developers. So much for voting for honest people whose primary concern should be people, not money."
   —*Sacramento Bee*

*"Money talks" is a cliché; "kowtow," though its original touch-the-forehead-to-the ground meaning is fading among all except those who read novels about the nineteenth century, still carries the sense of obsequious deference that brings it close to hyperbole here. The whole tone of the last sentence is slanted—it insinuates both that politicians are dishonest and that their primary concern is money (innuendo, and not very subtle).*

3. "Perhaps the 'religious leaders' who testified at the state Board of Education's public hearing on textbooks think they spoke for all Christians, but they did not."

*Note especially how quotation marks around "religious leaders" serves to question the credentials of those individuals.*

4. "The United States will not have an effective anti-terrorist force until the Army and the Air Force quit bickering about equipment and responsibilities."

*"Bickering" belittles the nature of the controversy.*

5. "Maybe it's possible, after all, to sympathize with the Internal Revenue Service. The woes that have piled up in its Philadelphia office make the IRS look almost human."

*"After all" suggests that the IRS usually deserves no sympathy; "almost human" implies that the IRS is actually inhuman.*

6. "We clearly can't trust the television networks, not when they've just spent two days interviewing young children on their feelings about the deaths of the astronauts. This attempt to wring every drop of human interest from the tragedy is either frighteningly cynical or criminally thoughtless regarding the damage that can be done both to the children interviewed and to children who see the interviews."

*"Wring every drop . . ." is a cliché and an exaggeration; the adverbs "frighteningly" and "criminally," approach hyperbole, especially the latter.*

7. "The anti-gun people think that just as soon as guns are outlawed crime will disappear and we'll all live together as one big, happy family."

*This trades on a stereotype; it's an excellent opening for a straw man.*

8. "Sam Goldwyn once said that an oral agreement isn't worth the paper it's written on. We wonder what he would have said about the Pennzoil-Texaco case."
—The Worcester, Mass., *Evening Gazette*

*(Background: In 1985 Pennzoil offered to buy out Getty Oil Co. for $5.3 billion. Although both parties agreed to the deal and press announcements were issued, Getty abruptly backed out when Texaco offered $10 billion for Getty. Getty accepted the Texaco offer, and Pennzoil sued for $14 billion in damages.) This is a persuasive comparison, of course.*

9. "Would you want to appoint my opponent as president of your company?"
—President Ferdinand Marcos of the Philippines, about his 1986 election opponent, Corazon Aquino, speaking to a group of Philippine businessmen

*Innuendo, based on a form of persuasive comparison*

10. "Early in the third phase of the Vietnam War the U.S. command recognized that the term 'search and destroy' had unfortunately become associated with 'aimless searches in the jungle and the destruction of property.' In April 1968 General Westmoreland therefore directed that the use of the term be discontinued. Operations thereafter were defined and discussed in basic military terms which described the type of operation, for example, reconnaissance in force."
—Lieutenant General John H. Hay, Jr., in *Vietnam Studies*

*Euphemism*

11. "Robert may be a pretty good gardener, all right, but you'll notice he lost nearly everything to the bugs this year."

*Innuendo, downplayer ("but")*

12. "The Soviet regime recently promulgated a law providing fines for motorists who alter their lights or grills or otherwise make their cars distinguishable. A regime that makes it a crime to personalize a car is apt to make it a crime to transmit a cultural heritage."
—George Will

*A persuasive comparison.*

13. "TO CHICO'S WHOLESALERS AND RETAILERS OF PORNOGRAPHY: DO YOU HONESTLY BELIEVE THAT PORNOGRAPHY HAS NO EFFECT ON THE BEHAVIOR OF PEOPLE?"
—From an ad in the *Chico Enterprise-Record*

*The phrase "do you honestly believe" is almost always used to establish without argument the claim that follows it. It isn't a type of slanter discussed in the text, though you might get away with calling it a proof surrogate.*

14. "Rodney Dangerfield? Yeah, he's about as funny as a terminal illness."

*Persuasive comparison*

15. "Within the context of total ignorance, you are absolutely correct."
—Caption in a *National Review* cartoon

*The height of downplaying, as it were, although the remark is clearly designed more to amuse than to persuade.*

16. "Handguns are made only for the purpose of killing people."

*This could be called stereotyping, an oversimplified generalization about a class of things, in this case, instead of people.*

17. "If we stop the shuttle program now, there are seven astronauts who will have died for nothing."
—An unidentified U.S. Congressman, after the Space Shuttle disaster of January 1986

*You'll recognize this primarily as a piece of pseudoreasoning (false dilemma), but the phrase "will have died for nothing [or in vain]" is a highly charged cliché.*

18. "It is, of course *conceivable* that the Khadafy regime has nothing to do with terrorist attacks on Israeli airports, but. . . ."

   *The downplaying "but" makes it almost certain that "conceivable" is functioning here as a weasler.*

19. "If the governor is so dedicated to civil rights, why is it that the black citizens of this state are worse off now than when he took office?"

   *Loaded question*

20. "Not only is chewing tobacco messy, it's unhealthy (just check the latest statistics)."

   *The parenthetical addition is a proof surrogate.*

21. "Once you've made our Day Planner a part of your business life there's a good chance you'll never miss or be late for another appointment."

   *"There's a good chance" is a weasler.*

22. ". . . despite the idealist yearnings in the body politic that this [the baby boom] generation supposedly epitomizes, the darker side of the lust for power is still present. Just witness the saga of the collapse of the once-promising career of Mayor Roger Hedgecock [former mayor of San Diego]."
   —Larry Remer and Gregory Dennis

   *The passage insinuates an almost obsessive desire for power on the part of Hedgecock.*

23. "If it ain't country, it ain't music"
   —Bumper sticker

   *Another hyperbolic false dilemma*

24. "Professor Jones, who normally confines his remarks to his own subject, ventured out on a high-wire to comment on the commission's findings."

   *Jones's credentials regarding evaluation of the commission's findings are impugned (innuendo) and the significance of his comments are downplayed.*

25. "I simply won't go into those cowboy bars; they're full of guys who disguise their insecurities with cowboy boots and hats."

   *Stereotyping*

26. "Can [Rep. Jack] Kemp or anyone believe that $27 million in 'humanitarian' aid would replace all that South Africa has done [to support Angolan rebels]?"
   —Anthony Lewis, *New York Times*

   *(Kemp sponsored a bill that gave $27 million in humanitarian aid to Jonas Savimbi's UNITA rebels for their fight against the government of Angola.) "Can anyone believe" suggests that the Kemp proposal is not to be taken seriously and is perhaps not taken seriously even by Kemp himself. The quotation marks around "humanitarian" serve to question whether the aid would be genuinely humanitarian.*

27. "Notre Dame people like to point out that, unlike other [college football] powerhouses, their players must face tough admissions standards, shoulder the regular course load and forget about being red-shirted to gain additional playing years. And, of course, it's a lot more fun to point out those things if your guys are out there stomping on 24-year-old golf-course management majors every Saturday, the way they used to."
—*Newsweek*

*Hyperbole; we expect there are football players for other teams who don't major in golf-course-management and are under twenty-four.*

28. "'Trivial pursuit' is the name of a game played by the California Supreme Court, which will seek any nit-picking excuse preventing murderers from receiving justice."

*Persuasive definition. Notice the switch in this one: Usually the slant is against the word or idea being defined; here the object of the attack occurs in the definition.*

29. "Any person who thinks that Libya is not involved in terrorism has the same kind of mentality as people who think that Hitler was not involved in persecuting Jews."
—Robert Oakley, U.S. Ambassador-at-Large for Counterterrorism, in an interview on National Public Radio's *All Things Considered*, in January 1986

*Persuasive comparison*

30. "Trivia question: In what comic strip does the following appear? 'A nation condemned to unrelenting cruelty by a clique of very cruel men, by a dictator in designer glasses and his comrades drunk with power and all its brutal applications'?

    "Answer: It does not appear in any real comic strip. It appeared in President Reagan's weekly radio address last Saturday. The nation is said to be Nicaragua. . . ."
—*Sacramento Bee*

*This one is pretty obvious. The* Bee *likens Reagan's description of Nicaragua to a comic strip (persuasive comparison) in order to discredit that description. Notice the powerful emotive language used in the description itself.*

31. "Although you were not selected to receive the award, I congratulate you for your achievements at California State University, Chico."
—Excerpt from a letter written by a university president and sent to an unsuccessful contender for a campus award.

*Downplayer: "Although"*

32. "Nazi propaganda chief Joseph Goebbels . . . justified the attack on thousands of Jews as a step toward removing an 'infection' contaminating Germany. 'It is impossible that, in a National Socialist state, which is anti-Jewish in its outlook, whose streets should continue to be occupied by Jewish shops.'"
— Reuters report in the *Sacramento Bee*, November 10, 1988

*Stereotype*

33. "Voting is the method for obtaining legal power to coerce others."
—From a commentary on a grocery bag urging citizens not to vote and thus not to encourage the majority to take away the life, liberty and the pursuit of happiness of the minority.

*Persuasive definition*

34. "To those who say that the analogy of Hitler is extremist and inflammatory in reference to abortion, I would contend that the comparison is legitimate. . . . The Supreme Court, by refusing to acknowledge their personhood, has relegated the entire class of unborn children to a subhuman legal status without protection under the law—the same accorded Jews under the Third Reich."
—Jerry Nims, writing in the Moral Majority's Liberty Report, October 1988

*Persuasive comparison*

35. "The beginning of the end of moral relativism was of course the landslide election of Ronald Reagan. He promised to bring the country back from its malaise, and in many ways he has succeeded, largely by speaking of and pursuing values the elite considers 'simple.' This is why symbolic issues ring with so many voters; whatever their narrow interests, they want to vote against relativism and for the values they share."
—Editorial, Wall Street Journal, October 3, 1988

*Dysphemism—opposite of euphemism—branding criticism of Reagan as well as public soul searching as "moral relativism" without examining its content*

36. To study the epidemiology of deaths involving firearms kept in the home, we reviewed all the gunshot deaths that occurred in King County, Washington (population 1,270,000), from 1978 through 1983. . . . A total of 743 firearm-related deaths occurred during this six-year period, 398 of which (54%) occurred in the residence where the firearm was kept. Only 2 of these 398 deaths (.5%) involved an intruder shot during attempted entry. Seven persons (1.8%) were killed in self-defense. For every case of self-protection homicide involving a firearm kept in the home, there were 1.3 accidental deaths, 4.6 criminal homicides. . . . Handguns were used in 70.5% of these deaths.

*We find this almost entirely free of slanters. "Only," in the fourth sentence from the end, downplays the number of intruders shot, but then it is a small number that's being downplayed.*

37. "Libya's strongman, Col. Moammar Khadafy, is the kingpin of Mideast terrorism, as Israeli and Western intelligence sources assert. Khadafy's 'who, me?' denials are as believable as would be his announcing conversion to Judaism."

*Both "strongman" and "kingpin" are slanters, and the second sentence is a persuasive comparison.*

38. "A political endorsement by the Rev. Jerry Falwell, the high-priest of holier-than-thou and 'let's hear it for apartheid,' would help a political candidate as much as an endorsement from the Ayatollah Khomeini."

*"Holier-than-thou" is a clichéd slanter; and the "let's hear it for apartheid" epithet is a jeer, regardless of the fact that Falwell supports apartheid in South Africa. The whole is, of course, a persuasive comparison.*

39. "As if they alone were concerned with clean air and pure water, these self-anointed environmentalists question whether there will be nitrate pollution from the new subdivision and whether Madrone Creek can accommodate storm runoff from the development. Their no-growth ideas are familiar to everyone in the community."

*"As if they alone were concerned" insinuates both that others are concerned and a smugness on the part of the people in question. "Self-anointed" is a standard slanter; nearly anybody who takes up a cause is self-anointed in a manner of speaking. "No-growth ideas" is probably exaggeration, although probably not hyperbole. If this entire passage were rewritten in neutral language, you couldn't tell which side of the issue the author was on.*

40. "The people who are fighting the Soviet-backed government in Nicaragua are freedom fighters just as George Washington was in our country."
   —Ronald Reagan

   *Persuasive comparison*

41. "He wants to talk positively, but that doesn't mean he won't continue to draw contrasts to his opponent."
   —Bush campaign chief of staff Craig Fuller, explaining that Bush's promise not to "talk on the negative side any more" did not mean that there would be a change in the Republican television campaign strategy.

   *Euphemism*

42. Just call him Zorba the Clerk
   — Joke about Michael Dukakis

   *Persuasive comparison*

43. "Who is to blame for this lackluster campaign?"
   —NBC's John Chancellor

   *Loaded question*

44. "The liberals — I'm sorry — but the liberals look at your paycheck the way Colonel Sanders looks at chicken."
   —George Bush

   *Stereotype; persuasive comparison, and (clever) innuendo in "I'm sorry"*

45. "When I saw the commercial, it came hard on the heels of a McDonald's commercial that was, compared to the Dukakis commercial, as informative as the Encyclopedia Britannica."
   —George Will

   *Will's persuasive comparison isn't any Encyclopedia Britannica of information, either.*

46. "I don't know what he's got against the Pledge of Allegiance."
   —George Bush, about Michael Dukakis

   *Assuming without argument something that needs argument. What should this be called, we wonder?*

47. "If they had been handling Gary Hart during the Donna Rice debacle, he would have been nominated for president — and he would be leading the race today."
   —Jesse Jackson campaign manager Gerald Austin, about the Bush campaign managers

   *One might have to explain the Donna Rice business for students to appreciate this piece of hyperbole.*

48. "Still, Bush may at least have the instinctive caution of a man without a compass."
—George Will

*A piece of innuendo*

49. "His wooden response to the obscene question whether he'd favor the death penalty if his wife were raped and murdered . . . called to mind Ogden Nash's Professor Twist, 'a conscientious scientist,' who is told, during a safari, that his bride has just been eaten by an alligator:
'Professor Twist could not but smile.
"'You mean," he said, 'a crocodile.'""
—Joseph Sobran, commenting on Michael Dukakis's response to a question in his television debate with George Bush

*Persuasive comparison (also could be called a horselaugh)*

50. "If Mr. Bush wanted someone against whom he could brightly shine, he could hardly have made a better choice."
—*New York Times*, about Bush's selection of Dan Quayle as his vice presidential running mate

*Sarcastic innuendo*

## Bank 5-2

These exercises are longer or more difficult. We'd ask students to discuss any instances of nonargumentative persuasion or pseudoreasoning and to explain any slanting techniques. As a further exercise they can be asked to rewrite the passage so that the informational content remains the same but the language is as emotively neutral as possible.

Since the following are filled with slanters and explaining them all would take up a great deal of space, we'll comment only on the ones we find obscure, unusual, or tricky.

51. "Citizens for a Clean Community caused quite a commotion the other day when it announced its campaign to end the sale or rent of so-called adult and X-rated videos and movies.
    "There immediately came the usual charges of censorship and free speech violations—as could have been predicted.
    "We certainly would be the first to defend someone's right to read or view whatever they please. But make no mistake, those who are offended by this smut have every right to express their frustration by protesting its distribution . . . . And this kind of material is completely debasing and has no redeeming value whatsoever . . . ."
—*Cascade News*

*Don't forget the downplaying role of "the usual charges . . . as could have been predicted."*

52. "What kind of crazy political system is it where a man who wants to run for president must begin by withdrawing from public life? It's become an American tradition, dating perhaps back to Richard Nixon in 1962. Gary Hart followed the pattern when he 'declared his "interest" in the presidency' (as the *Washington Post* chastely put it) by announcing that he won't run for reelection to the Senate this year. Good luck to Hart. I voted for him once before, and wouldn't mind voting for him again. But really. Is this necessary? . . . ."
—"TRB from Washington," in *The New Republic*

*There is a weak argument for withdrawal's having become a tradition, with Nixon the only example offered in evidence. What do you make of the reference to Hart's "'interest' in the presidency"?*

53. "The disbarment proceedings currently being conducted against New York Attorney Roy M. Cohn are the sickest example in recent memory of the sheer pettiness and vindictiveness of many liberals. Soundly and repeatedly trounced at the polls, they have retreated into their few remaining bastions and pulled up the drawbridges. Nationwide, their principal fortresses are the media and the academic faculties; in the case of New York, they also control the bar. It is this latter they are manipulating to wreak vengeance on Roy Cohn."
—William Rusher, in *The National Review*

54. Members of the baby boom generation, the generation that is now becoming yuppies instead of growing up, refuse to see the light. After being the center of the universe during the sixties and seventies, they expected to own it by the mid-eighties. They grew up believing they would have tremendous jobs, wonderful houses, exotic travel, great marriages, and beautiful children as well as European 'personal' cars, fancy music systems, high-tech kitchens and wine in the cellar. But it isn't turning out that way for most of them. Having glutted the professional marketplace, they live on depressed salaries; their dependence on immediate gratification causes them to spend like sailors—on the right stuff—driving prices of their playthings through the roof.

But they are addicted to their ways. Those who moved to Manhattan can't bear the thought of living anywhere else, but can't afford to live there. According to the *New York Times*, single-room-occupancy hotels that used to house the poor now contain tenants who cart in their stereos and tape decks, their button-down shirts, and their Adidas running shoes. One young woman says her bathroom is so filthy she showers with shoes on.

This insistence on doing it *right* bespeaks a refusal to grow up disguised as a commitment to—what?—"quality of life"? One no-longer-really-young professional says, 'It used to be you moved to the suburbs for the children. But on some level we still think of ourselves as children.' Peter Pan, call your office.
—*Very* freely adapted from George Will, "Reality Says You Can't Have It All," *Newsweek*

*This piece is very difficult to analyze on a part-by-part basis. Here and there you can identify a device (the last sentence reminds us of a horse laugh of sorts), but the entire piece is written with tongue at least in the direction of cheek. Exaggeration plays a role, with the activities of some baby boomers taken to represent those of an entire generation, but this is really an inductive argument. The choice of examples is prejudicial. You almost have to talk about the tone of the whole piece to do it justice.*

55. "Let's hear it for the Gross National Arsenal—and to hell with the pleadings of thousands of America's top law-enforcement officials, and with the recommendation of a Reagan task force on crime.

"The U.S. Senate has voted to gut what minimal protections have existed against interstate and quickie sales of handguns.

"The senators swallowed the arm-America philosophy of the National Rifle—make that read handgun—Association. The result is a dangerous bill that deserves prompt and lasting burial in the House. . . ."
—*Washington Post*

56. "The arms buildup that President Reagan promised us is now in its fifth year. We have spent a trillion dollars on it so far, and there is no end in sight, if the militarists continue to have their way. Do you realize how much a trillion dollars is? That's a one with twelve zeros after it. That's $4,000 for (or rather *from*) every man, woman, and child in the United States. And what is it all for? Are we any safer now for having spent all this

treasure?  Do you *feel* any safer now than you did five years ago?  Our children, who will eventually have to pay for all this because of the national debt, will look back on us as a generation of lunatics."
—Letter to the editor of the Bellevue (Ind.) *Star-Reporter*

57. "Britain has now confirmed that it will join the U.S. and withdraw from the United Nations Educational, Scientific and Cultural Organization at the end of 1985.  This decision by Prime Minister Margaret Thatcher, although condemned by the left-wing press, was an indication that the British have had their fill of UNESCO.

"Many UNESCO programs are widely regarded as reflecting a pro-Soviet bias.  UNESCO's proposed New World Information and Communication Order is considered by many experts to be a threat to freedom of the press.

"Primarily, however, it was the spare-no-expense budget of UNESCO, particularly in connection with its lavish Paris headquarters, that convinced the U.S. and Britain to pull out."
—Editorial, *Athens Courier*

58. "Well, it looks like the wimps are coming out of the woodwork all over the place.  If you're a man, the fashionable thing to be these days is 'sensitive.'  Articles with titles like 'Babies and Men,' 'The Divorced Father,' and— can you believe it?—'Men Cry Too' are cropping up all over the place.  You'd think today's males were unleashing the bottled up agonies of a couple of thousand generations from the way they like to step into the spotlight and bare their sensitive souls to anybody who'll listen.  They say there are more divorces today, and maybe because of the safety of numbers, a divorce is an excuse for a guy to become a softhead; the summons server may as well deliver a license to cry in public.

"If a kid wants his modern daddy to come out and toss a ball around, he'll have to drag him out of the kitchen first.  After making him take off the apron, of course, so he won't embarrass his kid in front of his buddies.

"It's a good thing the women are getting out there and learning to run the world.  Today's men are busily forgetting how to do it."

*This diatribe actually contains an rudimentary argument.  (The existence of the articles cited is offered as evidence for increased sensitivity among men.)*

59. "It [the feminist movement] was crazy.  The lunacy, unfortunately, wasn't confined to sex.  Male reviewers abased themselves before Miss [Susan] Brownmiller's book, *Against Our Will,* and the male editors of *Time* magazine, in a spasm of liberal gallantry, named her as one of its 12 Women of the Year, thereby atoning for five decades of Men of the Year."
—Joseph Sobran, "The End of Feminism"

*Not as "macho" as the previous one, but not without its slanters*

60. "The executives responsible for the recent corporate catastrophes popularly known as Agent Orange, asbestos, and the Dalkon Shield are not in jail and will not go to jail.  With the exception of informed victims, few of us describe these cases in the language of crime, even though in each case there is a wealth of evidence that victims were put at unacceptably high levels of risk of severe injury and death and that corporate executives knew of the risks, yet failed to take appropriate preventive action.  Even Morton Mintz, the award-winning *Washington Post* investigative reporter and author of *At Any Cost:  Corporate Greed, Women, and the Dalkon Shield,* a powerful indictment of the A.H. Robins pharmaceutical company, does not use the word 'crime' in telling the sordid tale of the Dalkon Shield."
—From Russell Mokhiber's "Criminals By Any Other Name," *The Washington Monthly*

*"Catastrophe," "powerful indictment,"* and *"sordid"* are obviously emotive; the rest is more subtle.

61. "Secretary of State George Shultz has never been accused of underreacting. In his latest poorly timed outburst, Shultz announced he would resign before submitting to lie detectors. The eruption was his response to a recent directive from President Reagan calling for polygraph tests for everyone with access to classified information. The idea for the directive is said to have originated with Defense Secretary Caspar Weinberger.

"It is easy to understand Shultz' reaction. As those who worked with him will tell you, he finds it easy to interpret any indication of White House support for Weinberger as an affront to his personal honor. Certainly the president was not thinking of Shultz when he issued the directive.

"The Secretary's temper has got him in trouble before. It is rumored that several top government officials would prefer to see him gone from the administration. Shultz's recent behavior can only solidify the opposition to him."
—Editorial, *Sierra Daily Journal*

*Notice the persuasive explanations.*

62. "Some of the ill will [at Dartmouth College] has been provoked by a student-run newspaper called The Dartmouth Review. Ten of the dirty dozen who destroyed the shanties [built on the Dartmouth campus as an antiapartheid protest] reportedly work for the six-year-old weekly, a New Right mouthpiece that is run independently of the college and has the support of such leading off-campus conservatives as William F. Buckley, Jr. Considered troublemakers by the administration and many faculty members, and disowned by former supporters such as Rep. Jack Kemp, the Review's editors traffic in outrage and offense .. ."
—*Newsweek*

63. The advertisement for Steven Spielberg's movie, "The Color Purple," shows a silhouette of a woman on a rocking chair, reading a book. Marlette, the political cartoonist for the Charlotte Observer, drew a cartoon take-off on this motif. In the "advertisement" for Marlette's "movie," which is entitled "The Colored People," Ronald Reagan is shown in silhouette on a rocking chair, reading a book entitled "Civil Rights Reversals." Beneath the picture is listed the "cast of characters": "Starring RONALD REAGAN as Whitey, EDWIN MEESE as Affirmative Action, and Introducing APARTHEID as The Good Old Days."

64. "Must the NFL—fat, sassy, the General Motors of professional sports—meet a similar crisis [to the one the National Basketball Association went through in 1983-84] before it tries to solve its own plague of drugs?

"For years, since Don Reese's personal revelation and charges of league-wide drug involvement, the NFL has lived under a cloud of suspicion. Initially, it seemed the front offices, deeply concerned that their image remain pristine, chose to look the other way. Now they've acknowledged the problem, and have chosen to push for testing; this year, eight franchises asked their players to undergo post-season analysis, but each was refused. . . ."
—Tom Jackson, *Sacramento Bee*

65. "It's past time that you and I and every other American asked some cold, hard questions.
"Who lost Iran?
"Who lost Afghanistan?
"Who lost Vietnam, Laos and Cambodia?

"Who crippled the FBI and the CIA?

"Who sold the Russians computers and other sophisticated equipment which have been used to stamp out freedom?

"Who is keeping our kids from praying in school?

"Who lets hardened criminals out on the street to kill, rape and rob again before their victims are buried or out of the hospital?

"Who says that America should do little if anything to help human beings who are daily being killed and beaten up by Marxist dictators?

"The answer in every case is LIBERALS.

"But America is waking up to what the liberals have been doing to it.

"To quote Michigan professor Stephen Tonsor, 'New Deal liberals are as dead as a dodo. The only problem is they don't know it.'"

—Richard Viguerie, *The New Right*


## Bank 5-3

Writing assignments: Construct seven sentences, each illustrating a use of the slanter indicated.

66. dysphemism

67. loaded question

68. proof surrogate

69. stereotype

70. euphemism

71. innuendo

72. hyperbole


Note: Items 31-35 were contributed by Dan Barnett; items 36 and 40 were contributed by Daniel Turner.

# Chapters 6 & 7
# Pseudoreasoning I & II

Our notion of pseudoreasoning is, more or less, the old notion of "informal fallacy." If you prefer that term, nothing we say about the subject in the text will cause any substantial difficulty. We prefer the pseudoreasoning label for a couple of reasons—it connects up nicely with "pseudoreason" and other "pseudo-" terminology, and it doesn't require distinguishing between an *informal* fallacy and a *formal* fallacy. Whether or not this traditional distinction has any practical value for a student, she would have to understand already the notion of valid argument in order to understand the formal/informal fallacy distinction. We do introduce the term *fallacy* right off in Chapter 6, in case you decide you need it.

Chapter 6 deals primarily with a particular kind of pseudoreasoning, the sort that makes appeals to our feelings, emotions, urges, drives, instincts, and so on; Chapter 7 covers much of what's left over. Together, they do not by any means exhaust the possibilities. As the text points out, many cases of pseudoreasoning simply have no standard names, and the number we and other writers have given names to would produce too long a list to deal with in a class. So we have to point out to students that a case of pseudoreasoning does not have to fit one of our patterns.

On the other hand, there are cases of *legitimate* reasoning that bear at least superficial likenesses to our patterns of pseudoreasoning, and students are often too quick to label as pseudoreasoning anything that resembles it. They tend to get tunnel vision and then combine that with a greater fear that they'll *miss* a case of pseudoreasoning than that they'll make a bad call the other way. One of these errors is not necessarily more important than the other— another thing we keep having to point out.

We tell students to think of the labeled patterns as "pseudoreasoning alert signals"—when a reader or listener encounters something that reminds her of one of these patterns, it should be looked at very closely to make sure it is not pseudoreasoning rather than immediately assuming that it is.

We've noticed a tendency on the part of students to confuse common practice pseudoreasoning (and, sometimes, two wrongs) with legitimate appeals to fair treatment. We get the first when $A$ thinks he can justify $X$ because some or lots of other people do $X$. But we get the second when $A$ says that, if he deserves criticism for doing $X$, so do all the other people who do it. Regarding the latter, of course, he's right, but students will often see legitimate appeal as more pseudoreasoning. Tunnel vision again.

We might also say once again that it is more important to be able to determine whether a given appeal or consideration is relevant to the issue at hand than to be able to determine which emotion the appeal is based on or which formula the consideration is an instance of. If you consider, say, #3 in Ex. 6-9 (about a brand of makeup designed to "bring out every woman's natural beauty"), you can call it apple polishing, since it flatters its intended victims, or appeal to vanity, or, at a deeper level, an appeal to insecurity. Like aftershave products with macho names for men, such ads play on our fears that we're not feminine enough, not masculine enough, not a good enough parent, that we don't have enough hair, or whatever. These fears can go pretty deep sometimes, and the ad makers certainly know that. But just how deeply you have to investigate before you know which label to apply to the pseudoreasoning is not crucial. As soon as we have *something* appropriate to call it, we can move on.

Concerning another matter, we've done some revision to the classification scheme, but nothing too dramatic. We've moved ad hominem from Chapter 10 and made it a general category, presiding over the subcategories of personal attack (under which we tuck circumstantial ad hominem, on the presumption that most of the "circumstances" that come into play are personal ones), pseudorefutation (which, in one of its forms, is what some call a "false charge of inconsistency"), and the genetic fallacy, which handles ad hominems that are aimed at groups, theories, histories, and so on, instead of individuals.

We've given a different name to the aubjectivist pseudorebuttal—it was too big a mouthful—calling it the "subjectivist fallacy." Besides the "true for me" version, we've included a variant we sometimes call the "just one opinion syndrome." We probably don't have to say more, but in case your students are unlike ours (who do this all the time), we get this version when someone discounts a claim as "just one (or his, or her, or their) opinion." We like to remind them that some opinions are a lot better than others—if their doctor tells them to stay off their broken leg or it will never heal, *that's* just his opinion too, but one they'd better heed.

We've also added a couple of new types, both sorely missed in the first edition, while resisting the urge to allow types to proliferate. New this time are burden of proof and slippery slope. About the latter, we imbed the pseudoreasoning in the failure to argue for the slipperiness of the slope; a good argument for the inevitability of the progression from one thing to another turns this into a legitimate slippery slope argument, with nothing "pseudo" about it.

Burden of proof is an elaboration on "argument from ignorance" (or "appeal to ignorance"), but is easier to remember and applies more clearly in many cases. For example, the conversation given at the bottom of page 182 and top of 183 in the text can be seen a subtle case of burden of proof, but would probably not be noticed as an example of argument from ignorance even by a careful reader (since it doesn't resemble the usual existence-of-ghosts cases). In order to capture these more subtle (but, we think, more prevalent) cases, we've given a broader characterization of burden of proof than is traditional for argument from ignorance. So, if one wishes to see the latter ("a lack of evidence *against* a claim is not evidence *for* that claim") as a special case of burden of proof, it shouldn't cause any trouble.

A second note on burden of proof has to do with its proper placement. The whole category comprises cases of *mis*placement of the burden, and we've given a rule of thumb about initial plausibility to serve as a guide against such misplacement. We realize that this is not the only way to do it. For example, in cases of whether Xs exist, one might say that the burden is always on the person who claims that they do exist rather than on one who says they don't. Sometimes this can conflict with the guide in the text: If the existence of Xs is a standard part of one's background knowledge, then, following our guide, he'd want to put the burden on the one who claims the nonexistence of Xs. (Who should be the first to have to make his case about the existence of external objects, Locke or Berkeley? The answer seems to depend on which guide you employ.) It may be, then, that in handling burden of proof in such a way as to make it more generally useful, we're asking for some trouble from the more philosophically astute. It's a chance we've decided to take.

You'll surely notice that the pattern we give in the text for false dilemma is also the pattern of the disjunctive argument, a valid form. Thus we have explained in the text when examples of the pattern amount to pseudoreasoning and when they do not—that is, when it is not reasonable to believe that the disjunctive premise is true and when it is reasonable to believe that it's true. It's wise to stress this point in class as well; one thing to say about it is that it points up the difference between logic (where we're concerned about the validity of the argument, and disjunctive argument is obviously valid) and critical thinking, where the soundness of the argument is what counts, including the truth of the premises. In cases of false dilemma, *we never get to the question of the argument's validity,* because, if we're familiar with false dilemma pseudoreasoning, we realize that the disjunctive premise has already tried to sell us a bill of goods. Unless we're considering an argument hypothetically (what would happen *if . . . ?*), we as critical thinkers are not ordinarily concerned about what follows from false premises.

While we're speaking of hypotheticals and false dilemmas, we want to mention that every false dilemma has a conditional variety, since, for every claim of the *Either P or Q* variety, there is an exact equivalent of the *If not-P, then Q* variety. So, since any claim of the latter type amounts to an equivalent claim of the former type, there is an "If . . . then . . . " version of every false dilemma. That is, if "Either X or Y" is a false dilemma, then so is "If not-X or Y." Students who have been through Appendix 2 pick up on this immediately.

Finally, we should remind you that some of the letters to editors and the "newspapers" they are alleged to have appeared in—those not credited in the acknowledgments section of the text—are fictitious. Any resemblance of such letters to those penned by actual people or of the publications to any that actually exist is (more or less) coincidental.

(Incidentally, you'll find that there is a total of exactly one problem bank for these two chapters. But it's enormous and should satisfy the needs of all but the most voracious of exercise consumers.)

## Exercises Unanswered in the Text

### Exercise 6-1

2. Two wrongs make a right
3. Appeal to consequences of belief
5. Scare tactics
6. Appeal to belief
8. Horse laugh
9. This looks like an appeal to pity, and it is. But it isn't pseudoreasoning. This is the sort of case that often gets tossed automatically into the pseudoreasoning category. But it doesn't belong there. "He" has given a perfectly good reason for patronizing the store; it just doesn't have anything to do with ice cream (although he does mention, in a separate claim, that the place "has the best"). This example illustrates the point that evaluation has less to do with classifying the emotion to which one appeals than with determining the relevance of the appeal.

### Exercise 6-2

2. Yes, unless it is known that the brand is a best-seller because of promotion or other facts that do not reflect on its quality
4. Yes
5. No
6. Yes
8. Yes. It would be relevant when you want to avoid disagreement, or, on the other hand, when you want to argue against their opinions.
9. Yes

### Exercise 6-3

2. Yes—she may not want to embarrass her parents (or she may wish to).
4. No

### Exercise 6-4

2. Yes, that the media are discourteous, that they distort the news, and that they will invent evidence to make a politician look bad
4. No, except for the one remark about distortion of the news—nothing in the passage addresses distortion of *this* kind of news, however

### Exercise 6-5

2. No, not on the basis of this ad
4. No, since not even pseudoreasons are given

### Exercise 6-6

2. No. Putting one in mind of the possibility is not giving a reason for anything.
4. No

### Exercise 6-7

2. Yes. Whether or not it is convincing is another matter.
4. No

### Exercise 6-8

2. No
4. No

### Exercise 6-9

2. (a) Whether he has earned an increase in his allowance
   (b) Pity
   (c) Not relevant to the question of whether he has *earned* an increase; the claims listed may support the conclusion that he should be given one anyway, however.
   (d) Appeal to pity

3. (a) Whether Limelight Blush will make you beautiful (if you're a woman)
   (b) Vanity (and, more subtly and more powerfully, to low self-esteem)
   (c) They are relevant, but, of course, unconvincing. There *is* an argument here: Any woman can be beautiful if her makeup does certain things; *this* make-up does those things; therefore this makeup can make any woman beautiful. Whether the premises of the argument hold any water is, of course, another question.
   (d) Appeal to vanity is not on our unofficial list.

*Items like the preceding can provoke interesting discussions about certain kinds of advertising, those that play on fears of not being sufficiently beautiful, intelligent, masculine, or whatever other features the advertisements themselves often dictate as desirable. (See Chapter 5 for further discussion of advertising.)*

5. (a) Whether continuing to jog will wreck your body
   (b) Fear of injury
   (c) The claims are relevant; if they were true they would make for good reasons for giving up jogging. They are most likely not true, however. (Notice the presence of hyperbole—see Chapter 5.)
   (d) Not pseudoreasoning (although it resembles scare tactics)

6. (a) Whether Israel should release the prisoners
   (b) The spokesman is trying to frighten Prime Minister Peres with the consequences on American public opinion of Israel's failure to release the prisoners.
   (c) Relevant. American public opinion is one of many factors that are relevant to the issue.
   (d) Not pseudoreasoning, given the issue as stated

   *Notice that we've given the issue the sense of a* practical *question for the Israelis. If it is seen as whether it would be morally right for them to release the prisoners, (c) would be "irrelevant" and (d) would be "scare tactics."*

8. (a) Whether the battery will last twenty-five years
   (b) Ridicule
   (c) Irrelevant (although the claim is really a nasty way of denying that the battery will last with no attempt at giving a reason)
   (d) Horse laugh

9. (a) Whether someone ought to "go in and kidnap some of the leaders of Lebanon and Iran."
   (b) This is an appeal to a sense of retribution, or, more charitably, a sense of fair play. Anger is clearly present too.
   (c) Irrelevant, especially if it is not known whether the Lebanese and Iranian leaders are responsible for the hostage taking.
   (d) Two wrongs, with maybe a dash of appeal to indignation thrown in

## Exercise 6-10

2. (a) Whether voting for Tomley will affect street crime
   (b) It sounds to us like a combination of fear and indignation.
   (c) The presence of widespread street crime may be relevant, but one person's fears are not much evidence. Further, it's worth noting that the person occupying the mayor's office is hardly in a position to make substantial reductions in street crime single-handedly. The sentiment is relevant only to the extent that such a person *can* have such effects.
   (d) Scare tactics, appeal to indignation

3. (a) Whether the student deserves a better grade.
   (b) This is not really an appeal to feelings or emotions but to subjectivity.
   (c) Not relevant
   (d) Subjectivist fallacy

5. (a) Whether Richard should be allowed to top off his tank
   (b) Not especially an appeal to feelings or emotions
   (c) Whatever we call it, Richard's claim is not relevant.
   (d) Your choice: Appeal to belief or common practice; some kind of case can be made for each.

6. (a) Whether they should slip in without paying.
   (b) The remark about lots of people doing it is not an appeal to a feeling, although the desire not to pay stems from greed.
   (c) The lots-of-people-do-it remark is not relevant. The desire not to pay is relevant, but:
   (d) We see this as a combination of selfish rationalizing, the greed being played down in favor of an appeal to common practice.

8. (a) Whether the Army Reserve disturbs the solitude of the park
   (b) Pride, patriotism carried a bit too far and in a silly context
   (c) Irrelevant
   (d) Not on our list, but we might call it "wrapping oneself in the flag."

9. We see this one just like number 6, above.


## Exercise 6-11

2. (a) Whether one ought to buy Sunquist grapefruit; whether Sunquist taste better than others
   (b) Greed
   (c) Relevant to the claim that Sunquist should continue to be successful, but clearly irrelevant to any claim about the quality of the fruit
   (d) Not on our list; greed, avarice, covetousness, lust for power, and so on, all operate similarly in cases like this.

3. (a) Whether readers should write to representatives in support of the MX
   (b) Fear of the Soviets' military strength
   (c) Relevant to the claim that danger from the Soviet Union should be decreased; but irrelevant to the claim that support of the MX missile is the best way to accomplish this
   (d) Scare tactics

5. (a) Whether Glen Haven Scotch will enhance your image (show that you've "made your mark")
   (b) Vanity, pride
   (c) Irrelevant. We figure that about the only thing one can infer from the brand of liquor somebody drinks is how much they spent for it; and this doesn't even tell you much about their financial status.
   (d) Apple polishing

6. (a) Whether prison guards' salaries should be increased
   (b) Sympathy; a sense of fair play
   (c) We find this perfectly relevant. Every consideration mentioned supports the main thesis.

8. (a) Whether the word *manpower* should have been replaced
   (b) Ridicule
   (c) Irrelevant. Whether there are other words that *could* be replaced for roughly similar reasons is irrelevant to the issue of whether *this* word should be replaced in this context. (Some words with apparent gender-specific parts may be more offensive than others to some people.)
   (d) Horse laugh

9. (a) There are two issues apparent: whether Jefferson's class is worth taking and whether "harping on the environment" is "a lot of hooey." There's actually a third implicit: whether the second of these should help settle the first.
   (b) The appeal is to the awfulness of the environmentalists' conclusions (as reported here).
   (c) Irrelevant to all of the issues
   (d) Appeal to the consequences of belief.

## Exercise 6-12

*This exercise, while a bit more complex, provides excellent practice in sorting out related issues and determining which considerations are relevant to which. There may be more ways to analyze the passages than ours; we invite you and your students to come up with alternatives.*

### Letter 2

*Issue:* Whether the magazine should run the ad
*Sentiment:* There are several appeals in this letter. The first is an attempt to arouse indignation toward people who have anything to do with or stand to gain by the promotion of tobacco use. Any such people, the letter claims, "have the blood of cancer victims" on their hands. The second appeal, less powerful perhaps than the first, is to one's sense of resentment at the power of the tobacco industry and its supporters. Finally, the comparison of tobacco workers with those who traffic in other drugs—marijuana, cocaine, and heroin—is designed to appeal to one's sense of proportion ("justice" may be too strong a word) in that, given the harm that tobacco causes, tobacco workers have no more claim to their jobs than those who deal in the other drugs.
*Relevance:* This letter brings at least one relevant consideration to bear on the issue. The claim is that every activity that promotes the use of tobacco (including running the ad) contributes to the serious detriment of people's health. This claim, if true, furnishes a reason for not running the ad, although it is not clear how much weight it should be given. The extent of the relevance of the consideration would be very difficult to determine, since it would be very nearly impossible to assess the effects of running the ad in *The Progressive*.

### Letter 3

*Issue:* Same as preceding letter
*Sentiment:* The last sentence of the first paragraph and the final paragraph both make the same appeal as letter 1 made, although it is done here with somewhat less vigorous language.
*Relevance:* Notice that the second paragraph and the first half of the first paragraph describe the ad but say nothing about whether it should be run—that the ad shows shrewdness on the part of the tobacco industry is not relevant to the issue. (Were the claim that the ad is fraudulent, on the other hand, it would be relevant.) The remainder of the letter can be treated much like the first letter.

### Letter 4

*Issue:* This letter addresses a different issue, namely, what would be an intelligent way to deal with the tobacco industry and similar industries that have hazardous effects.
*Sentiment:* There is much less in the way of emotional appeal in this letter. The first sentence begins such an appeal but then it is dropped and an entirely different approach is taken. The expression "kills people in wholesale lots" is emotively powerful, but appears

almost in isolation.

*Relevance:* We find this letter rather carefully conceived; it does not strike us as pseudoreasoning. You may find problems with it that we don't.

## Exercise 7-1

2. Straw man
5. Slippery slope
6. Burden of proof
8. Ad hominem: pseudorefutation
9. Straw man (in the second sentence; the first sentence may be false, but it isn't pseudoreasoning)

## Exercise 7-2

2. False dilemma
3. Ad hominem (pseudorefutation)
5. Straw man
6. Something here for everyone: ad hominem, straw man, and slippery slope
8. False dilemma (sneaked into the next-to-last sentence). There are other things going on in this one too: probably a loaded question near the beginning and another at the end.
9. Ad hominem (pseusdorefutation)

## Exercise 7-5

2. Ad hominem (pseudorefutation)
3. Straw man
5. Straw man
6. Ad hominem (pseudorefutation)
8. False dilemma
9. Ad hominem (pseudorefutation)

## Exercise 7-6

2. Clearly, *selfish* rationalizing won't do. Whether Edgerly is rationalizing about who properly should have the money is another matter, however.
3. Burden of proof, in Moe's second remark
5. Slippery slope
6. False dilemma. Clearly, there are other things going on in this passage too.
8. Ad hominem: personal attack (circumstantial)
9. Burden of proof (third sentence); ad hominem (personal attack), of a hypothetical sort that's easy enough to see

## Exercise 7-7

2. Such accounts could indeed be genuine explanations. Those we happened to read, however, were attempts to excuse the TWA hijackers—they were cases of two wrongs make a right. Whether any particular account is intended as a psychological explanation or a justification (and hence a potential piece of pseudoreasoning) can only be determined

through consideration of the total context and the emotive flavor of the language used.

3. There are obvious nonargumentative persuasion elements here; the whole thing smacks of straw man.

6. Reagan's remarks do count as something—if they are both true and indicative of his actual views, then they are evidence that he is personally not hostile to blacks. Beyond that, however, and especially with regard to the issue mentioned at the beginning of the passage, his remarks are a red herring (or, if you like, a smokescreen). They are clearly irrelevant to whether White House policy is hostile to black viewpoints, or whether it finds them unwelcome.

7. Straw man

8. The reference to the university is a red herring or smokescreen. The developers are in the business of making a buck, presumably, and one way to do that, if you're a developer, is to encourage people to stay around and buy a house.

10. We think there's a bit of false dilemma on both sides: The issue may be neither one that is *entirely* free speech nor one that "has nothing to do with free speech."


# Chapters 6 & 7 Test Question-Exercise Bank

*As mentioned at the beginning of this chapter division, there is only one bank of exercises for these two chapters. It should allow you to cover nearly any ground you like, however.*

Instances of pseudoreasoning in the following passages should be identified either by naming them or, where they seem not to conform to any of the patterns described in the text, by giving a brief explanation of why the pseudoreasons are irrelevant to the point at issue.

*For best results, as they say, we recommend that you mix these examples with cases of legitimate reasoning. Otherwise students come to expect that every item is pseudoreasoning, and they miss the most important kind of practice—distinguishing between real reasoning and its impostors. We've included an example of relevant support for a conclusion here and there, but those are easy enough to find or make up so we've left that mainly to you.*

1. "Free speech in the Soviet Union? Of course they have free speech in the Soviet Union. You are guaranteed the freedom to speak. You're just not guaranteed freedom after you've spoken!"

*A variation of the horse laugh*

2. Letter to the editor: "In rejoinder to your July 21 editorial, I certainly don't see how you can criticize the striking Springfield Unified School District teachers who carried their own signs. Let us not forget that you endorsed and supported City Council members Holt and Donazetti, who not only paraded up and down Main Street with their own placards, but

also got young children out of school to parade with them."
—*North State Record*

*Ad hominem (pseudorefutation)*

3. "No, I don't believe that Uncle Bob is really gone forever. He was like a father to me, and I believe that someday, somehow or other, we'll see one another again; I don't think I could go on if I didn't believe that."

*Appeal to the consequences of belief (wishful thinking)*

4. "No, I have not been to Russia, but I believe the President when he says that the Soviet Union is an evil empire. The Russians have but one goal—the enslavement of the rest of the world."

*Straw man*

5. "That, in sum, is my proposal, ladies and gentlemen. You know that I trust and value your judgment; and I am aware I could not find a more astute panel of experts to evaluate my suggestion. Thank you."

*Apple polishing*

6. "Why do I spend so much on clothes? Well, it's either that or look like a bum, and I know which of those I prefer."

*False dilemma*

7. "Hey Charley! Get a load of this: Frank thinks the Chargers will make it all the way to the Superbowl next year. Can you beat that?"

*Horse laugh*

8. "Sure, driving after you've been drinking can get you into trouble with the law, but if you're careful I don't think there's anything wrong with it. After all, everyone does it, right?"

*Appeal to common practice*

9. "You know very well I don't care what Mason says about investments or, for that matter, anything else. That guy is the most money-grubbing creep I've ever run into; all he ever cares about is where his next dollar is coming from. He can take his opinions and stick 'em in his ear."

*Ad hominem (personal attack)*

10. "Listen, friends, it's *our* money the Board of Supervisors wants to spend putting sewers and other improvements out there in that Antelope Creek development. And you know who's going to profit from it the most? The developers, who don't even live around here. I tell you, we have sat back and done nothing long enough! It's high time we told these out-of-town interlopers or antelopers or whatever they are to go mess with somebody else's town. I won't stand for it any more!"

*Appeal to indignation (There is a relevant appeal here, but the speaker is clearly trying to evoke outrage from his audience as well.)*

11. "I'll tell you why a hundred dollars is enough child support. You go into court and ask for more and I'll have my lawyer file a countersuit that will set you back a bundle in legal fees!"

*Scare tactics*

12. "I know it was not very nice to overcharge them like that for the room, but all's fair in love, war, and business, my dear. Besides, if the situation were reversed and *we* were desperate for lodging, they would have bled us for all we're worth."

*Two wrongs make a right*

13. "George, I speak for the rest of the neighbors on our street. Frankly, your front yard is a mess, and we'd appreciate it if you would do something about it. We put the time and money into making our places look nice, but the effort is largely ruined by one awful looking place right here in the middle of the block. We hope you'll do something about it."

*This might look like peer pressure or common practice, but we don't believe it's pseudoreasoning at all.*

14. Letter to the editor: "Your food section frequently features recipes with veal, and you say veal is a wholesome, nutritious dish. I disagree. Do you know how veal comes to be on your plate? At birth a newborn calf is separated from its mother, placed in a dark enclosure, and chained by its neck so that it cannot move freely. This limits muscular development so that the animal is tender. It is kept in the dark pen until the day it is cruelly slaughtered."
—*Cascade News*

*Appeal to pity*

15. Overheard: "When it comes to the issue of growth in this town, you're either part of the solution or you're part of the problem."

*False dilemma (Clever-sounding remarks like this one often disguise one type of pseudoreasoning or another.)*

16. Letter to the editor: "President Reagan continues to support Star Wars even though the Congressional Office of Technology Assessment Report has found that the Star Wars defense system risks a massive arms race. However, it is difficult to accept Reagan's pronouncements on the subject: He has publicly committed himself so strongly to Star Wars that it is impossible for him to reverse his position."
—*Chilton County Register*

*Ad hominem (circumstantial)*

17. "This business of American car manufacturers having joint ventures with foreign car makers really stinks. Think of the consequences of not being able to buy American-made cars. No jobs for American car workers, no big cars, no ready supply of parts, no consumption of American steel. I think we should prohibit joint ventures."

*Straw man*

18. "John, I just know you would make a wonderful and successful doctor. It's what your father wanted for you, and I know he would have been very proud if you were to go to medical school."

*Appeal to loyalty, or a variation on the theme*

19. "In spite of [Russian Premier] Gorbachev's hypocritical announcement that the Soviet Union has ceased underground nuclear testing, it is safe to assume that the Russians have done no such thing, for at present we have no means of verifying their so-called moratorium."

*Burden of proof*

20. Ad for a store that sells pianos: "Pianos are our *only* business. You'll get the best deal at the piano experts."

*Pseudoreasoning, although not of one of our patterns. (That they sell nothing but pianos is irrelevant to how much they sell them for.)*

21. "You bet I'll explain why FantasyLand [an adult bookstore] should be closed down! You go in there, and we'll send your license-plate number to the newspaper. You going to like people knowing what kind of stuff you read???"

*Scare tactics*

22. "This river has been changing its course every couple of years for the past few thousand years. Now they've decided that the banks need to be stabilized. Who does the Army Corps of Engineers think it is to come in here and decide they know something Mother Nature doesn't?"

*This kind of pseudoreasoning is of the "if it's been going on like this for a long time, then this is the way is should continue" variety—not one of our forms in the text. Sometimes the mere fact that something has happened in a certain way can provide reasons for leaving well enough alone, but the mere fact that this is the way it has happened is not itself such a reason.*

23. "Frankly, I don't think you would be satisfied with anything less than our Model 24, which allows for more expansion than any other personal computer in its class. The way you catch on to things—something I can tell just from the questions you've asked here in the store—you're not going to be happy with a machine whose limits you'll soon reach."

*Apple polishing*

24. "Are you telling me that you're twenty-one years old and you're still a virgin? I'd keep quiet about that if I were you—you'd be the laughing stock of the dorm if that were widely known."

*Peer pressure*

25. "I certainly don't think much of the Soviet form of government. A so-called 'free' election with only one candidate is not free at all.
    "Oh, I don't know. I don't think it's all that bad."
    "Why not?"
    "Because. Just look at our elections. Sure, we have more than one person running. But

the candidates are all alike. They might just as well be one person, for all the difference there is among them."

*Straw man, we trust*

26. "I say let's splurge and buy seats on the fifty-yard-line. I know a place we can get them for twenty-five dollars apiece."
   "Good grief! Maybe you want to spend every last cent we make on a football game, but not me. Are you nuts?"

*Straw man*

27. "Well! Finally, after all these years, the telephone company makes an error on my bill in my favor! And I'm surely not going to point it out to them. They've been gouging me since telephones first came into existence."

*Two wrongs make a right*

28. "So they came along and made me take my sign down because it was in violation of the city sign code. But look at the signs down in the next block, will you? They're under the same code and they're just like the one I had to take down."

*This may be an appeal to common practice, but there may be a reasonable appeal here as well, an appeal to fair play or equal treatment. (See Chapter 12 on treating like cases alike.)*

29. "Of course they have legal elections in Chicago. They just have to postpone certifying the results sometimes because the ballots get . . . uh . . . lost."

*Horse laugh, sort of*

30. "Hank 'Icebox' Gallagher, defensive lineman for the Tigers, knows his hamburgers—he orders them a half-dozen at a time. If *he* eats at Big Al's, then shouldn't you?"

*Pseudoreasoning as a result of a misuse of authority—see Chapter 3 on expertise*

31. When he was twelve, Walter Polovchak and his family were permitted to emigrate from the Soviet Union to the United States. Walter's father, however, eventually decided to return to Russia and was pressured by the Soviet Embassy to take Walter with him. The American Civil Liberties Union sided with Walter's father, rather than with Walter, who wished to remain in Chicago. When the case reached the courts, the legal arguments of the ACLU were criticized by some editorial writers on the grounds that in most other instances involving the rights of children, the ACLU had always sided with the child. Commented one law professor: "The ACLU's actions regarding Walter can be understood only in terms of 'an unwillingness to criticize communism.'"

*Ad hominem (pseudorefutation)*

32. "I don't see how you can possibly think Snellrod's Groceries has a good selection of fruit. Don't you remember how when he first moved here it was you who loaned him the money to get started? Sure, he paid you back, but did he ever do any favors for you? And now it's Snellrod, not you, who's getting all the business, all the attention."

*Appeal to spite*

33. "I don't like post-modern expressionism. It's another style spawned by the eastern art establishment, and, frankly, I'm tired of that group's dictating to the rest of the art world."

*Ad hominem (genetic fallacy)*

34. "Getting on Senator Davis' case about the propriety of some of his financial dealings strikes me as just plain carping. Davis made a considerable economic sacrifice when he left private industry and entered politics; the people of this district are lucky to have him there."

*Generic pseudoreasoning: Red herring*

35. From a letter to the editor: "They're wrong again, the doctors who say that the sun causes cancer. The four substances for all life are water, food, air, and sun. Everybody knows the sun opens the pores of your skin to release poisons; it cannot cause cancer. Cancer is caused by the toxins man puts in the air, not by sunlight."
—*Cascade News*

*Appeal to belief*

36. Overheard: "I don't know why Barbara won't go out with me. She must think I'm too intense for her."

*False dilemma (could be she finds him boring, if this remark is any hint)*

37. "Doesn't the fact that very few first-rank economists accept Marxist economic ideas suggest to you that there may be something wrong with those ideas?"
   "Not at all. Those economists are all tools of the ruling capitalist parties. I dismiss their views out of hand."

*Ad hominem (personal attack)*

38. "I just learned why all those theories about nonhumans building the Great Pyramids and the Easter Island statues and so on are full of baloney. The guy who wrote about them was once a hotel manager somewhere in Switzerland, and he was once convicted of embezzlement. No wonder those theories smelled fishy!"

*Ad hominem (personal attack)*

39. Letter to the editor: "On July 19, 1982, the Reagan administration announced it would not resume negotiations with the Soviet Union on a comprehensive nuclear test ban treaty, and in December of the same year Reagan ordered the U.S. to vote in the United Nations against a resolution outlawing all nuclear testing. Recently he has approved continuation of underground testing. For these actions the President has been harshly condemned by the bleeding-heart community.

   "Ultimately, however, Reagan is in the right. True, the Russians have just announced a moratorium on underground testing, no doubt as a propaganda ploy. But for a good many years they continued their own testing. Given this fact, it was fitting and appropriate that the United States did not discontinue its own testing program.
—*Tehama County Tribune*

*Two wrongs make a right? This is one of those cases, discussed in the text, that fits the formula but arguably is not pseudoreasoning but rather a case of "doing the same thing as the other guy for my own safety."*

40. After his return to India, Bhagwan Shree Rajneesh remarked that "the Soviet Union is far better than the United States." When the *New York Daily News* learned that the 53-year-old multimillionaire vowed never to leave India again, it said the following about his remark concerning the Soviet Union: "Shucks. It would have been a gas watching him accumulate umpteen Rolls-Royces and four battalions of aging flower children in the exurbs of Vladivostok." What technique was the *Daily News* using to "refute" the guru?

*Horse laugh*

41. From a defense attorney's concluding remarks at a trial: "This young man isn't guilty of a crime. No, ladies and gentlemen, it's *society* that's guilty of a crime, a crime against the very person on trial here. The society that wants to send him to prison for half his life is the same society that produced the rotten neighborhood in which he was born and grew up, that saw to it that he got a fifth-rate education, that gave him pimps and drug dealers for role models, and that offered him the choice between street crime or jobs nobody else would take. This jury—you—can do something to right the wrong that has been done to this young man. . . ."

*Red herring. The jury's job is to determine guilt or innocence; these remarks may be relevant to the kind of sentence that is deserved.*

42. "Listen. As long as you're going to live here at home and let your mother and me support you, you can rest assured that you're going to cooperate. And that goes for your opinions as well as for your behavior."

*Scare tactics*

43. What is the name of the mistake in reasoning committed by people who dismiss the policies of former President Reagan on the grounds that he is a former actor with a "cowboy mentality"?

*Ad hominem (pseudorefutation). The important thing is to notice that the reason given for dismissal of Reagan's policies is so very weak that it approaches irrelevance.*

44. "I know there are people who think that Sarah is too impetuous and flighty. But these qualities only make her exciting to me and make me love her all the more."

*This is really as much a case of self-induced self-deception as it is pseudoreasoning. We suppose wishful thinking is as close as our categories come to it. (Instances of this sort seem almost absurdly silly to most of us most of the time, but we must remember that reasoning about certain subjects becomes much more difficult when romance has one's brain chemistry temporarily, if pleasantly, out of kilter. It is part of the human condition that we are sometimes called upon to make crucial decisions at such times.)*

45. Letter to the editor: "Should people on welfare be allowed to play the lottery? I say no. It's time we did something about the welfare rip-off in this country. I believe in charity for the poor, but free-loading parasites who are too lazy to get out and do an honest day's work—I say cut them off at the knees!"
—*North State Record*

*This piece of vitriol is certainly pseudoreasoning; it seems to have one foot in straw man and one in appeal to spite or indignation, though it doesn't fit neatly into either category. There's plenty of Chapter 5 stuff here too!*

46. Another letter to the editor on the same subject: "It is positively disgraceful that welfare recipients can spend some of their checks on lottery tickets. If they can afford to spend their monthly allowances on the lottery instead of things that are essential such as food, shelter, and clothing, then they don't need public assistance. Why should I, a taxpayer, shell out my money to them for that purpose?
   —*North State Record*

   *False dilemma, with one horn of the dilemma a straw man*

47. "I know it probably puts me in the unfashionable minority these days, but I really don't care for Hank Williams's music. Ever since I learned that he drank a lot and took drugs I've felt that way."

   *While this may be ad hominem pseudoreasoning of the personal attack sort, it may also be a psychological explanation about somebody's reaction to Hank Williams and his music. It becomes more clearly the former if the person goes on to claim that the music in question is bad because of its creator's personal habits.*

48. "Because of [Abraham] Lincoln's policies the cemeteries of the nation were sown with 600,000 premature bodies, long turned to dust now, but in their time just as open to the promise of life as any young draft dodger of the 1960s."
   —From Tom Landess, "The Dark Side of Abraham Lincoln," *The Southern Partisan*

   *The reference to draft dodgers of the 1960s is an appeal to spite or indignation.*

49. In response to the woman who felt that Chicago Honeybear cheerleaders were being exploited by men who viewed the Honeybears as sex objects, *Chicago Tribune* columnist Mike Royko devoted a column to the subject, suggesting that such women are hypocrites. The most sexually motivated of all sports fans, he said, are females, who gather in front of the TV screen solely to gawk at the muscular thighs and lean hips of the "hunks."

   *Ad hominem (pseudorefutation)*

50. "*Revenge of the Nerds* is really a funny movie. I know, because I was a nerd myself, and that's really the way it was!"

   *Plain vanilla pseudoreasoning of no particular category. There may be two independent reasons here (see Chapter 8 on independent reasons) for seeing the movie, but neither of them supports the other. (Wonder what he means, "was" a nerd . . . ?)*

51. Theresa: "Hey! Take it easy with the salt. Don't you know too much of it is bad for you?"
    Daniel: "Aw, come on. They say that about everything."

   *The fact that many things are said to be bad for you is not relevant to the question of whether* this *thing is bad for you. When that is the association that's made, we have pseudoreasoning. On the other hand, if Daniel means, in effect, that since many of the claims about things being bad for you are false, this claim is probably false, then he is not guilty of pseudoreasoning; he has given an argument, although a weak one. Discussion of such arguments is found in Chapter 10.*

52. "Look, you can argue about it all day long, but I believe that Carmichael is the best person for the job and I hope he gets it. That's my opinion and it's as good as any other opinion, so we may as well change the subject."

*A version of the subjectivist fallacy. One person may be as good as another, and one may have as much right to an opinion as another, but not all opinions are created equal; those with better reasons are better opinions.*

53. "You can't trust the arguments you find in that magazine. It's well known as a right-wing apologist for the wealthy."

*Genetic fallacy. As noted in the text, arguments stand on their own feet; their origins are not important.*

54. "Toads do too cause warts. People have known that for centuries."

*A version of appeal to belief*

55. "It says here that smoke from wood-burning stoves, no matter how airtight they're supposed to be, gets into your house and is a health hazard."
"No way. We just spent close to a thousand on this new stove; what you're reading can't be true."

*Wishful thinking*

56. "It isn't so important how they're made or how long they last or how much they cost. These are the best jeans because they're incredibly popular right now. Sometimes I think you just don't understand style."

*Peer pressure (bandwagon), if the issue is whether the jeans are the best. There is also a danger of begging the question here (the question of what criteria should be used to determine the best jeans); see Chapter 9 for begging the question. If the issue is simply what jeans should you wear to be like everybody else, then of course there's no pseudoreasoning at all, and no real need for the remark in the first place. And it may be that, as the speaker says, your authors don't understand style.*

57. "Greyhound reminds you that when you travel by car, you take chances, especially if you are traveling alone. Anything can happen: dangerous thunderstorms [sound effect: thunder and lightening], engine trouble [sound of car failing to start], blowouts [tire blowing out, car screeching to a stop]. Next time [upbeat music] don't take chances. It's time to go Greyhound and leave the driving to us."
—Greyhound advertisement

*This may look like scare tactics, but the points made are relevant to the claim that alternatives to the automobile may be safer. Of course it doesn't follow that Greyhound is the best alternative.*

58. The Linberg's budget cannot really justify purchase of a new car, but they convince themselves that (a) they need a new car for reasons of safety [a debatable claim], and (b) they can afford a new car by "scrimping."

*Rationalizing*

59. "You shouldn't wear anything made out of white harp seal fur. Do you know how they get that fur? Baby harp seals, which are among the sweetest looking creatures on earth, are clubbed to death right in front of their mothers when they are just days or weeks old."

*This is not so clearly pseudoreasoning. Compare with item 14, which associates cruel treatment of calves with the value of veal as food. Truly, the killing of young harp seals arouses a great deal of pity, but, if the issue has something to do with whether they should be killed—including whatever uses their fur is put to—then the appeal to pity is quite relevant. Extended discussion of this item usually requires careful separation of the two issues (a) should harp seals be killed for human use? and (b) should harp seals be killed in this particularly brutal fashion?*

60. "Don't give me reasons where feelings are concerned; I can't be argued out of my feelings."

*This interesting remark is more complex than it looks. It's probably true that a person's feelings are at least sometimes things he or she can't do much about besides have them. But this is a different issue from the questions of whether a person should act on those feelings, or whether the feelings themselves are proper, appropriate, based on fact, and so on. That a person has certain feelings, and may be stuck with them, is irrelevant to the other two questions. To offer the former as a reason for a position on the latter issues is to commit pseudoreasoning of a form that at least vaguely resembles our subjectivist fallacy category.*

61. News Report: The city council's internal affairs committee voted to allow public access to the city's five creeks. But Councilwoman Shelly Harvard voiced strong opposition to the public access requirement. "Why do we want to allow access to the creek?" she asked. "Are we going to turn this into a town where anyone can walk across a person's lawn?"
Straw man

62. In a letter to the editor of a newspaper, a certified nutritionist criticized an editorial that had appeared earlier in the paper advocating a ban on raw milk. He wrote , "You call for an 'outright ban on commercial sales' of raw milk. Yet, by your own figures, you relate about 123 California cases of *salmonella dublin* [food poisoning], which represents a miniscule danger compared to the lives lost by smoking cigarettes."
—*Sacramento Bee*, August 12, 1985

*Ad hominem (pseudorefutation)*

63. "Did Amundsen beat Scott to the South Pole? Hardly, sir! 'Twould be disastrous indeed for the Empire if we allowed ourselves to believe Norwegians with dogs could ever best red-blooded English Males!"

*Appeal to the consequences of belief*

64. In an advertisement entitled "The second best smokescreen," the R.J. Reynolds Tobacco Company comments on the claim that cigarette smoke in the air may be harmful to nonsmokers. The ad first asks whether this charge is "wholly motivated by concern for the nonsmoker," or whether it is "the same old war on smoking in a new guise." It then goes on to quote a spokesperson for the American Lung Association who says that probably the only way we can reduce smoking is to make it nonacceptable socially. "Obviously," the ad concludes, "one way to make smoking 'nonacceptable socially' would be to suggest that second-hand smoke could cause disease."

*This doesn't seem to fit any of our categories precisely, except the generic one of red herring. Still, it's clear-cut (and rather clever) pseudoreasoning. Here's a way to spell it out: The cigarette company says, "If the Lung Association wanted to accomplish X (some rotten thing), then the way they would do it is by saying Y. And, sure enough, they're saying Y. Therefore, the reason they're doing Y is to accomplish X. Of course, the Lung Association may have other reasons for saying Y. In this case, the fact is that Y is pretty clearly true.*

65. Cheryl is deciding which of the girls who are rushing her sorority she wants most to join. Perl and Maria are trying to convince Cheryl that Debra is the best of the rushees and that Cheryl should vote for Debra when the time comes.

   "Debra has a wonderful personality, and she'll fit right in," Pearl says. "All the other sisters are going to vote for her."

   "And she'll be really hurt if you don't support her," Maria points out. "She thinks you like her a lot."

   "Besides," Pearl says, "she and I are very close. She's just about the best friend I ever had."

*In the last three speeches, we find (1) a bandwagon, (2) an appeal to pity, (3) some apple polishing, and (4) an appeal to loyalty.*

66. "Prop. 99 is a prejudiced proposition—flat out prejudiced. Takes one group of people and punishes them for their choice of lifestyle. You know Proposition 99 as the Cigarette and Tobacco Tax Initiative. But it doesn't punish tobacco companies—it punishes people who happen to smoke. Once we start passing propositions limiting people's freedom, we got a big problem. Suppose they start picking on you because of some choice you make—or the way you look. History tells us pretty soon that kind of thing gets out of hand . . . there are a lot of good reasons to vote no on 99. . . ."
—Text of political commercial urging no on Prop. 99 (which raised taxes on cigarettes) on the November 1988, California general election ballot. The ad was sponsored by the tobacco industry.

*There's an obvious slippery slope present, some nonargumentative persuasion ("punishing" people), and the business about who suffers, the smoker or the tobacco companies, is a red herring.*

67. "Politics, n., strife of interests masquerading as a contest of principles."
—Ambrose Bierce

*Persuasive definition*

68. "To the people who brought you 'The Great American Smokeout,' we make The Great American Challenge. We challenge the American Cancer Society to clean up the air in its 'smoke free' offices. We are willing to bet there isn't much cigarette smoking at American Cancer Society offices. But, according to a recent study from the National Institute for Occupational Safety and Health (NIOSH), cigarette smoke also wasn't the problem in 98 percent of 203 buildings reported to have indoor air problems. . . . Indoor air inspections resulting from worker complaints typically find viruses, fungal spores, bacteria, gases, closed fresh air ducts, and ventilation systems in need of maintenance."
—Full page ad in USA Today, November 17, 87, sponsored by the Tobacco Institute.

*A real, literal smokescreen! The Tobacco Institute is playing off reports of dangerous office environments, but the ad is meant to divert attention away from the even greater dangers of cigarette smoking. The ad may also hint that those who feel ill at the office should not blame the smoker; but the "Smokeout" was directed to actual smokers.*

69. Marty: "If we keep on the way we are going, we will destroy civilization on this planet."
    Tracy: "That's so depressing. I think we need to think well of things."

    *Appeal to the consequences of belief*

70. "Sure, driving after you've been drinking can get you into trouble with the law, but if you're careful I don't think there's anything wrong with it. After all, everyone does it."

    *Common practice in the last sentence; see the next item for more*

71. "Sure, driving after you've been drinking can get you into trouble with the law, but it you're careful and stay in control I don't think there's anything wrong with it. What makes something like that wrong is if you endanger others; so as long as you haven't drunk enough to impair your control you aren't doing anything wrong."

    *This is interesting. Regarding the issue of whether drinking and driving will get you into trouble with the law, the whole thing is irrelevant—a red herring. But, with regard to whether what's wrong is endangering others and that modest drinking doesn't do that (we can see this as whether such activity should be against the law), we have an actual argument. Given that most, or at least lots, of people find it difficult to tell when they've had too much to drink, it isn't a very good argument.*

72. Here's a "common practice" from the world of sports, overheard during the '88 Olympics: "Oh, I don't know. All athletes use some type of steroids in training and competition. "

73. In its July, 1988, issue, *Consumer Reports* criticized the Suzuki Samurai as unsafe and dangerously easy to roll over. A letter-writer in the next issue said in response: "In order to completely idiot-proof our society, we would have to surrender all freedom. Your suggestion that the Government protect us from this evil vehicle is just another step in a journey that could ultimately lead to an erosion of freedom in this country. "

    *This could be viewed as a slippery slope combined with a straw man, a false dilemma, or both.*

74. Evaluate the following: Rubwald went to the Saturday night fights. Outside the arena he ran into a man named "Bagan" that he knew. Bagan was taking bets on the main event bout between Svit Onion, a top-ranked contender, and Alf Granstan, an unknown fighter. Rubwald remembered that he went to high school with Granstan and so decided he should bet on his old schoolmate; he put down $100 against the favorite.

    *Appeal to loyalty, although it's less an "appeal" than a reliance on loyalty*

    And here, because we simply can't resist it, are a few more from the 1988 presidential campaign.

75. In the 1988 presidential campaign, Michael Dukakis's charge that Bush "is about to raid the Social Security trust fund." Scare tactics?

    *Dukakis wanted to frighten people of course. But he's not guilty of pseudoreasoning, since the charge, if true, is relevant to the issue of whether you should vote for Bush.*

76. Streetalk During the '88 Campaign: "It's obvious why George Bush picked Dan Quayle as his running mate. It's a foolproof defense against ever getting impeached."

*Horse laugh*

77. "The American people love boats, everybody has to relax, and I've got sunblock on but that light of yours is much too close to my face and it's burning me."
—Barbara Bush, when asked how George Bush could ride around in his fancy motorboat while people are starving

*The last phrase is a red herring (smokescreen, generic irrelevancy) known as Changing the Subject. Becoming indignant is THE recommended strategy for doing this effectively. The first two justifications are relevant, albeit marginally so.*

78. Letter to the Editor:
"George Bush says that he has not yet sorted out what the penalties for an illegal abortion should be. He does, however, believe that abortion should be illegal, except where the pregnancy results from rape or incest or where the mother's life is in danger. But unless abortion is legal for any women who thinks it is necessary for her own welfare, women will injure or even kill themselves trying to perform abortion on themselves or by going to illegal doctors. Abortion should not be illegal, and there should be no penalties to sort out."
—Letter, *Carton Falls News*

*False dilemma. This is not to say, of course, that the Bush proposal would not lead more women to injure themselves through back-alley- and self-abortion.*

79. INSTRUCTOR: On the basis of the vice-presidential debate, who do you think is most qualified to be vice-president, Quayle or Bentsen?
STUDENT: Bentsen. Quayle stumbled over his words, did not answer reporters' questions, was not as alert mentally as Bentsen, and did not have such a commanding presence.
*Question*: Is this ad hominem pseudoreasoning?

*Answer: Nope. What Quayle is here alleged to have done is relevant to the issue at hand. Of course it would be an ad hominem if the student had argued, say, that Quayle's taxation policy was unsound, based on the same reasons.*

80. During the 1988 presidential campaign, the Democratic vice-presidential candidate Lloyd Bentsen frequently dismissed the Reagan-Bush record on environmental issues by referring to Reagan appointees James Watt, head of the Department of Interior, and Anne Burford, head of the Environmental Protection Agency, as "the Bonnie and Clyde of the environment. " What pattern of pseudoreasoning is this?

*Horse laugh*

81. "Kid came to the door dressed up as President Quayle. Scared the hell out of me. "
—Johnny Carson

*Horse laugh*

82. By the end of the 1988 presidential campaign, opinion polls indicated that about 60 percent of the voting public thought that the campaign had been dirtier than most campaigns, and that the Bush campaign was primarily responsible for this. Answering this charge, Bush spokespeople frequently responded that the Democrats had instigated the negative campaign

at the Democratic convention, by ridiculing George Bush and by referring to the Reagan administration as a fish rotting from the head down.

*Two wrongs*

Note: Items 66-68 were contributed by Dan Barnett; items 69-71 and 74 were contributed by Daniel Turner.

# Chapter 8
# Understanding and Evaluating
# Arguments

This chapter is our principal introduction to argument. Instructors with backgrounds in logic will find this territory familiar; others will find that the basics come pretty easily.

As first edition users will have noticed, we've changed the diagramming method for this edition. Since it seems to have become nearly an industry standard, we've opted for the "Beardsley technique." For those instructors who do quite a bit of diagramming, we hope this will be helpful.

To clear up a couple of subtle glitches, we made some changes in a few definitions. These should cause no trouble. We've also changed "interdependent" to "dependent" when we talk about premises. Having two "I"-words was trouble-making, as it turned out. (Although it's pretty obvious, we should point out that whether we have dependent premises or independent premises tells us whether we have one argument or more than one argument.)

At least one of our correspondents noted that we shouldn't have rested the deductive/inductive distinction on the intentions of the person presenting an argument. But, aside from its being common practice, there are good reasons for resting it exactly there. The argument form, "If P then Q; Q; therefore P," is either an invalid deductive argument or a potentially useful inductive argument (it's the standard format for testing hypotheses in science). Whether the argument is any good, of course, does not depend upon its advocate's intentions, and that's the important point that is stressed in the text. If a person presents an argument he thinks is deductively valid, our readers, we hope, will notice both its invalidity and its potential strength as an inductive argument.

## Exercises Unanswered in the Text

### Exercise 8-2

2. Premise:     The Lakers almost couldn't beat the Jazz.
   Conclusion:  They'll never get past Dallas

3. Premises:    If the butler did it, he could not have locked the screen door.
                The door was locked.
   Conclusion:  The butler is in the clear.

5. However obvious this one may be, it requires some fiddling to get things explicit. The way we've done it here is to break it down into two arguments, with part of each unstated.
   Premise:     His mother's daughter only has one brother.
   Conclusion (from preceding) and Premise (for remainder): [Unstated:] He *is* his mother's daughter's brother.
   Premise:     [Unstated:] He can't be older than himself.
   Conclusion:  He can't be older than his mother's daughter's brother.

6. Premises: The state police have a weight limit.
Moscone is over the weight limit. (These two premises could be combined into a single conjunctive premise (see Appendix 2 about conjunctions).)
   Conclusion: Moscone will never make it into the state police.

8. Premises: He wastes his time watching daytime TV. (Although stated as a question, the claim is clear enough.)
   Conclusion: He doesn't have a thing to do.

9. Premises: There are more injuries in professional football today than there were twenty years ago.
If there are more injuries, then today's players suffer higher risks.
If players suffer higher risks, then they should be paid more.
   Conclusion: Today's players should be paid more.

## Exercise 8-3

We've left out the "probably"'s, and so on, that sometimes occur in the conclusions. These phrases tell us whether the person presenting the argument intends it to be taken inductively or deductively. They *could* have been included as introductory phrases to the conclusions. Your choice.

2. Premises: Kera, Sherry, and Bobby were all carded at JJ's.
They all look as though they're about thirty.
   Conclusion: I'll be carded too.

3. Premises: Seventy percent of the freshmen at Wharfton College come from wealthy families.
   Conclusion: About seventy percent of all Wharfton College students come from wealthy families.

5. Premises: She wears the finest clothes.
She orders the most expensive dishes.
When she goes on vacation, she stays at the best resorts.
[Unstated:] Anyone who wears the finest clothes. . .and so on, will be interested only in our top line
   Conclusion: She'll be interested only in our top line. (Show her the Ferraris.) *[The parenthetical remark can be taken as a further conclusion, with the unstated premise: Anyone interested only in our top line is someone to whom we should show the Ferraris.]*

6. Premises: According to *Nature,* today's thoroughbred racehorses do not run any faster than their grandparents did.
Human Olympic runners are at least twenty percent faster than their counterparts of fifty years ago.
   Conclusion: Racehorses have reached their physical limits but humans have not.

8. Premises: If this bucket has a hole in it, then it will leak.
It doesn't leak.
   Conclusion: It doesn't have a hole in it.

9.  Premises:   The last person we hired from Alamo Polytech was a rotten engineer and we had to fire him.
    Conclusion:  This new candidate (from Alamo Polytech, presumably) is somebody I won't take a chance on (that is, will not be a good engineer and will have to be fired).

## Exercise 8-4

2.  Independent
3.  Dependent
5.  Dependent
6.  Independent
8.  Dependent
9.  Independent

## Exercise 8-5

2.  Dependent
3.  Independent
5.  Dependent (in our opinion. Notice that the comparison of Hubbard with Jesus, even though it's preceded by an "also," is actually evidence for the differences in the views of Christians and cultists.)
6.  Dependent
8.  Dependent
9.  Independent (These may be related, depending on what the physicists' reasons are, but what we have here is a nutshell version of the teleological argument on one hand and an appeal to authority on the other.)

## Exercise 8-6

2.  False
3.  False
5.  False
6.  True
8.  True
9.  False

## Exercise 8-7

Note: Since there are occasions when a given argument could be either inductive or deductive, depending on what its presenter has in mind, we've sometimes had to indicate which is more likely given the way the argument is stated.

(Refer to Exercise 8-2)

2.  Inductive
3.  Deductive
5.  Deductive

6. Deductive
8. Inductive
9. Deductive

(Refer to Exercise 8-3)

2. Inductive
3. Inductive
5. Inductive
6. Inductive
8. Deductive
9. Inductive

### Exercise 8-8

(Refer to Exercise 8-2)

3, 5, 6, and 9 are valid

(Refer to Exercise 8-3)

3. Only 8 is valid.

### Exercise 8-9

Our opinions (which we hope agree with yours):

2. Probably true
3. Possibly true and possibly false
5. Probably true, but not something we'd bet on
6. Possibly true and possibly false. There are plenty of other reasons for the differences in GRE scores.
8. Probably true
9. Possibly true and possibly false. Ten years in a row is a lot of championships.

### Exercise 8-10

Note: For a conclusion of the sort $a$ is a $Y$, the type of premise we supply is All $Xs$ are $Ys$, where the other premise states that $a$ is an $X$. One could also make a truth functional inference by supplying the premise, "If $x$ is an $X$ then $x$ is a $Y$."

2. Everybody who is pretty sharp will get a good grade in this course.
3. There are puddles everywhere only when it has rained lately.
5. No party that produces tons of leftovers could have been very successful.
6. If the lights are bright, then the battery is in good condition.
8. All good senators would make good presidents.
9. All people who don't own guns are for gun control.

## Exercise 8-11

(Refer to Exercise 8-10)

2. Most people who are pretty sharp will get good grades in this course.
3. About the only times there are puddles everywhere is when it has rained lately.
5. Most parties that produce tons of leftovers are not very successful.
6. If the lights are bright, then the battery is probably in good condition.
8. Most good senators would make good presidents.
9. Most people who don't own guns are for gun control.

## Exercise 8-12

2. Everybody with a C going into the final and an A on the final will make at least a B in the course.
3. All students of Pepe Romero are good guitarists.
5. If the Federal Reserve Board chair is an experienced hand at monetary policy, then the board will make sure inflation doesn't reach 10 percent again.
6. Nobody with a well-known liberal policy on most matters stands a chance of getting elected in this county.
8. If half the people in the front row believe in God, then half the entire class believes in God.
9. If every Montezuma State student I ever met was career oriented, then so are all the rest of them. There are other possibilities—one is that the speaker has actually met every Montezuma State student.

## Exercise 8-13

(Refer to Exercise 12-12)

2. Most people with a C going into the final and an A on the final will make at least a B in the course.
3. Most of Pepe Romero's students are good guitarists.
5. It's very likely that, if the Federal Reserve Board chair is an experienced hand at monetary policy, then the board will make sure inflation doesn't reach 10 percent again.
6. Almost nobody with a well-known liberal policy on most matters stands a chance of getting elected in this county.
8. If half the people in the front row believe in God, then most likely half the entire class believes in God. Or, simply replace the premise with something like this: Of half the class (or more, depending on the size of the class) asked, half of them believed in God
9. If every Montezuma State student I ever met was career oriented, then it's very likely that all the rest of them are too. (Or: I've met most of the students at Montezuma State.)

**Exercise 8-14**

2.

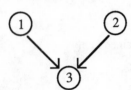

3.

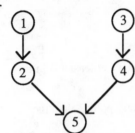

5.

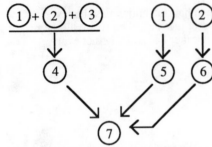

*We've duplicated (1) and (2) in order to keep lines from crossing up.*

**Exercise 8-15**

These exercises can be assigned with directions to include unstated claims or not to include them. We've diagrammed them as they are presented—that is, without any unstated claims. The unstated claims are given in the answers above and can be inserted as appropriate.

(Refer to Exercise 8-2)

2. (1) The Lakers almost couldn't beat the Jazz
   (2) They'll never get past Dallas

3. (1) If the butler had done it, he could not have locked the screen door.
   (2) The door was locked.
   (3) The butler is in the clear.

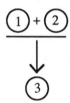

5. (1) He is not older than his mother's daughter's brother.
   (2) His mother's daughter only has one brother.

6. (1) Moscone will never make it into the state police.
   (2) The state police have a weight limit.
   (3) Moscone is over the weight limit.

8. (1) He doesn't have a thing to do.
   (2) He wastes his time watching daytime TV.

9. (1) There are more injuries in professional football today than there were twenty years ago.
   (2) If there are more injuries, then today's players suffer higher risks.
   (3) If [today's players] suffer higher risks, then they should be paid more.
   (4) Today's players should be paid more.

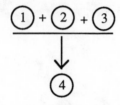

(Refer to Exercise 8-3)

2. (1) Kera, Sherry, and Bobby were all carded at JJ's.
   (2) They all look as though they're about thirty.
   (3) I'll be carded too.

3. (1) Seventy percent of freshmen at Wharfton College come from wealthy families.
   (2) Seventy percent of all Wharfton College students come from wealthy families.

5. (1) She wears the finest clothes.
   (2) She orders the most expensive dishes.
   (3) When she goes on vacation, she stays at the best resorts.
   (4) She'll be interested only in our top line. (Show her the Ferraris.)

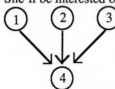

6. (1) According to *Nature,* today's thoroughbred racehorses do not run any faster than their grandparents did.
   (2) Human Olympic runners are at least twenty percent faster than their counterparts of fifty years ago.
   (3): Racehorses have reached their physical limits but humans have not.

8. (1) If this bucket has a hole in it, then it will leak.
   (2) It doesn't leak.
   (3) It doesn't have a hole in it.

9. (1) The last person we hired from Alamo Polytech was a rotten engineer and we had to fire him.
   (2): This new candidate (from Alamo Polytech, presumably) is somebody I won't take a chance on (that is, will not be a good engineer and will have to be fired).

(Refer to Exercise 8-4)

2. (1) You should drive me to the airport. *(Requires paraphrase)*
   (2) I'll pay you twice what it takes for gas.
   (3) You're my friend. *(Requires paraphrase)*

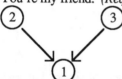

3. (1) If you drive too fast, you're more likely to get a ticket.
   (2) The more likely you are to get a ticket, the more likely you are to have your insurance premiums raised.
   (3) If you drive too fast, you are more likely to have your insurance premiums raised.

5. (1) If Jackson were president, he'd have lowered taxes by now.
   (2) If taxes were lowered, we'd have more money. *(Requires paraphrase)*
   (3) If we had more money, we'd be happier.
   (4) If Jackson were president, we'd be happier. *(Requires paraphrase)*

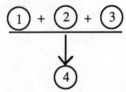

6. (1) The cat's food hasn't been touched in two days.
   (2) The cat's water hasn't been touched in two days.
   (3) The cat has run away.

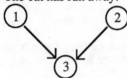

8. (1) By trying to eliminate Darwin from the curriculum, creationists are doing themselves a great disservice.
   (2) Darwin's discoveries only support the thesis that species change, not that they evolve into new species.
   (3) Darwin actually supports the creationist point of view.

9. (1) The Supreme Court's ruling that schools may have a moment of silence but not if it's designated for prayer is sound.
   (2) Nothing stops someone from saying a silent prayer at school or anywhere else.
   (3) A moment of silence will not favor one religion over any other.

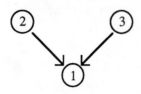

(Refer to Exercise 8-5)

2. (1) Jones won't plead guilty to a misdemeanor.
   (2) If he won't plead guilty, then he will be tried on a felony charge.
   (3) Jones will be tried on a felony charge.

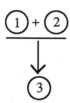

3. (1) John is taller than Bill.
   (2) Bill is taller than Margaret.
   (3) John is taller than Margaret.

5. (1) It is false (that all religions are basically the same and fraudulent).
   (2) The beliefs of Christianity and the cults are different.
   (3) There is a big difference between Ron Hubbard, who called himself God, and Jesus Christ, who said "Love your enemies, . . . ."

   *We can see doing this either of the following two ways:*

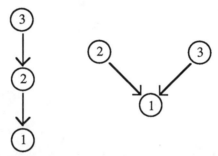

6. (1) We've interviewed two hundred professional football players.
   (2) Sixty percent of those interviewed favor expanding the season to twenty games.
   (3) Sixty percent of all professional football players favor expanding the season to twenty games.

   *Numbers (1) and (2) can be put together as a conjunction, as in the original passage.*

8. (1) Exercise may help chronic male smokers kick the habit.
   (2) Thirty young male smokers were put on a three-month program of vigorous exercise.
   (3) A year later only fourteen percent of them still smoked.
   (4) Thirty young male smokers who did not exercise were checked a year later and sixty percent still smoked.

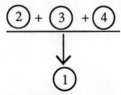

9. (1) God exists. (I believe in God.)
   (2) The universe couldn't have arisen by chance.
   (3) More and more physicists believe in God. . . .

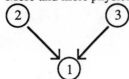

### Exercise 8-16

We've made the unstated claims in numbers 3 and 5 explicit.

2. (1) The federal deficit must be reduced.
   (2) It [the deficit] has contributed to inflation.
   (3) It [the deficit] has hurt American exports.

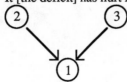

3. (1) Professional boxing should be outlawed.
   (2) Boxing almost always leads to brain damage.
   (3) Anything that leads to brain damage should be outlawed.
   (4) Boxing supports organized crime.
   (5) [Unstated:] Anything that supports organized crime should be outlawed.

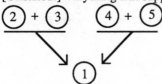

5. (1) One shouldn't vote for Jackson.
   (2) Jackson is too radical.
   (3) Jackson is too inexperienced.
   (4) Jackson's lack of experience would have made him a dangerous president.
   (5) [Unstated:] One shouldn't vote for anybody who is too radical.
   (6) [Unstated:] One shouldn't vote for anybody who would be a dangerous president.

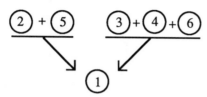

*Claim (3) is included, but, given (4), it's redundant.*

**Exercise 8-17**

2. (1) You should listen to loud music only when we are not at home.
   (2) It [loud music] bothers us.
   (3) We're your parents.
   (4) [Unstated:] You shouldn't do things that bother your parents.

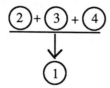

3. *There is more than one reasonable interpretation of this one. Here's ours:*
   (1) One cause of wasteful defense spending has been congressional boondoggling (members of Congress adding spending to benefit their districts).
   (2) There will be less boondoggling with Les Aspin as chair of the Armed Services Committee.
   (3) Aspin has an insider's knowledge of how the Pentagon operates.
   (4) Aspin will not have much patience with congressional boondoggling.
   (5) [Unstated:] There will be less wasteful defense spending with Aspin as chair of the Armed Services Committee.
   (6) [Unstated:] An Armed Services Committee Chair with an insider's knowledge of how the Pentagon operates can keep down wasteful defense spending.

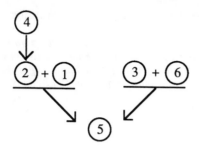

5. (1) The country cannot afford to celebrate about high growth and low inflation very long.
   (2) We have floated out of recession on a sea of red ink.
   (3) If some changes aren't made soon, we are in danger of being drowned in red ink.
   (4) The Reagan administration's tax breaks and defense spending increases also produced record-breaking federal deficits, which helped produce high interest rates.

(5) High interest rates must eventually take their toll.

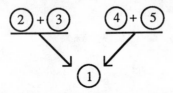

6. (1) ...The answer to both questions is no.
   (2) The veto spells disaster for . . . etc.
   (3) The veto may actually increase the federal deficit.
   (4) If large numbers of farms fail . . . the entire economy will be devastated.
   (5) Jobs will be lost, businesses will close, and tax revenues to help reduce the deficit will be lost.
   (6) We'll spend more money in the end . . . etc.

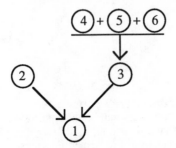

8. (1) Lugar's greatest attribute as the new chairman of the Senate Foreign Relations Committee is that he is not Jesse Helms.
   (2) That alone is plenty of reason for any rational American to breath a sigh of relief.
   (3) Lugar's words and actions show that he will work to bring bipartisanship and congressional independence to the conduct of U.S. foreign policy.
   (4) By pressing the administration for policy changes in South Africa and Nicaragua, Lugar has already sent a message to the White House. . . .
   (5) By scheduling a comprehensive committee review of foreign policy, Lugar furthers the hope that. . . .
   *There's more than one way to handle this one, obviously. (3) could be divided up into two claims, with one in support of the other; the same goes for (4). The conclusion of this argument is not really stated, but claim (2) gets pretty close, and that's what we've used. It would best be interpreted as something like, "It's a good thing that Richard Lugar is chairman of the Senate Foreign Relations Committee."*

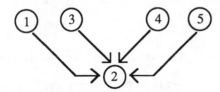

9. (1) Our right to move about freely is more important than having a check-point system for drunk drivers.
   (2) If the checkpoint system continues, there will be checkpoints for drugs, seat belts. . . .
   (3) We'll regret it later if we allow the system to continue.
   (4) [Unstated:] We'll regret it if we get checkpoints for drugs, seat belts . . . .

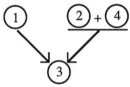

*Since no evidence is given for (2), this has the distinct aroma of Slippery Slope pseudoreasoning about it.*

11. (1) The constitutional guarantee of a speedy trial prevents crime.
    (2) More than a third of those with serious criminal records . . . are arrested for new offenses while free on bond awaiting . . . trial.
    (3) The longer the delay, the greater the likelihood of further violations.

12. *Clearly, this one requires some rephrasing to bring it down to size:*
    (1) A real town should be named after the one in which the *Andy Griffith Show* was set, Mayberry, only if some real town could live up to the image of Mayberry in the program
    (2) No real town could live up to that image.
    (3) No real town should be named after the fictional Mayberry.

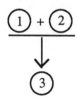

14. (1) Recycled water in automatic car washes may dump salt and dirt from one car to the next.
    (2) Brushes and drag cloths hurt the finish.
    (3) [Unstated:] ICA-sponsored tests don't really prove that automatic carwashes are easier on cars than home washes.
    (4) The home washes in the tests may not have been "average."

(5) The automatic washes in the tests were surely in perfect working order (that is, in better condition than the "average" automatic wash).
(6) Most automatic carwashes may not be properly maintained (we can't tell).
(7) If you follow a mud-caked pickup through the wash there may be dirt in the brushes or cloths that are dragged over your car.
(8) You should wash your own car. (Or: You're better off washing your own car; or: Home washing is easier on your car than automatic carwashes.)

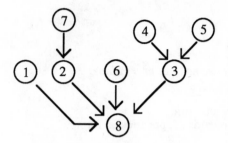

15. (1) The worst disease of the 1990s will be AIDS.
(2) AIDS has made surgery scary.
(3) In the last ten years several hundred Americans got AIDS from contaminated blood in surgery.
(4) It is predicted that within a few years more hundreds of people will receive AIDS blood each year.
(5) No one can feel safe receiving blood.
(6) We should be tested for AIDS (by a very sensitive test) before we give blood.

*There is more than one way to set this out. It's possible to leave out claims (1), (2), and (5) at no substantial loss to the argument.*

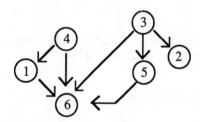

17. (1) A project with 3,000 houses and 7,000 new residents cannot properly be called a "village."
(2) Citizens of Chico will be better off if they vote no on Measure A [Vote no on Measure A].
(3) The project will not protect agricultural land.
(4) The Greenline protects valuable farmland.
(5) With the Greenline, there is enough land in the Chico area available to build 62,000 new homes.
(6) The project's park dedications will not reduce use of Bidwell Park.
(7) They developers want to attract 7,000 new residents . . . [who will use the park].
(8) The developers will not provide a school site [without cost to the taxpayers].
(9) The developers intend to sell the site to the school district, which will pay for it with taxpayers' money.

*One could include the claim "Chico does not need the Rancho Arroyo project" as the conclusion of a subargument (in the place of claim (2) in the diagram), and let it support the final conclusion: One should vote against Measure A. (Chapter 12 discusses getting "ought" conclusions from "is" premises—we won't complicate the example here by introducing an additional premise.)*

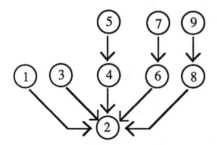

19. (1) My relative's client, who was serving a life sentence for murder, escaped and murdered someone else.
    (2) It's a waste of taxpayers' money to try this man [or others like him] again.
    (3) Murderers should be executed. [The death penalty should be restored.]
    (4) We are the most crime-ridden society in the world.
    (5) Someone is murdered every 27 minutes in the U.S.
    (6) There is a rape every 10 minutes.
    (7) There is an armed robbery every 82 seconds.
    (8) According to the FBI, there are 870,000 violent crimes a year, and the number is increasing.
    (9) Only 10 percent of those arrested are found guilty.
    (10) A large percentage of those found guilty are released on probation.
    (11) There aren't enough prisons to house the guilty.
    (12) The death penalty would create more room in prisons.
    (13) The death penalty would reduce the number of murders.
    (14) If a robber knew before he shot someone that if he was caught his own life would be taken, [he wouldn't do it; or would be less likely to do it].
    (15) [Murderers] deserve to die.
    (16) [Murderers] sacrificed their right to live when they murdered someone.

*We see the last claim in the passage as polemical window dressing. Also, we're not sure whether (11) is supposed to support (9) as well as (10).*

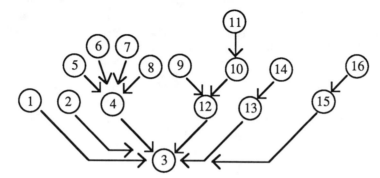

20. (1)   The Senate will (should) ratify the U.S.-Soviet treaty on intermediate-range nuclear missiles.
    (2)   The few Republican hardliners opposing it cannot prevail against the 90 Senators who [favor the treaty].
    (3)   The treaty . . . is an advance for Western security and a triumph of American diplomacy.
    (4)   The Senate should vote an end to the dilatory tactics of Helms, etc.
    (5)   If Helms, etc. continue their tactics, it would produce a needless source of friction at the summit.
    (6)   [Unstated:] Friction at the summit would be a bad thing.
    (7)   Since 1972, the U.S. has not ratified any of the four arms control agreements with the Soviets.
    (8)   If President Reagan cannot overcome the opposition . . . it will create doubt in Moscow about whether any American president can make his arms deals stick.
    (9)   [Unstated:] We don't want doubt in Moscow about whether . . . etc.
    (10)  The INF Treaty has been thoroughly examined by the Senate . . . and opponents have had a fair chance to make their case.

*Claims (1) and (4) are both conclusions; in the context of this passage, they amount to about the same thing. Hence, what looks like two separate main arguments is really a clutch of subarguments for essentially the same conclusion.*

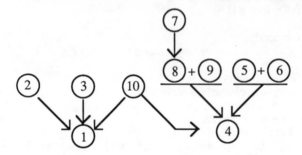

## Chapter 8 Test Question-Exercise Banks

These argument-passages can be treated in any number of ways: You can ask students to specify the issues they address; identify their premises and conclusions; classify them as inductive or deductive; determine whether their premises are dependent or independent; supply missing premises; separate the arguments themselves from their window dressing; or diagram them. You can also return to them from later chapters or appendices for examples or exercises. We've grouped them into some rough groups and included diagrams for some. Claims that we suggest leaving as unstated are given in square brackets.

**Bank 8-1**

Deductive arguments with dependent premises. There are more deductive arguments with dependent premises in the Chapter 9 banks.

1. We'll be better off in the dark than driving on ice in the fog. So let's wait a while. [If we're better off in the dark than driving on ice in the fog, then we should wait a while.]

2. It isn't too late. The bars haven't closed. [If the bars haven't closed, then it isn't too late.]

3. I'd advise you not to vote for Melton. Melton is very radical. [You shouldn't vote for radicals.]

4. The almond trees have not blossomed. It is not yet the middle of February. [The almond trees do not blossom before the middle of February.]

5. Computer networks are immune from computer viruses only if they're completely isolated from other machines and stray software. So, like I told you, this network is not safe from viruses. [This network is not completely isolated from other machines and stray software.]

6. No floor with 2x4 joists on two foot centers is strong enough. So this floor isn't stong enough. [This floor has 2x4 joists on two foot centers.]

7. The only time you can count on dry weather in Seattle is the first week of August. So, since you need to count on dry weather for your trip, you'll have to plan it for next week. [Next week is the first week of August.]

**Bank 8-2**

Deductive arguments with independent premises (or independent sets of premises). Diagrams are provided for some items.

8. If your shoes are too small, then you shouldn't wear them, and those are much too small. Besides, they're worn out. [If the shoes are worn out, then you shouldn't wear them.]

9. You shouldn't buy a television set that costs over $300, and that one costs $450. And that television set is much too big for your living room anyway. [You shouldn't buy any television set that's too big for your living room.]

10. Tony's car is dangerous. It has bad brakes and the tires are nearly worn out. [Unstated premises: Any car that has bad brakes is dangerous. Any car with tires that are nearly worn out is dangerous.]

11. Look, (1) there's no sign of smoke from the cabin. (2) If he were there, he'd have a fire and we'd see the smoke, unless he couldn't find any dry wood. (3) But there's a lot of dry wood around. Notice also that (4) you don't hear his dog. (5) He's not there. [(6) If you don't hear his dog he's not there.]

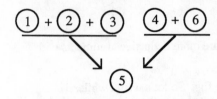

12. If she really thought those clothes were unflattering, she wouldn't be caught dead in them. Anyway, she told me herself she thought she looked good in them, and she wouldn't say that unless she believed it, so she obviously does. [Unstated premise: She wears those clothes.]

13. You've got to take Math 3. First of all, it's a required part of the general education program. Second, it's a prerequisite for several courses in your major. [Unstated premises: You've got to take all required parts of the general education program. You've got to take all prerequisites for courses in your major.]

14. (1) Toyota is raising its prices by three percent on January 1, and (2) we won't be able to afford one if we wait until then. Besides that, (3) the old heap won't make it to the first of the year. (4) We'll have to buy now. [(5) If we cannot afford a Toyota after January 1, we'll have to buy now. (6) If the old heap won't make it to the first of the year, we'll have to buy now.]

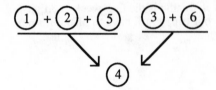

15. (1) Either there's a burglar outside or there's a dog in the garbage. (2) There can't be a dog in the garbage because of the fence. So (3) it must be a burglar. Besides,(4) I think I saw a flashlight beam, and (5) it could only be a burglar that would make such a light.

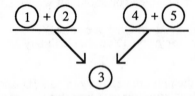

16. (1) Congress will allow the construction of more than 50 MX missiles only if the Air Force finds a way to protect them, otherwise we'll get more Midgetman missiles. Furthermore, a study has just been done that shows that (2) the Midgetman is more efficient than the MX, and it's clear that (3) Congress will allow building more of whichever of the two missiles is more efficient. And (4) the Air Force could never protect the MXs anyhow. Therefore (5) Congress is going to authorize building more Midgetmen rather than more MXs.

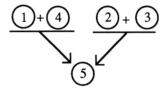

## Bank 8-3

Inductive arguments with dependent premises.

17. I've already won $100 in the state lottery, and hardly anyone wins that much twice. So I'm not likely to win that much again.

18. It's Monday, so the mail carrier will probably arrive after noon today. He usually comes in the early afternoon on Mondays.

19. The blasted hedge-clippers aren't working again. Must be the switch. That's usually the problem.

20. *60 Minutes* has been in the top ten in the Neilson ratings for the last ten years. It's a safe bet to be there this coming season as well.

21. I'll bet a dollar that (1) Booth picks Chapman as his new Vice-President. (2) Booth and Chapman have been on a first name basis for a long time, and (3) Booth usually rewards his friends.

*Note: Booth's picking Chapman is the latter's reward, of course. You may want to make this clear with additional premises.*

22. I've been looking at the available literature on the trial of Julius and Ethyl Rosenberg, and the great majority of writers on the subject have grave doubts about the Rosenbergs' guilt. It seems clear that they may well have been innocent.

23. (1) I'm pretty certain she wouldn't be happy as a police officer. (2) Just watching a crime movie makes her nervous, and (3) if she can't tolerate simulated violence, (1) she most likely won't like the real thing.

*Note: The way we've chosen to indicate that the first and last claim are essentially the same is simply to assign them the same number in the passage. Another way to do this would be to give them different numbers and indicate their sameness in the diagram.*

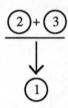

24. (1) People who read more tend to have better vocabularies than those who don't, and (2) having a good vocabulary makes you a better speaker and writer. Since (3) good speaking and writing are important job skills, (4) you are probably a better job candidate if you read a lot.

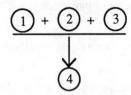

25. (1)    It seems pretty likely that all the smaller food stores around town are going to have trouble staying open. (2) Jack's Market has closed, and the 5th Street Market has closed, and now I hear that the Cash And Carry across town is going to fold up too. (3) You'd best get used to the idea of shopping at the big supermarkets since (4) those are probably going to be all that's left in another six months.

**Bank 8-4**

Inductive arguments with independent premises

26. Sal is probably going to be late, since the traffic is so bad. And he said he had an errand to run on his way over here.

27. The MiniMax Video camera: It's the lightest in weight, the least expensive, and it comes with the longest warranty in the business. All good reasons for making it the one you take home.

28. For one thing, (1) every movie Stallone has made in the past decade has made money. For another, (2) blood-and-guts patriotism is selling big these days. So (3) the combination of a second film of that kind from Stallone is very nearly a certain money-maker.

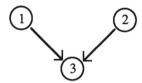

29. (1) Automobile air bags substantially reduce the chances of being hurt in a crash, and, (2) unlike safety devices like seat belts you can't forget to use them. What's more, (3) there is not one case on record of a bag inflating when it shouldn't have and causing an accident. So (4) you're much safer buying a car with air bags than one without them.

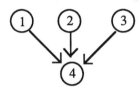

30. Let's see. (1) I know our policy covers us if our car is stolen or the windows are broken, so (2) chances are it'll cover us if someone steals the stereo, too. Besides that, (3) our homeowners policy covers stereos, and (4) our car policy seems to cover a lot of the same stuff the homeowners policy covers.

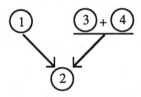

**Bank 8-5**

Miscellaneous problems

31. (1) The competition employs a sliding mechanism. (1) But a hinged door is lighter, easier to operate, and (2) ensures a better fit and seal with the body than a sliding mechanism, thus (3) keeping the cabin's interior noise level to a minimum. And (4) it allows for greater freedom in the shape of the vehicle. [Unstated conclusion: A hinged door is better than a sliding door.]
—Mazda truck product manager Bernie Chaisson, arguing that the new Mazda MPV's door set-up is superior to that of Chrysler minivans.

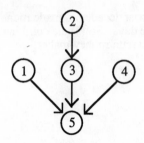

32. (1) The Gallup people estimate that most Americans believe that physicians' fees are excessive, so (2) probably most of them do. I know (3) everyone I talk to thinks that. But (4) we'll never have socialized medicine in this country. (5) Americans will pay any amount for the freedom to choose their own doctors; (6) that's what history tells us. *Note that this one has arguments for two separate conclusions.*

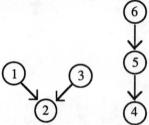

33. (1) I think we should ask Bill to take care of the house while we're gone. (2) He took good care of Kent's house, according to Kent. In addition, (3) he's always been responsible about other things. (1) I'm sure he'll do a good job.

34. Editor: Does George Bush represent the mainstream in American political thought? Let's consider some facts.

(1) Bush supports supplying military aid to the Contras, but (2) most Americans oppose this. (3) He is against a woman's right to decide for herself if she wants an abortion; (4) however, a great majority of Americans are pro-choice, according to opinion polls. (5) Bush is also against the ERA, in contrast with most people, and (7) he favors prayers in public schools, which (8) most Americans oppose.

(9) Bush also cast votes in the Senate to continue production of chemical and biological weapons, and (10) supported the Reagan administration's cuts on education spending. (11) Most Americans strongly oppose chemical and biological weapons production and (12) the cuts in federal spending for education were very unpopular.

Clearly, Bush does not really represent mainstream American values.

—*North State Record*

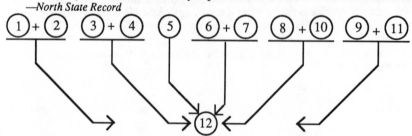

The following three items are from a letters to the editor column of the *Sacramento Bee*, October 17, 1988, three weeks before the presidential election.

35. If Michael Dukakis wants to play on the audience's emotion, he shouldn't use the poor little kid in Texas who wants to play Little League but whose parents can't afford the insurance. (2) Little League provides its own insurance program and covers anyone, whether he can pay or not.

(3) He shouldn't act tough on crime. (4) Anyone who has commuted the life sentences of 28 first-degree murderers can't be too tough. (5) His prison furlough program proves that too. (6) Nor should he act tough on drugs. (7) He rejected mandatory sentencing of drug dealers. (8) He rejects the death penalty for narcotic kingpins (or for anyone, for that matter). (9) His prison furlough for drug offenders has gone up 103 percent in just three years. This is tough?

(10) He shouldn't keep saying "I care deeply." (11) There are many victims of crime and drugs who are hurt deeply by his policies.

[Unstated conclusion: (12) Dukakis should not be elected president.]

—Jeanine Corbin

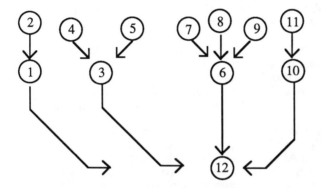

36. ...(1) The Union of Concerned Scientists says Star Wars is too vague, too expensive and 20 years before construction could start. (2) I disagree.

(3) We already have nuclear bombs. (4) We know how to launch satellites. (5) SDI, phase one, admittedly consists of launching 4,000 "killer rockets" aboard 400 satellites into polar orbits. (6) If we have any citizens dumb enough to believe that those "killer rockets" won't be nuclear bombs that can be brought down onto targets by radio command, then we are really in trouble.

(7) With our missiles (bombs) already in orbit, we won't have to fear a surprise Soviet pre-emptive strike. (8) We can stop looking for expensive ways to base our missiles or harden our missile silos. (9) We have the technology in place, ready to go, and it will provide employment for a lot of people.

(10) The only problem, as I see it, is that the Soviets will have no choice but to set up a similar system, and they are miles ahead of us in satellite-launching expertise.

[Unstated conclusion: (11) We should start on Star Wars right away.]

—Mel Vercoe

*In the following diagram, we've put claims (1) and (2) together thus: (1/2), which can be read: "The Union of Concerned Scientists is wrong about . . . etc."*

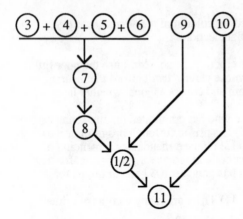

37. A footnote is in order to political editor Martin Smith's excellent October 4 commentary, "Bush's overblown rhetoric." (1) One of the vice president's numerous misleading statements during the first presidential debate was his claim that advocates of a nuclear freeze wished to cut U.S. nuclear forces unilaterally, "hoping against hope that they [the Soviets] would match our bid. . ."

(2) This is a lie. (3) No responsible or leading member of the freeze movement has urged such unilateral cuts. (4) The nuclear freeze proposal, as George Bush well knew, was aimed at Soviet nuclear forces as much as American nuclear forces. (5) Had it been adopted in 1982 or 1983, when numerous U.S. citizens made clear they wanted it, our nation would be more secure in part because the Soviet nuclear weaponry program would have been dramatically curtailed.

(6) It is not hard to fathom the Bush campaign strategy: (7) Since his anti-civil liberties and pro-nuclear arms race positions fly in the face of public opinion, he must smear both those organizations that support the First Amendment as well as those that use First Amendment guarantees to urge the adoption of meaningful arms control.

(8) In an honest debate over the merits of these issues, Bush and his supporters wouldn't stand a chance.

—Daniel Galpern, Executive Director, Sacramento Nuclear Weapons Freeze

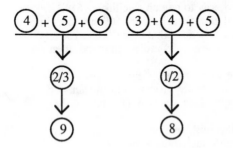

**Bank 8-6**

Fill in the blanks

38. Arguments whose premises are intended to provide absolutely conclusive reasons for accepting the conclusion are _*deductive*_, and arguments whose premises are intended to provide some support but less than absolutely conclusive support for the conclusion are _*inductive*_.

39. Sound arguments are _*deductive*_ arguments that are _*valid*_ and whose premises are all _*true*_.

True/False

40. A valid argument cannot have any false premises.
*False*

41. If a strong argument has a false conclusion, then not all its premises can be true.
*False*

42. If a valid argument has a false conclusion, then not all its premises can be true.
*True*

# Chapter 9
# Common Patterns
# of Deductive Arguments

This chapter of *Critical Thinking* provides an introduction to a handful of common deductive argument patterns from categorical and truth-functional logic. Neither of these logics is developed systematically. So, if you wish to teach a fully clothed component in elementary deductive logic, including truth-functional derivations, we recommend that you go to the Appendices and forget Chapter 9. (Well, you might remember it for the exercises that occur there; the latter make good practice even if you substitute the Appendices for the material in the text.)

## Exercises Unanswered in the Text

### Exercise 9-1

*In this and the following exercises we're arbitrarily assigning "P" (or, where appropriate, "not-P") to whatever claim occurs first in the argument and "Q" to whatever is left. Students sometimes get the idea that "P" has to be assigned to the antecedent of a conditional claim simply because that's the way they first saw it done. They disabused of this notion.*

1.  P = Baffin Island is larger than Sumatra.
    Q = Two of the five largest islands in the world are in the Arctic Ocean.

    If P then Q.
    P.
    Therefore, Q.          Modus ponens (valid)

3.  P = The alternator is not working properly.
    Q = The ampmeter shows a negative reading.

    If Q then P.
    Q.
    Therefore, P.          Modus ponens (valid)

5.  P = The danger of range fires is greater this year than last.
    Q = State and federal officials will hire a greater number of firefighters to cope with the danger.

    If P then Q.
    Q.
    Therefore, P.          Affirming the consequent (invalid)

# Exercise 9-2

1.  P = Jack Davis robbed the Central Pacific Express in 1870.
    Q = The authorities imprisoned the right person.

    If P then Q.
    Not-Q.
    Therefore, not-P.       Modus tollens (valid)

3.  P = The recent tax cuts were self-financing.
    Q = There would have been no substantial increase in the federal deficit.

    If P then Q.
    Not-P.
    Therefore, not-Q.       Denying the antecedent (invalid)

    *Note that the change in tense in Q from premise to conclusion does not affect the argument's validity.*

5.  P = The public would have reacted favorably to most of the policies Reagan has recommended during his second term.
    Q = Reagan's electoral landslide in 1984 was a mandate for more conservative policies.

    Not-P.
    If Q then P.
    Therefore, not-Q.       Modus tollens (valid)

    *Reminder to students: Arguments do not require that the premises occur in any particular order. The above is as good a case of modus tollens as any other.*

# Exercise 9-3

1.  P = Paul attends the ceremony.
    Q = Charles attends the ceremony.
    R = Charles will take Susan.

    If P then Q.
    If Q then R.
    Therefore, if P then R.          Chain argument (valid)

3.  P = Juniors are eligible to take the examination.
    Q = Seniors are eligible to take the examination.
    R = Sophomores are eligible to take the examination.

    If Q then P.
    If P then R.
    Therefore, If Q then R.          Chain argument (valid)

5.  P = The commission will extend bow-hunting season.
    Q = The commission cuts back on the rest of the primitive-arms season.
    R = The commission is fair.

If P then Q.
If R then P.
Therefore, if R then Q.          Chain argument (valid)

*Note: "P only if Q" means the same as "If P then Q." Some students can take two weeks getting this straight. We tell them that "if," by itself, always introduces the antecedent of a conditional claim and that "only if" always introduces the consequent of a conditional claim. They can always memorize this rule of thumb if nothing else works. (The only confusion that might result occurs when they run into "if and only if." This becomes "If P then Q and if Q then P," in which Q is both antecedent and consequent. Since logicians and mathematicians are about the only ones to use "if and only if," students are probably safe from it.)*

## Exercise 9-4

*Note: Here, rather than using "P" and "Q" we'll assign the letters that come to mind most naturally.*

2. If W then C.
   Not-C.
   Therefore, not-W.          Modus tollens (valid)

3. If L then Q.
   If Q then F.
   Therefore, if L then F.          Chain argument (valid)

5. If A then S.
   S.
   Therefore, A.          Affirming the consequent (invalid)

6. If A then C.
   Not-A.
   Therefore, not-C.          Denying the antecedent (invalid)

7. If T then P.
   Not-T.
   Therefore, not-P.          Denying the antecedent (invalid)

8. If P then S.
   Not-S.
   Therefore, not-P.          Modus tollens (valid)

10. L = You lift weights once every other day.
    M = You get a larger muscle mass.
    D = You desire to lift more frequently.

    If L then M.
    If M then D.
    Therefore, if L then D.          Chain argument (valid)

**Exercise 9-5**

2. Some criminals are not gamblers.

3. All exceptional employees are recipients of rewards.

5. Some Democrats are conservatives.

6. All places where there is smoke are places where there is fire.

8. All voters are members.

9. No things are angels.

**Exercise 9-6**

1. Original claim (rewritten): All people with tickets are people who will be admitted.

   The converse is claim (b), which does *not* follow from the original.

3. Original claim: Some of the most boring aquarium animals are *Limulus*.

   The converse is "Some Limulus are members of the class of the most boring aquarium animals," and this claim follows from the original. Claim (b) is not the precise converse, but it certainly follows from the converse.

5. Original claim: Some high-technology stocks are not stocks that have been part of the recent rally in the stock market.

   The converse is claim (a), which does *not* follow from the original.

**Exercise 9-7**

2. S = sportcasters
   A = athletes
   C = college professors

   All S are A.
   No A are C.
   Therefore, No S are C.          Syllogism 2.

3. D = Dukakis voters
   F = people who favor explanations of medical services for the needy
   H = people who favor higher taxes

   All D are F.
   All F are H.
   Therefore, All D are H.          Syllogism 1.

5. C = conservationsists
   R = Republican voters
   E = environmentalists

No C are R.
All E are C.
Therefore, No E are R.     Syllogism 2 (Switch order of premises).

6.  P = philosophers
    S = skeptics
    T = theologians

    All P are S.
    No P are T.
    Therefore, No S are T.     Invalid syllogism 2 (Convert last premise).

8.  P = peddlars
    S = salesmen
    C = confidence men

    All P are S.
    All C are S.
    Therefore, All P are C.     Invalid syllogism 1.

9.  A = addicts
    D = decent people
    C = criminals

    No A are A.
    All C are D.
    Therefore, No A are C.     Syllogism 2 (Switch order of premises, and
                               then convert second premise and conclusion).

## Exercise 9-8

1.  M = Mohawk Indians
    A = Algonquins
    C = Cheyenne

    All M are A.
    All C are A.
    Therefore, All C are M.     Invalid syllogism 1.

3.  M = moas
    D = Dinornithidae
    E = creatures that still exist

    All M are D.
    No M are E.
    Therefore, No D are E.     Invalid syllogism 2 (Convert second premise).

5.  M = madmen
    G = people who would gamble on launching a nuclear first strike
    L = leaders of the Soviet Union

All G are M.
No L are M.
Therefore, No L are G.     Valid syllogism 2 (Convert last premise and
                           conclusion).

7. A = cases of aesthetic surgery
   L = surgery designed to make a patient look better
   R = reconstructive surgery

   All A are L.
   No A are R.
   Therefore, No R are L.     Invalid syllogism 2 (Convert last premise and
                              conclusion).

9. W = stockholders' information about a company's worth
   M = information that must come from the managers of a company
   B = information that must come from the very people who are trying to buy the stock from
   stockholders

   All W are M
   All M are B
   Therefore, All W are B     Valid syllogism 1

*Getting students to represent this one correctly can be instructive, but it resembles pulling
teeth.*

**Exercise 9-9**

1. E = evergreen trees
   H = hardwood trees
   D = deciduous trees

   No E are D.
   All H are D.
   Therefore, No E are H.     Valid syllogism 2 (Switch premises; convert
                              last premise and conclusion).

3. P = The animal laboratories at the university would allow spot inspections.
   Q = They [at the animal laboratories] are living up to the standards of the Animal Welfare
   Act.

   If Q then P.
   Not-P.
   Therefore, not-Q.     Modus tollens (valid)

6. Begging the question. The premise merely restates the conclusion.

7. P = The dairy interests are satisfied.
   Q = The Air Force must turn down the bid from a Seattle dairy.
   R = The taxpayers will pay an extra quarter of a million dollars in milk costs.

161

If P then Q.
If Q then R.
Therefore, if P then R.       Chain argument (valid)

9. RAA. Though at a deeper level it begs the question.

12. P = Junk bonds are a good deal.
Q = The default rate of junk bonds would outweigh their higher than normal yields.

If not-P then Q.
Not-Q.
Therefore, P.       Modus tollens (valid)

*This is modus tollens even though the "not-" occurs in the antecedent of the conditional premise rather than in the conclusion. Doesn't matter: P and not-P are each the denial of the other.*

14. P = Russell's theory had a chance of success.
Q = Russell's theory could escape from the paradox of inherence.
R = Russell's theory contains a solution to the problem of asymmetrical relations.

If P then Q.
If Q then R.
Not-R.
Therefore, not-P.

Setting out the subarguments:

If P then Q.
If Q then R.
[Therefore, if P then R.] (unstated)      Chain argument (valid)

[If P then R.] (unstated)
Not-R.
Therefore, not-P.       Modus tollens (valid)

Since both subarguments are valid, the entire argument is valid.

**Exercise 9-10**

1. Claims required:

P = Greater efficiency is to be had from our communication systems.
Q = Fiber optic technology replaces the current cable system.
R = A great many communications workers lose their jobs.

Argument structure:

If P then Q.
If Q then R.
Therefore, if not-R then not-P.

Subarguments:

step 1:    If P then Q.
           If Q then R.
           [Therefore, if P then R.]          (unstated)
           Chain argument (valid)

step 2:    [If P then R.] (unstated)
           If not-R then not-P.

This last form is equivalent to:

           If P then R.
           Not-R.
           Therefore, not-P          Modus tollens (valid)

The argument as a whole is then valid.

3. Classes required:

L = Large travel agencies
H = Agencies that can handle the travel business of major corporations
S = Agencies that can survive the shakeout in the travel industry

Claims required:    P = All agencies that can survive the shakeout in the travel industry are
                    going to be large agencies.
                    Q = There will be a lot of mergers in the travel industry in the near
                    future.

Argument structure:

step 1:    All H are L.
           All S are H.
           [Therefore, All S are L.]    (unstated)
           Valid syllogism

step 2:    If P then Q.
           [P.] (unstated conclusion from above subargument)
           Therefore, Q.                    Modus ponens (valid)

5. Classes required:

C = cases we ought to be concerned about
S = cases of enlisted men selling information to the Russians
M = material sold in recent cases
N = material that's dangerous to our national security when in Russian hands
R = material that's been classified secret by our ridiculous classification system
D = routine drivel . . . etc.

Claims required:

P = All cases of enlisted men selling information to the Russians are cases we ought to be concerned about.
Q = All material sold in recent cases is material that's dangerous to our national security when in Russian hands.

Argument structure: This one is complicated enough to warrant numbering the various lines to make reference easier.

(1)  If P then Q.
(2)  All M is R.
(3)  All D is R.
(4)  [No D is N]             unstated premise assumed by author of the argument
(5)  [All M is D]            unstated conclusion of invalid syllogism which has (2)
                             and (3) as premises
(6)  [No M is N]
(7)  [not-Q]                 line (6) denies Q; they cannot both be true
(8)  Not-P                   Modus tollens, from lines (7) and (1)

*Since line (5) is achieved by means of an invalid syllogism, and since the original argument requires this line in order to reach the eventual conclusion, the argument as a whole is invalid.*

*The main reason the analysis of this argument looks as long and complicated as it does—apparently longer and more complicated than the original argument—is that the original version took a good bit for granted. When the author of the argument claims that all M is R and all D is R (see the appropriate claim in the text), he seems to think this establishes that the material sold in recent spy cases is all harmless stuff, not dangerous to national security. But it establishes no such claim, even if we allow the reasonable extra premise (line 4) the author needs. The inference requires an invalid syllogism as well.*

# Chapter 9 Test Question-Exercise Bank

All the argument patterns in the text are illustrated in the following. You'll know best what to do with them.

1.  Letter to the editor: "The General Accounting Office says that the average ocean voyage taken by State Department and U.S. Information Agency employees costs the taxpayer on the average of $6,084. GAO investigators were told by foreign service officers that ocean travel is a 'fringe benefit.' If that is true, and I believe the GAO, it's time to trim the fringes."

*Modus ponens, without restatement of the conclusion, "It's time to trim the fringes."*

2.  "The band raised enough money to make it to the Rose Parade. They were only going to be able to go if they could get the funds together, and I read in the paper that they left this morning."

*Modus ponens*

3. "A universal opportunity to have an education implies 100 percent literacy, and 100 percent literacy, or close to it, is exactly what you find in Denmark, according to the almanac. So everyone there has the opportunity for an education."

   *Affirming the consequent. Note that this could be interpreted as an inductive argument.*

4. "It's got to be a reasonably short drive from out where Hal lives to downtown Denver, because, if it's short, you know you'd find lots of commuters living out there. And look at Hal's subdivision—it's full of commuters."

   *Affirming the consequent*

5. "If war is inevitable, then spies are necessary. They aren't, so it isn't."

   *Modus tollens*

6. "At the station bookstall, Jim bought himself a *Rude Pravo* and boarded the Brno train. If they had wanted to arrest him, they would have done so by now."
   —John Le Carré, *Tinker, Tailor, Soldier, Spy*

   *Modus tollens, with one premise, "They haven't yet arrested him," and the conclusion, "They must not have wanted to arrest him," both unstated.*

7. "If cutting the federal budget were simply a matter of arithmetic and not one of politics, we would never see the more draconian provisions of the Gramm-Rudman bill put into effect. Unfortunately, though, cutting the budget is much more politics than arithmetic. That means that, somewhere down the line, we're going to see Gramm-Rudman's harsh side."

   *Denying the antecedent*

8. "He won't get the tax credit unless he filed before the first, but fortunately he did file before the first."

   *Unstated conclusion: "He'll get the tax credit." If the first premise is interpreted as "If he didn't file before the first, then he won't get the credit" (and this is a correct interpretation), then the argument is a case of denying the antecedent. If the first premise is interpreted as "If he gets the tax credit, then he filed before the first" (and this is also a correct interpretation), then the argument is affirming the consequent.*

9. Overheard: "If drunk driving checkpoints continue, then next there will be checkpoints for driver's licenses, infant car seats, you name it. And if we have checkpoints for all those things, we're going to wish we hadn't allowed drunk driving checkpoints in the first place."

   *Unstated conclusion: "If drunk driving checkpoints continue, then we're going to wish we had not allowed them in the first place." Chain argument*

10. "You can't get from here to New Orleans without taking the Pontchartrain Causeway, and taking the causeway will bring you in through Jefferson Parish. So you've got to go in through Jefferson Parish in order to get from here to New Orleans."

    *Chain argument*

11. "Jan will start work as an assistant director next fall if she finishes her degree by that time; and she can finish her degree this summer if she goes to summer school. This means she's going to be an assistant director in the fall, but only if she goes to summer school."

*Reversed chain argument*

12. "If Kirkpatrick got his work done before the deadline, he'd have been paid before Phyllis left for Hawaii, and if that had happened, they'd be skiing right now. So if they're skiing, he got his work done before the deadline."

*Reversed chain argument*

13. "There were some people who were disappointed when Ted Kennedy announced he wouldn't run for president in '86, but they aren't what you'd call the old-school liberals. So none of the old-school liberals were disappointed."

*Valid conversion*

14. "Nothing that happens is inevitable; therefore no inevitable events ever happen."

*Valid conversion*

15. "It really ought to be evident," he lectured. "Wherever that particular type of beetle is present, you'll find exactly that kind of hole in the trees. Therefore, when you see that kind of hole, you know that type of beetle is present."

*Invalid conversion*

16. "All the office people who went to Mexico during the holiday came back with great tans. So anybody you see around here with a tan was one of the lucky ones who went to Mexico."

*Invalid conversion*

17. "There are a few actors who work for humanitarian causes, so some humanitarians are actors."

*Valid conversion*

18. "A small percentage of the boards he nailed into his fence are nailed so close together they'll buckle when they get good and wet. Therefore, you can count on some of the fence boards that buckle when the rains come being boards he nailed so close together."

*Valid conversion*

19. "At least a few members of the Fatah Revolutionary Council are not terrorists." Does it follow that at least a few terrorists are not members of the FRC?

*Nope. Invalid conversion*

20. "Some people who find logic difficult are not good mathematicians, because some good mathematicians are not people who find logic difficult."

*Invalid conversion*

21. "Jackson won't take the Democratic nomination in '92. He's the front runner, and the front runner never captures the nomination."

*Valid syllogism. In effect, it says: "All H are F, and No F are C; therefore No H are C," where "H," "F," and "C" each denote a one-member class: Jackson, the front runner, and the capturer of the Democratic nomination.*

22. "Nobody who showed up had any money left, and everybody who had been to the casino showed up. My earlier estimate of this crowd's luck must have proved to be correct: None of the folk who had been to the casino had any money left."

*Valid syllogism: No S are M, and All C are M; therefore No C are M.*

23. From an editorial: "Any instance of censorship is wrong, and the Soviet attempt to squelch the ABC miniseries, *Amerika*, is the worst kind of censorship—that imposed by another country. ABC executives should not cave-in to the Soviet pressure . . . ."

*Valid syllogism: All C are W, and All S are C; therefore All S are W.*

24. "Everybody who knows about the violence attending last year's election in the Philippines knows that the election couldn't have been fair, and anybody who read the papers knows about that violence."

*Unstated conclusion: "Anybody who read the papers knows that the election couldn't have been fair." Valid syllogism: All K are F, and All P are K; [therefore, All P are F].*

25. "Freddy's gone completely whacko. He's nuts."
"Yeah? Why do you say that?"
"Because he thinks he's a rock star, and these days all the crazies think they're rock stars."

*Invalid syllogism: All F are R, and All C are R; therefore, All F are C.*

26. "I'm telling you that every club member can vote. Here are the rules: The only people who can vote are those who are subscribers to the newsletter, and you're automatically a subscriber if you're a member of the club."

*Invalid syllogism: All V are S, and All M are S; therefore, All M are V.*

27. Letter to the editor: "I would just like to say, in response to the blatantly anti-Christian letter that appeared on your editorial page on March 11, in which it was alleged that Christians aren't racists but are bigots, just how is that supposed to be? All racists are bigots, so if we Christians aren't racists, then it follows that we aren't bigots either. The writer is not only anti-Christian, he's anti-logic."

*Invalid syllogism: All R are B, and No C are R; therefore, No C are B.*

28. "Anybody who can speak the local dialect of the Khmer language would have to have been a Cambodian resident at some time, but we believe that none of the new settlers along the Tonle Sap [or Great Lake] are genuine former residents of Cambodia, because but none of these new settlers can speak that dialect."

*Invalid syllogism: All D are R, and No S are D; therefore, No S are R.*

29. From a letter to the editor: "The counties of Michigan clearly need the ability to raise additional sources of revenue, not only to meet the demands of growth but also to maintain existing levels of service. For without these sources those demands will not be met, and it will be impossible to maintain services even at present levels."

    *Begging the question*

30. "It doesn't make any sense to speak of tracing an individual human life back past the moment of conception. After all, that's the beginning, and you can't go back past the beginning."

    *Begging the question*

31. Opponents to PROPOSITION 102 say that contact tracing will lead to 'witch hunts'. We say it's time to stop peddling such fear and panic."
    —Rebuttal to Argument Against Proposition 102, 1988 *California Ballot Pamphlet*

    *Begging the question*

32. Reconstruction of a remark heard at a faculty meeting: "The quality of teaching performance cannot be measured. No matter what administrators at campuses around the country might say, teaching performance is simply not the kind of thing to which you can assign measurable variables and then compare a bunch of numbers at the beginning of a course and again at its end. That isn't the way it works."

    *Begging the question*

33. "If the Syrians really shot down two American jets, then American pilots are not as good as we thought they were. Therefore, the Syrians couldn't really have shot down the American jets, since American pilots are every bit as good as we thought they were.

    *Modus tollens*

34. "No performances at which the audience maintains a fixed apparent distance from the performers can be as dramatically powerful as film, in which the audience gets a variety of views, from long, panoramic shots to extreme close ups. Unfortunately for the theater, stage productions are necessarily perfomances that keep the audience fixed in the middle distance. For that reason, a play can never be as powerful as a movie. It just doesn't have the equipment."

    *Valid syllogism: No P [performances . . . fixed apparent distance . . .] are F [performances as powerful as film], and All S [stage productions; plays] are P. Therefore, No S are F.*

35. ASPIRING STUDENT: "I'm going to get an A in this course."
    SKEPTICAL FRIEND: "But I thought you got a D on your first quiz."
    ASPIRING STUDENT: "I did. But I got As on my last three quizzes, and Mr. Garbez said that you get an A for the course if you get one on each of the last three quizzes."

    *Modus ponens*

36. "Sure, Prof. Bumstead will give you passing marks on all your papers. I know she said she wouldn't pass any papers that didn't analyze the issues, but look: I read your papers and every one of them contained an analysis of the issues."

*Invalid syllogism: All P [passing papers] are A [papers that analyze issues], and All Y [your papers] are A; therefore, All Y are P.*

37. "Your honor, I can prove that I'm not guilty."

    "I'm listening."

    "Okay. Well, if I had broken into the egg chamber, well, I'd really be sweating it now. I mean, I'd really be nervous, right?"

    "I have no idea, but go ahead."

    "Right. Well, I'm not nervous. So I *couldn't* have broken into the egg chamber."

*Valid, even if unconvincing (modus tollens)*

38. "I'm know that all tracks like these in the sand are made by rattlesnakes; my reptile book says that a rattlesnake *always* makes marks just like these."

*Invalid conversion*

39. "Let's start at the top. It had to be Libya that fired at us if it was the Russians who gave them the surface-to-air missiles. And it *was* Libya that fired at us, right? So the Russians had to be the ones who gave them the surface-to-air missiles."

*Affirming the consequent*

40. "Let me explain why beefed-up law enforcement against drug smugglers will be counterproductive. First, if a smuggler has to contend with more enforcement, he's going to turn more to a drug that is easily smuggled into the country than one that's more difficult. That's only good business. Second, if he's looking for a more easily smuggled drug, he's going to choose one with a high value per unit volume, and that means his choice is going to be cocaine, not marijuana. So, in the long run, putting the heat on with more law enforcement will result in cocaine becoming the drug more often brought into the country rather than marijuana."

*Chain argument*

41. "Obviously the next summit, coming as it will around election time, might be politically damaging if the United States breaks the arms control pact. But Reagan assures us that the United States will not break any arms agreements prior to the summit—and he knows. So it is nonsense to say, as conservatives are inclined to do, that the next summit will be politically damaging."

*Denying the antecedent*

42. "Clearly Mexico desperately needs financial help in handling its $96 billion foreign debt, since without any aid Mexico cannot possibly reduce that enormous sum, and it is urgent that it be reduced."

*Valid, but it begs the question*

43. "We sympathize with the 3,000 airport workers who staged a strike last week against the Vienna airport. They wanted to have more security. The truth is, the best way to protect airport workers is with an attack against the terrorists themselves. But you can attack terrorists only if you know where they are. And if you know where they are then you know what government is protecting them. So you can attack terrorists only if you know what government is protecting them—a tall order."

*Chain argument*

44. "We checked all the cheese in the store, and none of it came from the plant that the FDA said may be producing contaminated dairy products. So, even if the management and the customers and whoever else want to worry about it, I'm perfectly confident that none of the cheese from the problem dairy plant made it into our store."

*Valid conversion*

45. "Coffee drinkers shouldn't become surgeons. They all have jittery nerves, and anyone with jittery nerves shouldn't become a surgeon."

*Valid syllogism*

46. "It's got to be a case of bad rings if the compression goes up when oil is squirted into the cylinders. And look: The pressure is up by twenty pounds since we squirted in the oil. I'm afraid your fears were well founded; it's sure enough bad rings."

*Modus ponens*

47. "The drug situation poses a real dilemma. If legalization of certain narcotics would not broaden the population of drug users, then we could decrease the crime and violence that is associated with drug traffic. Most every expert in the field, however, is certain that legalization would certainly increase the number of drug users. That means we can't get at the problem of violence and crime."

*Denying the antecedent*

48. "If your teeth or gums hurt, then you've got a serious dental problem, and if you've got a serious dental problem, then it must be a problem of tooth decay or gum disease. Therefore, if you have a problem of decay or gum disease, then your teeth or gums hurt."

*Reversed chain argument*

49. From a letter to the editor: ". . . Mr. Weller, like all ultraliberals, can only find harsh things to say about America. But Weller is something besides an ultraliberal. There is another type of person who can only find harsh things to say about America. I am talking about people who allow themselves to be the dupes of the Politburo. . . ."

*Invalid syllogism with an unstated conclusion: "Mr. Weller is a dupe of the Politburo." All W [Weller] are H [people with only harsh things to say...], and All D [dupes of the Politburo] are H; therefore, All W are D.*

50. "The Chinese themselves must pronounce the name of their capital 'PAY-KING' if indeed that's the way it's really supposed to be pronounced."
"Well, that's exactly the way the Chinese say it."
"See there, that must be the correct pronunciation."

*Affirming the consequent*

51. "Now, let me see if I've got this straight: If your brother is moving to Chatooga, then he's moving to Georgia, right? And if he's moving to Georgia, then he's not moving to Chattanooga, which is in Tennessee. So, if he's not moving to Chattanooga, then he's moving to Chatooga. Is that it?"

*Reversed chain argument*

52. "I had a friend who was in Port-au-Prince last January during all the uproar. He told me that some news reporters were fooled by the reports that the Haitian government could not fall. So, even though I realize you have all kinds of faith in your fellow correspondents, it appears that at least some of those taken in by the reports were among your colleagues."

*Valid conversion*

53. "I've heard your silly theory before. But if fusil oils and all that other stuff you were talking about were really what gave people hangovers, then they wouldn't get them from vodka, for instance, which doesn't have that stuff in it. However, as you well know, people do get hangovers from vodka. I conclude that your fusil oil theory is just so much bunk."

*Modus tollens*

54. "The rise of the initiatives on state ballots represents an increased demand on the part of the voters for accountability from government. Clearly, therefore, people are demanding, through increased use of initiatives, more accountability from their elected officials."

*Valid, but it begs the question*

55. "All oil is produced from organic matter. For some reason I find this somewhat depressing. Maybe it's the idea of all the world's living things winding up as potential fuel for motor homes and chain saws."

*Invalid conversion*

56. "Sweden has claim to the largest impact structure in Europe, it appears. The area—a twenty-six-mile-wide area about 150 miles northwest of Stockholm—is the largest one in any European country; provided, of course, that the formation known as the Siljan Ring was indeed created by the impact of a meteor, a claim nobody doubts."

*Modus ponens*

57. From a letter to the editor: "Wood burning stoves are warm and attractive, and are a primary source of energy conservation. The Wood Heating Alliance estimates that wood stoves save about 100 million barrels of oil a year. Yet there is a hidden cost for the savings in oil—our health. The EPA estimates that by the turn of the century wood stoves will be sending 7 million tons of particulate matter into the air. Even now, according to the EPA, residential wood combustion causes 'almost as much airborne particulate matter as all U.S. coal-fired power plants, and more particulate matter than the coal mining, metalic ore mining, iron and steel, cement, and pulpwood industries combined.'

Clearly, something must be done. Residential wood-burning causes heavy pollution, and sources of heavy pollution, no matter what their other benefits, must be strictly regulated . . . ."

*Valid syllogism: All W [residential wood-burning] are P [causes of pollution], and All P are R [activities that should be regulated]; therefore, All W are R. The statement of the conclusion is implicit.*

58. "You could have gotten an A in that critical thinking course if you had just read over the chapters assigned; since you blew the course, don't tell me you read the chapters!"

*Modus tollens*

59. "If the Soviets build their version of Star Wars, the United States will redouble its efforts on SDI. But if that happens it will mean less money for important social programs. So if the Soviets build their system, Americans will go hungry. It's a crazy world!"

*Chain argument*

60. "Every politician wants approval, and so does every network anchor. Those anchors better remember that the next time they snicker at those who lead our country -- newtork anchors are all politicians, too!"

*Invalid syllogism*

61. "All professional counselors here in Georgia are licensed, so you can be certain that if the man your mother recommended has a license, he's a professional."

*Invalid conversion*

62. "Betty, if you were a good girl, you could go outside and play."
"But, Mommy, you know I got into a fight with my sister."
"That's right, Betty. And that's why you have to stay inside."

*Denying the antecedent*

63. "With steroids you become very injury prone. Your muscle insurgents can't take that kind of potential strength and start to give. That's why you see a lot of minor injuries with players on steroids. And that's why I suspect Jerry uses them. He has a lot of minor injuries."

*Invalid syllogism*

64. "In 1988 each presidential candidate could spent up to $23 million in primaries and caucuses. General Foods, by comparison, spent $32 million just advertising Jell-O in 1987. If the American people continue to believe that presidential races are too expensive, then they continue to believe a myth."

*This is best analyzed as modus ponens. Students may require a hint, namely, that the last sentence is just a way of saying that presidential races are not too expensive: More is spent advertising such things as Jell-O than the presidential candidates could spend in the primaries and caucuses; [Unstated: If more is spent advertising such things as Jell-O than the presidential candidates could spend in primaries and caucuses, then the presidential races are not too expensive]; Therefore, presidential races are not too expensive.*

65. "When we let the fossil record speak, its testimony is not evolution-oriented. Instead, the testimony of the fossil record is creation-oriented. It shows that many different kinds of living things suddenly appeared. While there was great variety within each kind, these had no links to evolutionary ancestors before them. Nor did they have any evolutionary links to different kinds of living things that came after them. Various kinds of living things persisted with little change for long periods of time before some of them became extinct, while others survive down to this day."
—*Life—How Did It Get Here? By Evolution or by Creation?*

*Modus tollens is perhaps the best analysis, since the topic sentence asserts that the fossil record does not support evolution. Thus: If the fossile record supported evolution, then it would not be as the rest of the paragraph asserts. The fossil record is as the rest of the paragraph asserts. Therefore, the fossil record does not support evolution.*

66. "Before 1917, the United States had a decentralized democracy, the most decentralized government in the West. However, when we entered the war, Woodrow Wilson galvanized the nation into a highly centralized state, in which railroads, shipping lines, and munitions factories were nationalized, other corporations were regulated, and the states turned to the federal government for their instructions. After the war it became accepted wisdom that if centralization could solve the problems of war it could help solve peace-time problems as well. Given the sweep of history, it is manifest that we cannot now return to decentralized government. We cannot do so, because the 1980s cannot be the 1900s."

    *Looks like question begging to us.*

67. "For Dukakis, the Wake Forest wordfest was the badly needed moment. Given his limited emotional range and his earnest, smartest-boy-in-the-class presentation, his command of the debate was his strongest performance since the Atlanta Convention. If the exchange, watched by 100 million viewers, did not help him rebound in the polls, it was not because of his lack of debating skills."

    *Modus ponens: If the exchange didn't help him rebound, it wasn't because of his lack of debating skills. [It didn't help him rebound.] [Therefore, it was not because of his lack of debating skills.]*

68. "Professor Regan thinks that animals can feel pain, and that therefore they have the right not to be experimented on to promote someone else's happiness."

    *Valid syllogism: Professor Regan thinks: All animals are pain feelers; [no pain feelers should be experimented on to promote someone else's happiness]; therefore no animals should be experimented on to promote someone else's happiness.*

69. "The new Pakistani administration will have to stay clear of the type of Islamization that Zia and his supporters sought to promote, if they want Pakistan to return to democracy. Unfortunately, after Zia's death the new regime sounded a loud message that its own design to stay in power involves a scheme of Islamization that is a duplicate of Zias. We are saddened by the failing prospects of democracy in Pakistan. So much was expected when Zia died in the plane crash."

    *Modus tollens*

70. "After Bush became president, my taxes didn't go up, but my Social Security payments did, and when that happened I had less take-home income. Less money for me to spend was therefore the result of the Bush election."

    *Valid syllogism: When Bush became president, my Social Security payments went up; when those went up I had less take-home income. Therefore, when Bush became president I had less take-home income. Or, in syllogism-ese: All occasions identical with Bush's being elected are occasions identical with my Social Security payments going up. All occasions identical with my social-security payments going up are occasions identical with my having less take-home income. Etc.*

Items 58-62 courtesy of Dan Barnett

# Chapter 10
# Generalization and
# Related Inductive Reasoning

This chapter of the text presents a series of questions that we think a reasonable person should consider when the types of argument described in the chapter are encountered. Not all of the arguments in the text's exercises or in the ones below—or in daily life—respond tractably to all the questions. So students should not be led to think that the questions should be applied unthinkingly and mechanically, as if the result of doing so will be an easy final evaluation of the argument at issue. The purpose of the questions is to help students deal thoughtfully with these types of arguments—to help them understand the arguments (which is crucial to everything else, of course) and to help uncover their strengths and weaknesses.

There's a small change in terminology in this edition: We use the phrase "error margin" instead of "confidence interval." Students hear about error margins (or "margins of error") all the time, nearly every time they see a poll or survey in the newspaper or hear the regular Louis Harris report on PBS's *Morning Edition;* but the words "confidence interval" almost never turn up in everyday life. So, we've left the latter in, so that students will recognize it if they take statistics, but we've used the former throughout as the principal term.

In the discussion of analogical arguments (pp. 286ff.) we stress that diversity of the sample is important to the strength of the argument. There is an obvious exception to this that is pointed out in a parenthetical remark near the middle of page 287. We thought we might put it another way here: Regarding an *unknown* characteristic of the target individual (if we don't know whether the target is a sedan, a wagon, or a sports model, for example), we want diversity in the sample; if the characteristic is *known* (e.g., we know the target is a sedan), then we want as little diversity in this respect as we can get (we want as many of the sample as possible to be sedans). This way of putting it seems to work well with most students.

## Exercises Unanswered in the Text

### Exercise 10-1

2. Universal. If someone said, "Lame ones don't, ha ha," the generalizer would probably say that he was not talking about lame ones.
3. Nonuniversal
5. Nonuniversal
6. Nonuniversal (probably, you'll recall)
8. Universal
9. Universal
11. Universal
13. Nonuniversal
14. Nonuniversal

## Exercise 10-2

2. (a) Yes, as far as what it means, but how does one know when he's at risk?
   (b) Yes, even though *what* appropriate exam is not specified
   (c) Yes

3. (a) No (Would "fan" include people moderately interested in the game?)
   (b) No ("Thug" is as vague as "British soccer fan.")
   (c) No, not given the vagueness mentioned above

5. (a) Yes
   (b) Yes
   (c) Yes, at least "in principle"

6. (a) Yes
   (b) Yes, although clarification of which sport would make it more clear
   (c) Yes

8. (a) "Feminists" is somewhat vague.
   (b) Yes, essentially
   (c) Yes, in principle

9. (a) Yes
   (b) Yes
   (c) Yes

## Exercise 10-3

2. The overall superiority of one defense to another is not quantitatively measurable.
3. Once again, the overall superiority of a current player to one of thirty-five years ago would be very difficult to measure because of changes in rules, stadiums, length of season, and such.
5. "Mood of the country" could mean a lot of things; so could "more conservative."
6. Better in what way? Is decaffeinated coffee included? Better for *every*body?
8. Both "tolerate" and "pain" are vague: tolerate before crying out? before succumbing? psychological as well as physical pain?
9. Maybe "harmful effects" is clear enough, but *up to* 50 percent includes as little as a tenth of a percent. And we'd like to know what it would reduce them *from*—from those when no protection at all is used? When our old car wax is used?

## Exercise 10-4

2. (a) "Blonde" is a term that's vague in several obvious ways. (b) By what standard do you measure how much fun a person has? More *intense* fun? Fun more of the time?
3. (a) How do we know what the "average" chimp and monkey are? (Halfway between a really smart chimp and a really dumb one?) (b) How is smartness being measured here? The standard is not a clear one.
5. (a) The most that can be said is that *reported* crime is up. (b) The claim doesn't spell out a location for the increase. (c) It also doesn't say what kind of crime. Without this information the 160 percent figure would be meaningless even if some base figure had been given.

6.  What counts as a classical musician? As a rock musician? (There are musicians who play both classical music and rock, after all.) And what does "more talented" mean? More *native* talent? Better trained? We're sure something can be made of this claim, but it certainly isn't clear quite what.

8.  Suppose you compared December 1-7, 1978 with December 1-7, 1979 (the claim doesn't contain any evidence that the periods discussed were really comparable) with respect to profanity on the networks. What would you count as profane? Individual words or phrases? Where does one profanity end and another begin? How do you compare the incidence of phrases with the incidence of single words? Equally? Were any "profanities" in news reports? If so, their occurrences are due to external events, not a simple choice of the networks. What is the difference between hard and soft profanity? A meaningless statistic.

9.  (a) One flaw here is the terms of the comparison. If a married couple is mugged, do we count it as two crimes or one? What if the couple had been two single people—is it counted the same? (b) The statistic could be misleading if one took it to mean that being married all by itself made for some difference in being a victim of crime. It may be that married couples tend to live in more affluent neighborhoods and are better protected against crime, and that *that* is what accounts for the difference.

### Exercise 10-6

Answers may be found in the glossary.

### Exercise 10-7

2.  Students from Tulare State
3.  A belief in God
5.  Yes. They should diminish our confidence.
6.  Yes. It should diminish our confidence, because many people may change their views (either way) during the course of their college careers. Such changes might result from their college experience, from other kinds of experience, or simply because they become older or more mature.
8.  Yes. It should increase our confidence.
9.  Yes. It should diminish our confidence (since more people with one view may choose to respond).

### Exercise 10-13

2.  No (At the 95 percent confidence level that Smitty requires, he can depend on only somewhere between 24 and 36 percent holding the belief. See table at the top of p. 277.)
3.  Yes
5.  No
6.  No
8.  No
9.  No

### Exercise 10-14

2. Students in Professor Ludlum's history classes
3. That a majority find him lacking
5. Yes. Students with an animus toward Ludlum may be more likely to write evaluations.
6. No
8. It is much too small.

### Exercise 10-15

2. Hasty generalization
3. Anecdotal evidence
5. Biased generalization
6. Anecdotal evidence
8. Hasty generalization, biased generalization
9. Biased generalization

### Exercise 10-16

2. The next deadlift
3. Accompanied by back pain.
8. Yes. It weakens the argument.
9. No
10. Yes. It strengthens the argument.

### Exercise 10-17

4. Yes
5. None are given in the passage.
6. No information about diversity is given.

### Exercise 10-18

2. Relevant, stronger
3. Relevant, stronger
5. Relevant, weaker
6. Not relevant, as far as we can see.
8. Relevant, weaker
9. Not relevant

### Exercise 10-19

3. No
5. 100 percent. This strengthens the argument.

**Exercise 10-20**

The numbers in parentheses refer to the questions used in the evaluation scheme for Exercise 10-19.

1. (1) Yes: Cranston's senatorial performance is the sample; his potential presidential performance is the target.
   (2) Yes, assuming that the speaker understands what he or she means by "excellent."
   (3) Yes
   (4) Yes, the sample is likely to be diverse, assuming that the speaker has paid enough mind to Cranston's performance as a senator to warrant an endorsement of that performance.
   (5) The premise is, presumably, that in *many* of his activities he has acted as I would want him to, but what counts as many is left unclear.

3. (1) Yes: Homer's appearance is the sample; the state of the Barnes's house upon their return is the target.
   (2) Yes
   (3) Yes, enough to call the argument into serious question
   (4) No
   (5) 100 percent of the sample items have the characteristic, but this isn't saying very much since there is only one of them—Homer's personal appearance.

4. This is best analyzed as a persuasive comparison (nonargumentative persuasion) or an instance of horse laugh pseudoreasoning. It's very doubtful that the egg/chicken and milk/cow analogues are offered as *premises*.

6. (1) A highly qualified "yes" to the first part of the question. The federal budget is too complicated for any one person to have a detailed idea of it and it isn't clear whether the speaker means just *any* household budget. "No" to the second part of the question: The characteristic that's being attributed to the sample and target is simply "trouble." This is much too vague to be of any use.
   (2) What kind of trouble an unbalanced federal budget might cause is very complicated, although it is knowable to some extent in terms of certain of its presumed effects.
   (3) Yes, enormous differences
   (4) No.
   (5) This isn't clear. It looks as though the characteristic is being claimed for all household budgets, though certainly a temporarily unbalanced budget in some households does not produce the "trouble" that seems to be claimed here.

7. (1) Yes: Wilbur's gastric circumstance is the sample; Mark's are the target.
   (2) Yes. Notice that it is the presence of a stomach problem (actual in Wilbur's case; potential in Mark's) that is the characteristic in question, not any causal claim about how the meat may cause stomach problems.
   (3) Yes. A dog's digestion and a human's are hardly the same, yet the differences are likely to affect the case somewhat less than one might think. We suspect that something that would cause a dog to become ill is more likely to cause a human to grow ill than would be the case vice versa.
   (4) Only one item in the sample

9. (1) Yes: Oregon's bottle law and its effects and California's proposed law and its possible effects
   (2) Yes
   (3) Some: Oregon has less urban area than California and fewer freeways and other highways; some claim significant differences in personality between the two populations, but we're not sure what to make of that.
   (4) Sample of one
   (5) Not applicable

10. (1)-(5) The sample is personalities in fish bodies. The target is personalities in non material "bodies" or environments. Both are members of the class we can describe as "personalities in radically altered environments." The argument is basically this: Human personalities cannot survive in bodies of fish; therefore, they cannot survive in a nonmaterial environment. The claim about the sample could not be known in any ordinary way, though it could be inferred (analogically) from, say, the results of sensory deprivation experiments. The claim about the target could not be known in any ordinary way either. Questions (4) and (5) seem not to be applicable to this case. In any event, the strength of the argument turns on question 3, concerning possible differences between the cases. Those who believe in a disembodied afterlife will see enormous differences (e.g., the desire and support of God for the disembodied survivors), and those who don't, won't. This item could also be analyzed as a persuasive comparison, though we think that analysis overlooks a considerable bit.

## Exercise 10-21

3. Ad hominem, if the conservationist's claim is being rejected in this passage. Whether it is actually being rejected is not clear, however.
4. Appeal to illegitimate authority
6. Ad hominem
8. This is an appeal to *legitimate* authority
11. Ad hominem, although it's close to nonargumentative persuasion
13. Ad hominem
15. Ad hominem, followed by an appeal to *legitimate* authority

# Chapter 10 Test Question-Exercise Bank

## Bank 10-1

These general claims are for evaluation. Students should keep the criteria noted in Exercise 10-2 in mind, but they should not confine their remarks to these criteria if other comments are called for.

1. "Professional sports? Never watch 'em. They're all fixed."

   *It's theoretically possible but very unlikely. Even if the claim were true, how would anybody go about establishing it? We'd like to hear the proof.*

2. "My liberal colleagues in the Congress are all big spenders."

   *How do you identify "liberals" (or "conservatives," for that matter)? The class is too vaguely defined, as is that of "big spenders." Note: If the speaker defines "liberals" as those who vote to spend the most money, he has begged the question—he has, possibly surreptitiously, turned it into an analytic claim.*

3. "The world and everything in it was created fifteen minutes ago complete with fictitious memories and false records."

   *As Bertrand Russell noted, there's no way to disprove this claim.*

4. "I'm not very photogenic—no photograph anybody has ever made of me really looks like me."

   *"Photogenic" is not a clearly defined notion, but there probably isn't anything that can be done about it. We doubt that no photograph resembles him; it's more likely that he just doesn't like the way he looks in the photographs. Maybe he just doesn't like the way he looks.*

5. "Bomb threats on abortion clinics are called in by the clinics themselves to gain sympathy and support from the public and news media."

   *The general claim would be very difficult to know, though one might know of a particular instance in which this happened.*

6. "Digital recordings may be all the rage these days, but every serious audiophile knows that a good analogue disk played on a music system of high quality is better than even the best digital version."

   *"Serious audiophile" isn't clear—could the speaker mean those people who prefer analogue recordings and hence be begging the question? Some of the other phrases are vague too—"good analogue disc," "system of high quality"—it may or may not be possible to specify more clearly what's intended by such terms.*

7. "The universe and everything in it doubled in size last night."

   *Unknowable claim—although this is controversial among philosophers.*

8. "Every account that Delwood has worked on has come back with computational errors in it."

   *We don't find anything wrong with this one. "Computational errors" could be spelled out precisely, but the context probably does not require such precision.*

9. From a letter to the editor: "It appears that the administration's foreign policy is increasingly far out."

   *What's being said about the administration's foreign policy? Who knows?*

10. "In no previous epoch were adversaries so continuously and totally mobilized for instant war. It is a statistical certainty that hair-trigger readiness cannot endure as a permanent condition."
—Nobel Peace Prize winner Dr. Bernard Lown, cofounder of International Physicians for the Prevention of Nuclear War

*"Continuously and totally mobilized for instant war" is not too vague; everyone understands what Lown means. "A statistical certainty" is apt to be less clear to many listeners. These claims would pass muster in many contexts, however. Note that only the first one is a general claim.*

11. "Conservative Christians are a politically sophisticated voting bloc."

*This may be an expression of praise; then again it may not. Measured against the three questions in Exercise 10-2, the claim is deficient in making clear what is being said about conservative Christians. It's not even totally clear who conservative Christians are.*

12. "Of the over 100,000 aliens who married U.S. citizens last year, 40 percent did so only to bypass immigration laws."

*We're skeptical whether such a precise percentage could be known in a matter like this.*

13. "It is prudent to assume that all nations attempt to spy on other nations to the extent that their capacities and interests dictate."
—Baltimore Sun

*It is known that many nations employ spies, and it is a reasonable inference from what is known about history and human nature to believe that most do. Further, the assumption is prudent.*

14. "Every Communist country in the world has been a violator of the fundamental human rights of individuals."

*We recognize clear-cut cases of Communist countries and violations of fundamental human rights, but both terms have very fuzzy edges indeed; general claims like this one require more precision if they're to be acceptable.*

15. "Caution: cigarette smoking is hazardous to your health."

*Vague, but knowable. And known.*

16. "Most voters in the 1988 presidential election believed that the Republican candidate better represented traditional values than did the Democratic candidate."

*It would be hard to know whether this was true even if we could identify just what "traditional values" meant. There may be something to this claim, but it would take someone more willing to go out on a limb than we to say exactly what it is.*

17. "All of the last three years have been extremely dry."

*"Extremely dry" is pretty vague, but it isn't that bad; this could still be a useful claim.*

18. "Obscene movies available at movie rental outlets are harmful to children who watch them."

   *Defining "obscene" is notoriously difficult, but there are surely items most of would agree fit the term. What counts as harmful to children may be just as difficult to determine. This is a pretty vague claim.*

19. "Nobody under seventeen is permitted unless accompanied by an adult."

   *This is clear enough, provided we know what counts as an adult.*

20. "The great majority of the science books in the high school library were published before 1960."

   *What's a science book? This probably isn't as important as whatever inference is likely to be drawn from it. We presume that, since it's a high school library, this means an awful lot of the library's science books are seriously out of date.*

## Bank 10-2

Comparative general claims for criticism

21. "A new anti-lock rear brake system has reduced the distance required to stop from fifty miles per hour by 11 percent."

   *We presume that the car stops 11 percent quicker than the same car did without the new brake system. It is possible that there's some weaseling going on here if the context leads one to believe that the car stops 11 percent faster than the competition.*

22. "Reagan was a better president than Nixon was."

   *How so? In what way?*

23. "The county unemployment rate went up 40 percent during our opponent's administration, but since we took the reins it has risen only 35 percent in the same length of time. Clearly, we have done the better job."

   *Probably not, as a matter of fact. It's wise to remember that events at the national level affect the rate of unemployment at least as much as county administration. More to the immediate point: If the number of unemployed at the beginning of the speaker's administration was the same as it was at the end of the opponent's, the latter did the better job. (Say that the number of jobless in the county was 5,000 at the beginning of the opponent's administration and 7,000 at the end of it—an increase of 40 percent. If the number of jobless increased by 35 percent during the speaker's administration, a total of 2,450 were added to the unemployment rolls during that time while only 2,000 were added during the opponent's.)*

24. "The pride is back."

   *As compared with before, presumably. This Chrysler advertising slogan, taken from a popular song, "Born in America," strives to stir patriotic sentiment for Chrysler products (note pseudoreasoning). There is no definitive way to measure national pride, of course.*

25. "The office has become more productive since we changed from typewriters to word processors, although it took about half a year for the staff to learn how to use them well enough to produce the gain."

*"Productive" is somewhat vague, although it can be made quite clear.*

26. The increase in the number and support of conservative think tanks has been substantial since the mid-1970s. The American Enterprise had twelve resident thinkers when Jimmy Carter was elected; today it has forty-five. The Heritage Foundation has sprung from nothing to command an annual budget of $11 million. The budget of the Center for Strategic and International Studies has grown from $975,000 ten years ago to $8.6 million today. Over a somewhat longer period the endowment of the Hoover Institution has increased from $2 million to $70 million.
—Adapted from Gregg Easterbrook, "Ideas Move Nations"

*Although some of the language may sound vague—for example, "sprung from nothing"—these are all straightforward comparisons with relatively well identified times in the past.*

27. "You'd be better off if you got more sleep."

*Unclear terms of comparison: better off than what? Also, the comparison itself is obscure: In what way better off—looks, health, attitude, or what? The terms of the second comparison are clearer, but it's still pretty unclear how much additional sleep counts as more.*

28. "Reading novels is a more productive use of one's time than going to movies."

*Just any old novel? More productive of what? Just any old movie?*

29. "I'd much rather stay home and read a novel than go to a movie."

*This is a different kind of remark from #28. The speaker is describing a preference that is clear enough for nearly any context in which the claim might be made.*

30. "Doctor Mohanty is younger than I."

*Clear comparison unless the context is unusual.*

31. "The best American film of the decade is *Out of Africa*."

*In what way best?*

32. "More people were killed by handguns in the United States in 1985 than in Great Britain."

*Clear comparison (The score, for the record, was 10,728 to 8.)*

33. "Beer drinkers are 23.2 times more likely than teetotalers to have unhappy marriages."

*What's a beer drinker? Anybody who ever drinks a beer? How are unhappy marriages distinguished from happy ones (or so-so ones)? Could such a comparison really be accurate to a decimal place? This isn't a very helpful statistic.*

34. "The answer to the question, 'How are blacks doing in America?' is 'Better than ever before.'"
    —Ronald Reagan, on the first national observation of Martin Luther King Jr.'s birthday.

    *In what way better? Income? (The median family income for black families was higher when Reagan made his comment than it was in 1968, the year Martin Luther King, Jr., was killed. It was also further behind the median family income for whites than in that year.)*

35. "George Bush ran a more negative campaign in 1988 than did Michael Dukakis."

    *"Negative campaign" is vague. And it may be that the speaker means that Bush was negative for more of the campaign than was Dukakis, since the latter is generally thought of as having slung mud only near the end.*

36. "NCAA rules for recruiting athletes are broken more frequently by Division 1 schools than by Division 2 schools."

    *This could mean either that the typical Division 1 school breaks rules more frequently than the typical Division 2 school or that the aggregate of Division 1 violations is greater than the aggregate of Division 2 violations.*

37. "Chrysanthemums that have been pinched back produce bigger blooms than those that have not."

    *This seems clear and reasonable. Most people who would be interested in it would know what "pinched back" means.*

38. "The Soviets still have a stronger force in Europe than the NATO allies."

    *"Stronger" could mean either bigger, in terms of more troops, or better armed, or both, or maybe something else yet.*

39. "Compact discs produce a clearer sound than vinyl records."

    *We don't have any trouble with this, although what counts as a "clearer sound" may be different for different listeners. (Some music critics find vinyl records "warmer" than CDs. We don't know what that means either.)*

40. [Background: "Aspartame" is the generic term for the sweetener known as "NutraSweet®" and manufactured by G. D. Searle & Co. Ellen Ruppell Shell wrote an article for the *Atlantic Monthly* ("Sweetness and Health," August 1985) in which she stated that claims made by Searle & Co. that aspartame's component amino acids (aspartic acid and phenylalanine) occur naturally in many foods as "somewhat misleading." The following are brief excerpts from a letter and reply in the January 1986 edition of the magazine.]

    "Shell alleges that aspartame 'delivers . . . amino acids in a much more concentrated form than a person would normally consume.' Aspartic acid and phenylalanine occur naturally in protein-containing foods, and the normal diet provides quantities far exceeding those derived from aspartame in aspartame-sweetened foods. . . . "
    —John P. Heybach, Director, Scientific Affairs, NutraSweet Group, G. D. Searle & Co.

"As a scientist, Dr. Heybach surely understands that concentration and quantity are two very different things. Aspartame delivers aspartic acid and phenylalanine in a much more concentrated form than do normal proteins, which contain up to eighteen other amino acids to balance the load."
—Ellen Ruppell Shell

*These brief excerpts are not intended to settle the aspartame issue, of course, but to give students an opportunity to sort out just what issue the two writers differ on; what is being compared to what?*


## Bank 10-3

Passages for the identification of fallacies

41. "Housing is far too expensive in this country. Why, the median price of a home in San Francisco is now over $152,000."

    *If the speaker is generalizing from San Francisco to the entire country, then the argument is hasty generalization, and, if you are aware of typical housing costs in San Francisco you could also call it a biased generalization. But perhaps the speaker only means something like, "When the median price of a home has gone over $152,000 in some place or other, San Francisco or wherever, then housing has just gotten too darn expensive in this country." Viewed this way, it's not clear that the speaker is even offering an argument.*

42. "I certainly did not enjoy the first meeting of that class. I think I'll drop it; I don't want a whole semester of meetings like that."

    *Whether this is a hasty generalization depends upon what it is the student didn't like about the first class. There are some things, such as an instructor's manner of presentation, that a person can reach legitimate conclusions about after only a small sample. Further, were the student to refer to the instructor's overview of what the course was going to be about, he may have a good inductive argument: "She said she was going to cover such-and-such material; instructors usually cover about what they say they're going to cover; therefore she will probably cover the material she said she was going to cover. And I have neither need nor inclination to study that material."*

43. "Political repression is so widespread in the Soviet bloc that those who monitor human rights in the world may sometimes wonder whether it is worth recording one more injustice. After all, the suffering of as great a human being as Andrei Sakharov goes on. On January 22, it will be six years since the KGB seized him on the streets of Moscow. . . ."
    —Anthony Lewis, *New York Times*

    *Is Lewis trying to support the first claim by the latter two? If so, it's a hasty generalization.*

44. Remark made while driving on the Pennsylvania Turnpike: "We've seen nine cars with license plates from west of the Mississippi today, and six of them have been from Texas. Texans must travel more than other people."

45. FIRST BICYCLE RIDER: "How come when we coast downhill you always go so much faster than I?"
SECOND BICYCLE RIDER: "Cause I'm heavier. Heavier things fall faster."
THIRD BICYCLE RIDER: "Wait a minute. I thought that was what Galileo proved wrong."
SECOND BICYCLE RIDER: "C'mon! That's only common sense. Heavy things are bound to fall faster. Just look at how fast I coast—and I'm the heaviest."

*This is something between hasty generalization and anecdotal evidence. Begging the question would also be a straightforward analysis.*

46. "If you think the people of Phoenix are going to give up their rights to water from the Colorado River to Los Angelinos, you'd better think about it some more. Read the letters to the editors of the Phoenix newspapers and you'll see what I mean. People are really hot under the collar about the issue."

*Biased generalization*

47. One western town (which we won't name) was found in a reliable state-wide study to have an unusually high cancer death rate. The study, done during the 1970s, showed the cancer death rate for white females to be 175.4 per 100,000 compared to 154.9 for the state. One resident dismissed the finding as follows: "Statistics! You can prove anything you want with statistics! There's no more cancer here than anywhere."

*Hasty generalization: Some statistical conclusions aren't trustworthy, so none of them are.*

48. "I went into that office supply store on Jackson Avenue the other day and I can tell you that I'm not ever going back. They're the rudest people I've ever seen in a retail business. The guy who waited on me griped constantly about it being inventory time and he was of no help at all in finding what I wanted to buy."

*Biased and hasty generalization*

49. From a letter to the editor: "The news media can never be trusted. Shortly before the Geneva summit the *Washington Post* decided that a news scoop concerning a confidential letter from Defense Secretary Weinberger to President Reagan was more important news than a coordinated posture by our negotiating team. . . ."

*Hasty generalization*

50. "Goldman may have won the Supervisor of the Year award, but that just means they didn't look very hard for a winner. I know a couple of people who work in Goldman's division and they say that he's a real pain to work for. I'd sooner trust my friends than some awards committee."

*Anecdotal evidence*

51. "I watched *Nova* on public television the other night, and it was great! I'm going to be in front of the tube every week for it from now on."

*If one Nova was good, that's not a bad reason for believing that they're generally pretty good. Still, this may be just a bit hasty.*

"I've seen brochures depicting the scenery in the Ozark Mountains, and it's beautiful. I'm even thinking of retiring to Arkansas, since it's clearly such a beautiful state."

*Hasty generalization*

52 "The photographs from the first roll of that new Kodak film were really good. I'll tell you, that film is good stuff."

*This is okay, since one roll of Kodak film can be expected to be much like every other roll of the same type.*

53. "Bill bought one of those Burn-Rite wood stoves last year, and it smoked up his house all winter. Those stoves are not worth the high prices they get for them."

*Hasty generalization*

54. "According to one of the leading consumer magazines, the best built cars these days are Japanese. Cars built by foreign manufacturers have just outclassed those built in the U.S., it appears."

*Biased generalization: What holds for Japanese cars may not hold for all foreign-built cars.*

55. "Sharon's father thinks the idea of a space-based laser missile defense is entirely feasible, and he should know, since he's a physicist who specializes in laser technology and has a degree in computer science."
    "Yeah, well he may be right, but he also works for the defense industry. There's a pot of gold in it for him if people believe that. He's probably not the most reliable source."

*No fallacy*

56. "*A Prairie Home Companion* must be a pretty popular radio program around here. About half my friends have copies of the book the program's host recently published."

*A hasty, and quite likely biased, generalization. The speaker's friends may not resemble the general population in its taste in radio programs.*

57. "Hello Mom? Yeah, it's me. . . . Fine. Great, in fact. Massachusetts is super—I've never had so much fun. . . . No. . . . Yes! And listen, I've just met the most wonderful guy. And I'm *sure* he's rich. You should just *see* the expensive car he drives. . . ."

*Hasty generalization*

**Bank 10-4**

Generalizations for evaluation. Identify sample, target, attributed characteristic, and the extent to which the claims involved are knowable. Consider carefully the size and diversification of the sample, and how different from the target the sample is or may be. Remember that what's important is a representative sample.

58. SUSANVILLE — Less than 20 percent of college professors consider themselves shy, according to a new study by two psychologists. "We were surprised by this result because other studies have reported that almost 50 percent of adult Americans think of themselves as shy," said Elliot Smalley, professor at Colusa State University. "College professors are sometimes thought to be an introverted lot and so we expected perhaps a majority to think of themselves as shy," he said.

    Smalley and his associate, John Mahmoud, interviewed 150 college professors who were identified by administrators at twenty-five American universities as typical faculty. The universities were selected by a random procedure from a list of American colleges and universities, Smalley said.

    *This is a poor generalization. University administrators might be apt to state the first professors who come to mind, and professors selected in this manner might tend to be among the more outspoken faculty. Truly shy, introverted faculty might well be unknown to most administrators at a large university.*

59. A random survey of 1,000 callers to a drug hotline number produced the following results: 535 of the callers were heavy users of either cocaine freebase, amphetamines, or heroin; 220 were "recreational" users of cocaine or hashish, 92 were not drug users at all, and the remainder refused to answer the survey questions. This should put to rest the claim that most people who take drugs are of the occasional, "recreational" type.

    *The sample in this argument is badly biased. It's much more likely that a typical heavy user of a drug will get into a crisis situation and thus call a hotline number than that a typical "recreational" user will have reason to call a hotline.*

60. ATLANTA (UPI) — A long-term federal study by the National Centers for Disease Control of 13 million U.S. births shows increases in the rate of eleven different types of birth defects, including a 17.5 percent yearly average increase in patent ductus ateriosus and a 10.8 percent increase for ventricular septal defects over a fourteen year period. The study was conducted by the Birth Defects Monitoring Program of the CDC, which collected its data from hospitals across the country. From 1970 to 1983 over 13 million births were monitored. [An adaptation]

    *"Hospitals across the country" is vague, but this is almost certainly a reputable scientific study, and the sample is extremely large. A generalization from these results to the American population as a whole should be sound.*

61. A survey was made in 1948 in which a large number of names were randomly selected from the telephone book of a large city. The individuals called were asked whether they preferred Truman or Dewey in the presidential race. Over half of the respondents named Dewey, so the poll-takers concluded that Dewey would carry the city and region.

    *The principal problem with this survey is that in 1948 many voters did not have telephones and thus had no chance of being selected. Since possession of a telephone was linked with a person's economic status, and economic status helps determine political views, the sample was badly biased.*

62. As part of his work for NASA, Dr. Murdock was asked to find out what percentage of Americans saw Halley's comet when it was visible in 1985-86. He randomly selected three cities, Seattle, Cleveland, and Boston, and polled several hundred randomly selected individuals from these cities. His findings are that less than 5 percent of Americans saw the comet.

*It makes no difference whether the cities and the individuals were randomly selected. Inhabitants of large cities, especially northern big cities, would be less likely to see the comet because of city lights, clouds, air pollution, and latitude.*

63. Haslett wanted to know what percentage of students at his college vote in local elections. He asked each of his professors (he was a political science major) to ask for a show of hands in his classes so he could make a count. He found that 45 percent of the 120 classmates polled vote in local elections. He concludes that about 45 percent of the students at his college vote in those elections.

*The sample is large enough to be somewhat reliable, although Haslett should not be surprised by a substantial deviation from his 45 percent projection. A more serious problem is that, so it appears from the story, Haslett's poll may have been taken in political science classes, or at least mainly in political science classes, and it may be that people who take such classes—especially political science majors like Haslett himself, are more interested in political matters and hence more likely to vote in any election. The possibility of bias is substantial.*

64. Seventy-two percent of those interviewed at a luncheon sponsored by the Camellia Chamber of Commerce favored local tax incentives to attract new businesses. Would this finding generalize to the Camellia population?

*No. This is not likely to be a representative sample.*

65. Let's say that state wide studies have been done in Montana and Virginia and the infant mortality rate for these two states averaged 10.5 per thousand live births. Could this figure be generalized to the infant mortality rate in the United States? What factors might be relevant to the generalization?

*Montana and Virginia provide a large and reasonably good sample, although there may be a bias toward rural and small town areas compared to large urban areas. We would want to know about Montana's and Virginia's resident-to-doctor ratio, its resident-to-hospital bed ratio, the level of prenatal education available in the two states, and similar matters. The more similar these possibly relevant factors are in Montana and Virginia to the remainder of the country, the stronger the argument.*

66. A majority of Americans think that tobacco companies should be prohibited from advertising their products. In a survey of 1,213 adults, 86 percent said that prohibiting tobacco advertising would lower smoking rates. The results of the nationwide telephone survey, conducted by American Opinion Research, Inc., were published in this week's edition of *Research Fact*. Spokespersons for the American Tobacco Council had no immediate comment on the findings.

*It is not clear from this passage whether a majority of the respondents actually think that tobacco advertising should be prohibited. The 86 percent said something else, that doing so would lower smoking rates. Whether or not they would outlaw tobacco advertising is not known.*

67. Osteoporosis is a degeneration of bone tissue that afflicts between fifteen and twenty million Americans and leads to approximately 1.3 million bone fractures every year. The condition is found mainly among women. A conference sponsored by the National Institutes of Health in 1984 reported that calcium was one of the "mainstays of prevention and management of osteoporosis." In a localized study designed to help predict the future incidence of osteoporosis in women in a midwestern community, a county hospital did a survey on calcium intake. It selected 500 women at random and asked them to keep a record of their food and dietary supplements for one month. The data was analyzed to determine the amounts of calcium each woman received. It was determined that 85 percent of the surveyed women received less calcium than the recommended amount of 1,000 to 1,500 milligrams a day. County medical people concluded that about 85 percent of the community's women were getting less than the recommended intake of calcium. They also concluded that local medical facilities would soon see an increase in the number of cases of osteoporosis as the calcium deficiency had its effects. Given just the information presented here, how much confidence would you have in these conclusions?

*The first conclusion is less solid than it might appear. The survey was done during one month, and diets change during the course of a year. Some dairy products may be consumed more during one time of the year than others; certainly some vegetables are consumed on a varying seasonal basis. Hence the study may accurately reflect only the calcium intake in the population during that month of the year. Another problem with the survey is that women were not sorted into age categories. Women of different ages may consume different amounts of calcium, and , since osteoporosis is a degenerative condition, it is likely to affect women of different ages much differently. (Women who take too little calcium at age 24 but who increase their intake by the time they are 35 may be no more likely to suffer osteoporosis than those whose intake is high during their entire lives.)*

*The second conclusion does not follow at all. The insufficient intake of calcium may have been going on for years, hence the incidence of osteoporosis may remain exactly the same in the future.*

68. FRESNO — In a new study of dangerous Halloween pranks, Fresno State University sociologist Joel Best has documented the exact number of American children killed or seriously injured by anonymously given, booby-trapped Halloween treats. Best reviewed supposedly real Halloween horror stories appearing from 1958 to 1984 in the *New York Times*, the *Chicago Tribune*, the *Los Angeles Times*, and the *Fresno Bee*. He did not find a single case in which a Halloween treat anonymously given to a child caused serious harm. He concluded that the infamous Halloween sadist is an "urban myth."
—Adapted from a McClatchy News Service release

*The question is whether the "exact number" of American children killed or seriously injured by anonymously given Halloween tricks can be determined by looking at the incidents reported in the five newspapers mentioned. There may have been a few incidents not reported in these newspapers, but we'd be surprised if there were many. Events of this type tend to attract too much attention not to be reported in at least one of these sources.*

69. A poll of fifty weight-lifters at a Southern California gym determined that thirty-three payed close attention to their diets as well as to their exercise. Of those thirty-three, twenty-five (50 percent of the original fifty) made it a point to eat more than the minimum daily amount of protein for large adults, and twenty (40 percent of the original fifty) took vitamin pills and other dietary supplements. The chain of health food stores that took the poll concluded that weight-lifters constitute a substantial market for its products, since most likely 40 percent of all weight-lifters across the country take vitamin pills and supplements, and an additional 10 percent are at least highly conscious of their diets.

*The health food chain had best not invest too much in trying to attract this new market. The first flaw in the survey is technical: The sample is too small to give a very detailed picture of weight-lifters' habits—even if nothing else were wrong with the survey, strong confidence (95 percent) would be justified only in the claim that from about 36 to 64 percent of weight-lifters nationwide make sure to eat more than the usual amount of protein—not a very precise conclusion (see the confidence interval chart in the text, p. 244). More important, the survey is flawed in confining the interviews to clients of only one gym. Information is often passed around among people who frequent the same establishments, and there may be trends or fads or a particular bit of useful information that is current at one gym but not in others. The sample is biased, in other words.*

70. "NEW YORK (AP) — Women who read 'bodice-rippers,' a sexy, violent genre of historical romance novel, have sex 74 percent more often than nonreaders, according to a survey by two psychologists from the Emory Medical School in Atlanta, who interviewed 72 middle-class women in Atlanta, an equal number of them housewives, working women and college students. Women who read the romances reported making love an average of 3.04 times a week, compared to 1.75 for nonreaders."

*How significant "74 percent more often" is is something we'll take up in the next chapter. Our concern here is whether the "3.04 and 1.75 times a week" figures generalize from the Atlanta sample. First, we'd not be at all surprised if there were an important discrepancy between reports of frequency and actual frequency (the article runs the two together). Further, a sampling of Atlanta women may not be representative of American women even in regard to reporting the frequency of sex. There may be, for example, cultural differences between urban and nonurban areas, southern and other areas of the country, and so forth, that affect attitudes about sex and reports about sexual activity. Also, does the distribution in the sample between housewives, working women, and college students reflect that in the population as a whole? Are one-third of American women college students, for instance? Only if they were would this sample be representative.*

(The following four exercises are all based on the two paragraphs in item 71.)

71. A college professor converted one room of her house into a home office and intended to deduct her home office expenses on her federal income tax return. She wondered how many other college faculty had done the same, thinking that the more who deducted home offices the less likely her own return would be noticed by the IRS, hence the less likely it would be that she would be audited. So she decided to do her own informal survey of her colleagues to see how many of them had home offices. She sent out a questionnaire of three questions to all 1,200 instructors at her campus, and she received 950 responses. (She promised to share the results of the survey, something that apparently motivated faculty to respond.)

   As it turned out, 32 percent of her respondents answered "yes" to the question, "Do you maintain an office at home?" Half of these also answered "yes" to the question, "Do you deduct your home office expenses on your federal income tax return?" And 24 percent of the entire group of respondents answered "yes" to the question, "Is your campus office adequate?"

Would our professor's conclusion, "About 32 percent of college faculty nationwide maintain home offices," be more likely if she had included faculty from other institutions among her survey? Why?

*It would be much more likely to be accurate. Faculty at different kinds of colleges (community colleges, state colleges, state universities, and private universities) have different requirements, and hence a different level of need for offices at home—the more research a faculty does, the more likely the home office phenomenon.*

72. Would our professor's conclusion, "Sixteen percent of faculty nationwide deduct home office expenses on their federal income tax return," be more accurate if she restricted it to faculty in her own state?

*Yes. Different states may have different state income tax rules, and it may be more worthwhile, for tax reasons, to have a home office in some states than in others. A faculty member who does not find it worthwhile to have a home office in one state may find it advantageous in another.*

73. Is it reasonable for our professor to conclude that faculty office space on the campus is inadequate?

*Yes, at least it is reasonable for her to conclude that her faculty colleagues believe it is inadequate, and by a large majority. Her sample is not only large enough to guarantee reliability in such a conclusion, but also it includes almost all of the target population.*

74. Do you find any flaw in our professor's reasoning about the usefulness of the survey for her own purposes? That is, should she believe that, the more people who have home offices, the more likely her own is to escape attention from the IRS?

*This is not a question about the criteria for evaluating statistical generalizations, but rather about the assumption that motivated the study. It does us no good to produce studies to answer questions if they are the wrong questions to begin with. In this case, it may be that the IRS will turn more attention to home office deductions if there are enough of them to constitute a large total of deductions. Our professor has done a good job of answering some questions (about office space, about the number of home offices maintained by her colleagues and at other campuses similar to hers) but she had best be careful not to let her enthusiasm at having produced some reliable figures rub off on her initial assumption; such a mistake could be costly at tax time.*

75. "Seventeen percent of Winchell State students intend to pursue careers as computer programmers or analysts. That's what a recent survey of WSU students conducted by psychology major Jack Nafarik shows. Nafarik passed out questionnaires to students who voted in the March student election as they exited from the polling stations in the student union. 'The results didn't surprise me,' Nafarik said. 'The figure may seem fairly high, but you'd expect that in a technical school like Winchell State.'"

*Do student voters comprise a representative sample of the students at Winchell State? Probably not. Upper division students may vote in larger numbers than freshmen and sophomores, and there may be correlations between class standing and career goals.*

*There may also be a direct correlation between types of major and participation in student elections. Can you think of any other possible sources of bias?*

76. Thirty percent of American women ages 19 to 39 diet at least once a month, according to a news syndicate poll released last November. These findings, based on telephone interviews with a random sample of women listed in the Los Angeles telephone directory. . . .

    *We'd not trust a generalization about this subject based on a sample of women who list themselves as women in the telephone book, perhaps especially if they live in Southern California, which may have more than its fair share of aspiring models and actresses, beach-goers and other figure-conscious women.*

77. According to a study published by Dr. William P. Newman III of Louisiana State University Medical Center in the January 16, 1986, edition of the *New England Journal of Medicine*, physicians in Bogalusa, Louisiana, conducted autopsies on thirty-five youngsters, ranging in age from seven to twenty-four with an average age of eighteen, who had died mostly from accidents, homicides, or suicides. They found that all but six of the young people had fatty streaks on their aortas, the body's main artery. Fatty streaks are the earliest gross recognizable lesions of atherosclerosis (hardening of the arteries), according to Newman. Since there was a direct link between the number of fatty streaks and the cholesterol levels in the young people, Newman recommended that all schoolchildren be checked for high cholesterol levels.

    *Newman is generalizing from the sample of thirty-five young people to all schoolchildren. However, he probably would not say that the sample indicates that a majority of all young people have the early signs of atherosclerosis. Rather, he would say that the sample suggests that a sufficient number of young people may have that disease for it to be worthwhile to monitor the cholesterol levels of all children. Interpreted this way, this is a reasonable generalization: The Bogalusa study does warrant concern and further investigation.*

78. Ronald is driving across the country when his car develops a minor mechanical problem. He can fix the trouble himself, but he'll need a wrench of a size he doesn't have. He resolves to stop at the next Sears retail store he sees to purchase one. He's been in four or five Sears retail stores in the past, and all of them have carried automotive tools. So he is confident that all Sears retail outlets stock them.

    *His sample is small, but very representative: Ronald has made a sound generalization. Note that the argument could also be construed as analogical.*

79. "Well, I did rotten in Algebra I last semester, so I expect I'll do poorly in the rest of the math classes I'll have to take."

    *There may be enough differences between last semester and the rest—we'd like to think— to make the argument a weak one: different instructor, new study habits, etc. Still, we'd bet against him doing well before we'd bet against somebody who did well in Algebra I.*

80. "Don't buy any Australian wine. I've had Australian wine before and, believe me, you won't like it."

193

*Well, maybe she will. This is too hasty. That one kind of Australian wine was not very good doesn't mean that there aren't good varieties. Every country that makes wine makes at least a little bad wine.*

81. "Mr. Smythe has closed each of the last four contracts with France International. Seems to me he'd be likely to do well with the rest of our overseas deals."

*This may be a biased sample. Did Mr. Smythe work with the same people on the four France International contracts? More diversity in the sample would make this a stronger argument.*

82. Hamilton City was considering annexing a portion of land adjacent to the city limits where construction of a subdivision was planned. In order to determine what the residents of the town thought about this annexation and about municipal growth in general, the city council had a poll taken. One thousand of the city's fifteen thousand registered voters were randomly selected and asked three questions: (1) Do you favor no growth, modest growth, or accelerated growth for Hamilton City? (2) Do you favor annexation of the 800-acre Brodnax parcel north of town and its planned subdivision? (3) Should the city enter into agreements with developers promising to supply city services like sewers and street maintenance in return for the added tax revenue the developer's projects will produce? The results of this survey were taken to be the "official" opinion of the voters of Hamilton City.

*There is clearly nothing wrong with the sample size, and, if the selection was indeed random, this poll can be taken as indicating pretty much what the voters of Hamilton City think about the questions asked. The problem is with the questions: The first is much too vague (we'd bet the great majority of responses favored modest growth, whatever that means); the second can be intelligently answered only by voters who understand the implications of annexation—we can imagine a voter responding "yes" to the question and living to regret the annexation later (or responding "no" and living to regret that). The third question is also too vague to be helpful. How expensive will the services be? How much tax revenue will be generated? What kinds of commitments would the agreements involve over how long a period? Without carefully thought out questions, no adherence to the rules of statistical generalization can produce a reliable result.*

83. MEMO: "We interviewed Haddow and found that she could handle each of the problems we gave her. I recommend we hire her."

*The speaker is betting that because Haddow can solve certain kinds of problems, she'll be able to solve all those she's given. If the problems she solved really are representative of the problems she will encounter, then it's a good bet. If they're not, it's not.*

84. A New York newspaper stopped theater goers as they exited from a performance of *La Tragédie de Carmen* and asked them whether they thought that Broadway theater was better or worse than it was ten years ago. When the majority of the respondents answered that they thought it was worse, the paper printed an article with the headline "Public Thinks Broadway Is Going Downhill." Does the poll justify the headline?

*No. "Public" is misleading, since it could be taken to refer to the general public and not just the theater-going public. More important, the poll is highly biased in at least two ways: it may be that the production mentioned does not draw a typical theater audience, and hence the sample may be biased; and the effects of the performance attended may bias an individual respondent (whether he liked* this *performance may have undue influence on his answer).*

85. Readers of *Consumer Reports* can write in their opinions of movies they have seen. Each month *CR* reports the total number of opinion votes it receives in this way. In the February 1986 issue, the average rating of the movie *Explorers* is 4 on a scale of 1 to 5, with 5 the bad end of the scale. The total vote on the movie is 107. How sound would a generalization from this sample to American movie goers in general be?

*Not very. We know that* maybe *107 people who know about the* CR *movie poll didn't like the movie very much ("maybe" because some may have voted more than once), but that's about all we know. There is no assurance that the sample is representative of the population mentioned in the question.*

## Bank 10-5

Analogical arguments for evaluation

86. HE:    "Let's leave Cincinnati for the golden west!  Why don't we move to Los Angeles?"
    SHE:    "Well, for one thing, we couldn't afford to buy a house there."
    HE:    "Don't be such a pessimist.  We bought this house here, didn't we? How much more expensive can houses be in LA?"

*Even if he is not aware of the difference in the cost of housing in the two cities he should realize there are important relevant differences between such different parts of the country that could profoundly affect housing costs. Furthermore, if they bought their Cincinnati house quite a while ago there is a relevant difference in time between the two occasions as well as the geographical difference. Note that the argument would be just as shaky if the inference were from Los Angeles to Cincinnati. (The fact that housing costs are currently higher in LA than in Cincinnati is irrelevant to the strength of the argument, though it proves that the implied conclusion is false.)*

87. "The Chicago Bears made it into last year's Superbowl with about as little trouble as a team could have.  They'll have almost the same personnel next year, so I'm putting my money on the Bears to be back next year."

*The Bears having almost the same personnel next year helps the analogy some, but there are way too many other relevant factors that have to be considered before this argument would be a safe one—the other twenty-five teams may not have the same personnel they had last year, for instance. Notice that it's easy to confuse what a person is betting on in cases like this: It's one thing for the Bears to be more likely than any other team to be in the championship game, but it's another thing for it to be more likely that they'll be there than that they won't.*

88. Six months ago several of Molly's friends joined the Trimtime Fitness Center. Each of them participated in Trimtime's weight-reduction and fitness regimen. All reported substantial weight reduction and all are visibly slimmer. Molly is convinced. She joins Trimtime and enrolls in the same program, hoping and expecting to see the same results. She is especially delighted to learn that Trimtime has adjusted its program to make it even more effective in a shorter period of time.

*Molly should consider potential differences between her and her friends, but from our outsider's point of view we would have to say that, if she followed the original program just as they did then we would expect her to get similar results. But without knowing the details of the changes in the program or the evidence for believing that the changes will be an improvement, Molly should not be delighted to learn that the program has been "adjusted"; the change in the program weakens the argument. (Trimtime might, of course, be able to give Molly good reason for thinking that the change will be an improvement.)*

[Items 89-92 are based on the paragraph in item 89.]

89. Juanita has taken six courses at Valley Community College, and she has a grade average of B so far. All the courses she has taken have been in sociology and psychology. She's thinking of enrolling in another course next term, and she expects to make at least a B in whatever she takes. If we don't know yet what subject she will take, would her argument be stronger, weaker, or neither if her previous six courses had been in four different subjects rather than two?

   *Stronger. The more diversification among the sample, the more likely it is that at least some of its members will resemble the new course.*

90. Would Juanita's argument be stronger, weaker, or neither if we knew that the new course will be in psychology (compared to not knowing what it will be in)?

   *Stronger. If her new course is in a subject that we know is included in the sample, that tells us of at least one relevant similarity.*

91. Would you assess Juanita's argument as stronger, weaker, or neither if you knew that Juanita had made a B in each of her previous courses and not just that she has a B average?

   *Stronger. She could have a B average even though she has made Cs in several of her previous courses, and such a possibility weakens the argument.*

92. What if, when she took the previous courses, Juanita had done all her studying alone because she didn't know any of the other students at Valley, but now she knows several good students and plans to study with them when she takes her next course? Would her argument be stronger or weaker.

   *Weaker. If this seems paradoxical, it's because we're thinking of a separate argument (which might go something like this: Juanita studies better when she studies with other good students; she did not study with other students for her previous courses but she'll study with other good students for the next course; therefore she'll study better for the next course). This other argument would support the conclusion, provided that its premises are true. But the original analogical argument is weakened because of the addition of a relevant difference between the target and the sample.*

93. Mr. Naphal has read in an authoritative science report that a dye commonly injected into Florida oranges is carcinogenic. He resolves not only to avoid Florida oranges until he learns that they no longer are dyed with the same chemical, but to avoid California oranges and all grapefruit as well.

*We'd avoid California oranges too, unless we had some reason to think they weren't dyed with the same dye. Concerning the grapefruit, certainly the fact that oranges are orange and grapefruit are yellow (and thus would require different colored dyes) weakens the argument.*

94. In Great Britain savings of between 20 and 40 percent in costs have resulted from selling government-run programs and business to individuals and companies in the private sector. This argues well for the administration's interest in selling such U.S. government entities as the Bonneville Power Administration, the Tennessee Valley Authority, and various parts of the postal service.

    *The terms of the analogy are not clear: Which (or at least what kind of) British programs and businesses were sold off? Would the sales be handled similarly (with regard to terms of payments, for example)? Would the government subsidize private ownership for a period of time after the sale? How would general differences in the economic structures of the U.S. and Great Britain affect the argument? There are too many differences between the sample and the target to put too much confidence in this argument.*

95. Wolfgang's friend has an opportunity to visit New Orleans and wants to know what Wolfgang's recommendation is, since he has been to America, once visiting New York and once visiting Columbus. *(Why is it always "Columbus, Ohio"?)* Wolfgang tells her to stay away from New Orleans. "Based on my experience, it will be awful—you'll find crime, violence, poverty, rude people, drug addicts—every kind of unpleasantness."

    *Wolfgang's reasoning is really to this effect: I didn't like New York or Columbus, so I wouldn't like the next U.S. city I visited—and she won't either. And we would expect Wolfgang not to like New Orleans, even though there are tremendous differences among the cities mentioned in the exercise.*

96. "He won the Silver Medal of Honor, has a Purple Heart, and was an Eagle Scout. I find it difficult to believe that it was he who committed the robbery."

    *Even though few of us know people who have won all these awards, most of us do have experience with people who have earned acknowledgment for dedication, respect for others, courage, conscientiousness, and so on. These people are the "sample." Because we know (and know of) few such people who also commit deeds that seem to deny these virtues, we reason that this individual is unlikely to have done so either. The analogical reasoning encountered here is inherently weaker than any direct evidence that bears on the person's evidence.*

97. A conversation:
    "You going to vote for Spankey or Howard in the City Council election?"
    "Howard. As far as I can make out, their experience is the same, and they both take about the same position on the issues. But Spankey was a student of mine. I caught him cheating once."

    *Our experience tells us that most people who are dishonest in one situation are more apt to be dishonest in another, so, everything else being equal between the two candidates, it is reasonable to give the nod to Howard. (Seldom is everything else equal, of course.)*

98. Hank ("The Flailin' Australian") Kingscote has won every one of his fifteen previous prizefights by knockouts. The chances are this poor fellow who's going to fight him next will wind up stretched out on the canvas.

    *Prizefights are a lot like snowflakes and political elections: The next one is not necessarily going to look like the last one(s). We know nothing about the quality of opponent in Hank's previous fights (the sample) nor about his upcoming opponent (the fight with who is the target).*

99. Washburn has read that it is good to include cabbage in one's diet. He doesn't care much for cabbage, but he likes Brussels sprouts. Since the latter look like small cabbages, he assumes that their nutritional benefits will be about the same as those of cabbage.

    *Obviously there may be differences between cabbages and Brussels sprouts that are highly important from a nutritional standpoint. Nevertheless, the clear physical similarities between the two vegetable make this a fair analogical argument.*

100. From a letter to the editor: "Tom Bradley lost the last election because he supported handgun control. So now he's changed his tune and claims he'll be the first one to oppose handgun control. I voted for him last time, but I won't vote for him this time, and it's not because I favor handgun control. I just don't want a governor who can talk out of both sides of his mouth like that. . . ."

    *This is similar to item 97. Incidentally, this is not an ad hominem. The argument goes like this: Our experience tells us that most people who are unprincipled in one way are apt to be unprincipled in others; therefore Bradley, who is a member of this class, is apt to be unprincipled in other ways, too. Given the premises, the argument is not a weak one; however, a premise that assigns a person to a class of unprincipled people because of a change in position is one that needs close examination. Is the change due to a lack of principle? Or was it occasioned by legitimate, nonself-serving reasoning?*

**Bank 10-6**

The following items each contain an example of appeal to illegitimate authority.

101. "Donald Westlake's novel, *Kahawa,* points up how incredibly brutal the Ugandan regime of Idi Amin was. It's hard to believe how someone with such a perverse bloodthirstiness could actually have run an important country like Uganda."
    "Now wait a minute. You've got to remember that Westlake's book is a piece of fiction. You can't tell the difference between what he's dug up and what he's made up."

    *The second speaker is right. There may be evidence that Amin is what Westlake makes him out to be, but such a picture in a novel is not evidence. The first speaker appeals to illegitimate authority.*

102. "We decided to design and build our own house, one that would suit our needs as perfectly as possible but would be expandable later. We knew we were going to need help because we'd never done anything like that before. But, fortunately, my cousin Sid is a carpenter and has had years of hands-on experience at house building. We've hired him to do the design, and we're delighted to have a professional working with us."

    *Appeal to illegitimate authority: Sid may know house building, but that does not make him an expert at designing a custom house beyond giving advice on what is technically feasible.*

103. "I went to my Uncle Stan for advice all the time I was growing up, and he never once failed me. So it was natural to turn to him when I found myself facing the dilemma of doing what was best for my career or trying to save a deteriorating marriage."

*Uncle Stan may have been a help to a young man or woman with the problems most young people encounter, but this does not make him an expert at more "grown-up" problems—he may not have any experience in matters of careers and problematic marriages. So, even though our speaker may feel comfortable talking to his Uncle Stan— and that is worth something, of course—we'd count this as an appeal to illegitimate authority unless we knew that Stan was offering advice that's within his experience.*

104. SHE: "Let's start adding calcium supplements to our diet, okay?"
HE: "Listen, those things are expensive. Why bother?"
SHE: "Well, the sports physiologist out at Trimtime suggested that it might be a good idea."
HE: "Ha! What does he know about it? He's no nutritionist."

*He's probably guilty of an ad hominem. We don't think she's really guilty of an appeal to illegitimate authority, although it may look like it at first. A physiologist's opinions on nutritional matters are less creditable than those of a nutritionist, but they are more credible than those of a layperson.*

## Bank 10-7

Here are some more ad hominems, useful here and in the pseudoreasoning chapters as well.

105. Lottery director Mark Michalko said Thursday that allegations that Californians are squandering money they once used for food to buy lottery tickets 'are just not correct.' California Grocers Association president Don Beaver raised the issue earlier in the week, saying five supermarket chains had complained that grocery sales dropped about 5 percent after lottery tickets went on sale October 3. Michalko rejected Beaver's assessment at a news conference held to announce a new lottery game. He suggested that Beaver's comments may stem from his group's failure to talk the Lottery Commission into an increase in the commission for selling lottery tickets.
—Adapted from an article by Steve Gibson in the *Sacramento Bee*

*As presented here, Milchalko is guilty of an ad hominem.*

106. MS. STONEWALL: "I believe we ought to think about buying a house. I talked to George Stakarkis the other day, and he says this is a really good time to buy because interest rates are down but home prices have not yet started up."
MR. STONEWALL: "I'm perfectly happy here, my dear. Besides, Stakarkis may be in the real estate business and worth a fortune, but he inherited most of that money from his father—he doesn't know any more about real estate than I do."

*Ms. Stonewall's appeal is as much to Stakarkis's reasons as to his authority. Unless Mr. Stonewall is or has been in the real estate business himself, it's unlikely that he knows as much about it as someone who has. Mr. Stonewall commits an ad hominem.*

107. Adapted from an editorial:  The local antidevelopment environmentalists are at it once again.  Now they're questioning whether the proposed Wildwood development will interfere with deer migration patterns.  But their opposition to every development proposal that has appeared in recent years makes their concern highly suspicious.  One is led to believe that their true motivation is to keep Wildwood Canyon as their own special preserve.

*A straightforward ad hominem*

108. "No, I don't want to hear what our British expert has to say about the subject.  The British have been on the economic slide since World War II, and I wouldn't trust any advice that came with a British accent."

*Ad hominem*

109. "In a full-page ad in the *Washington Post*, the organization [Planned Parenthood] declared that 'What [anti-abortion leaders] want is a return to the days when a woman had few choices in controlling her future.  They think that the abortion option gives too much freedom.  That even contraception is too liberating.  That women cannot be trusted to make their own decisions.'
      "Whew!  Pretty strong language, even from a group that makes its living partly by cutting babies into little pieces."
—Richard Viguerie

*Ad hominem*

110. "I'm convinced by the arguments given in the *National Review* that supply-side economics have been a success after all."
      "For crying out loud, you can't make up your mind based on something you've read in a right-wing magazine like that; of *course* the *National Review* would claim success for the administration's conservative policies."

*Ad hominem*

111. A cogitation: "She said I paid too much for this watch, and she ought to know, since she owns a jewelry store herself.  But then she probably just said that to get my goat for not having bought it at her store."

*Ad hominem*

112. "Gas prices are going to drop sharply.  Ted Missick said so, and he owns a Lincoln dealership.  He ought to know."
      "He doesn't know anything of the kind.  He just wants people to buy his gas hogs."

*Ad hominem*


**Bank 10-8**

Fill in the blank; true-false; miscellaneous

113. When you add a group of quantities together and divide the result by the number of quantities you get an average known as *the mean*.

114. In the premises of an inductive generalization, a thing is said to be characteristic of a *sample* of a class of things. And in the conclusion the same thing is said to be a characteristic of the entire class, or __*target*__.

115. No generalization based on an unrepresentative sample is trustworthy.
*True*

116. A statistical inductive generalization cannot establish that some precise percentage of a target population has a given characteristic.
*True*

Evalutate the following quotations from a local newspaper:

117. "Sexual offenses are becoming native to our culture."

118. "Dangerous offenders incorporate pornography into their preparatory stimulation before seeking a victim."

119. "Pornography interferes with interpersonal relationships in everyone who uses it."

*We would like to see discussion emphasize the obscurity of #117, the vagueness of #119, and the question of the knowability of both #118 and #119.*

120. "In a study done by a University of Pennsylvania psychologist, 29 suburban and 38 inner-city children from the Philadelphia area, ranging in age from 3 to 12 years, were asked to consume foods mixed with 'disgusting' substances, like apple juice stirred with a used comb or containing a dead grasshopper. Almost two-thirds of the children from 3 to 6 sipped juice in which a grasshopper floated. There were no differences between city and suburban children."
—published in *Developmental Psychology*

Would it be safe to say, given this study, that the same percentage of *all* American children from 3 to 6 would be willing to sip juice in which a disgusting object floats? Explain in a brief essay.

*We'd think a good essay would make it clear what the sample and target classes are and what characteristic is attributed to each (note the shift from "apple juice in which a grasshopper floats" to "juice in which a disgusting object floats"). It would address the "knowability" of the thesis, given the latter's vagueness, and would show that the writer remembered the cautions in the chapter about inferences in statistical inductive generalizations to "the same percentage." It would also consider the size, diversification, and representativeness of the sample.*

121. Critically discuss the following analogical argument.

Economic sanctions simply do not work. As a weapon on international persuasion, they are about as effective as popguns.

The United Nations imposed drastic sanctions upon Rhodesia; they failed utterly.

We imposed sanctions upon Poland; nothing happened.

Our government has forbidden trade with Cuba for the past 25 years; Cuba goes its way.

Most recently the president has laid heavy sanctions upon Libya; our noble allies have pooh-poohed the effort.

You can count on the same kind of results if economic sanctions are imposed on South Africa.
—Adapted from a column by James Kilpatrick

*We think that a good evaluation should identify the sample, the target, and the characteristic attributed to both. The last of these is vague in this example—the phrases "failed utterly," "nothing happened," and "goes its own way" are not clear. The claim that "our noble allies pooh-poohed the effort" attributes a different characteristic to the Libyan case than was attributed to the others. Is the author trying to say that economic sanctions never have any effect whatsoever? His remarks don't say so (Cuba may "go its own way," but American sanctions were very detrimental to the Cuban economy), and how knowable is such a claim? Does he mean that sanctions don't destroy a country? Are we talking about American sanctions or sanctions imposed by all of America's allies as well? Any relevant differences between South Africa and the other countries mentioned would add to a critical evaluation.*

# Chapter 11
# Causal Arguments

Experience has convinced us that the great bulk of causal reasoning among specific events can be sorted into the two patterns we call "Common Thread" and "X is the Difference." As a result, we have simplified our treatment in this edition so as to deal just with these patterns. Nearly anything that can be dealt with by Mill's Methods fits one or the other of these, and we find that much less confusion results from problematic cases.

Also in this edition, *post hoc, ergo propter hoc* has been eliminated as an "official" pattern of reasoning—albeit a specious one—and installed as one of several fallacies of causal reasoning. The others are assuming (or ignoring) a common cause and reversed causation. As the text points out, the last of these is only occasionally helpful in understanding what is the matter with a causal argument, and we've not burdened these pages with many examples.

Finally, don't forget the treatment of causal explanations in Chapter 4. Often causal explanations are set forth without supports. When this is the case our idea is for students to keep in mind the principles and questions discussed in Chapter 4 (circularity, testability, and so on). When they are offered with supporting argumentation, then the *supporting arguments* are to be analyzed and evaluated in accordance with the guidelines in the current chapter, although the claims the arguments support should still be reviewed with an eye to the questions and principles discussed in the earlier chapter.

## Exercises Unanswered in the Text

### Exercise 11-2

2. (a) Water brings the worms out of the earth.
   (b) X is the common thread; thus it should be asked.
   (c) If the heavy watering is the only relevant common factor preceding the emergence of the critters; if the various occurrences of the worms' emergence could have been occasioned by independent causes; and if the phenomenon and the heavy watering came about coincidentally or as the result of a common cause.
   (d) We don't think of any.
   (e) None appears.
   (f) Yes. That the various occurrences of the worms' emergence could have been occasioned by independent causes is possible, but the fact that they *always* come out after a rain *or* heavy watering seems to make this possibility remote, and these same considerations also make unlikely the possibility of the events being coincidental. That the water and the worms' appearance are both the result of some third cause is most unlikely, since sometimes the water comes from rain and sometimes from Mr. Mahlman's faucets. There could be another relevant common factor—that is, perhaps Mr. Mahlman always fertilizes before he waters and before it rains. But, assuming that the combination of events has been observed by Mrs. Mahlman over a long period of time, these possibilities seem unlikely too. (Of course, if he fertilized every time he watered he wouldn't water long—he'd kill everything. We presume nobody is running an electrical charge through the ground—somebody told us this would bring out the worms too.)

3. (a) Getting into a lane causes the other to go faster.
   (b) This is a feeble attempt at common thread
   (c) The important question, clearly, is whether the events are purely coincidental.
   (d) There are as many accountings for the changes in speed as there are variables in traffic, which are practically without end.
   (e) Post hoc
   (f) No good at all, of course, 'though we'll bet we're not the only ones who've wondered about it when we're in a hurry to get someplace.

5. (a) The cat isn't hungry because it has been catching and eating mice.
   (b) X is the difference.
   (c) Are there other events or circumstances that might have made the difference?
   (d) Cats just go off feed sometimes, for reasons known only to cats. Could be the cat has been working up an appetite chasing those mice around in the attic: When they left, the cat stopped getting exercise. We're grasping at straws here, of course.
   (e) Sounds like post hoc to us.
   (f) No. It *may* be that the cat ate the mice. But we think this is a long shot.

6. (a) El Niño caused the abnormally wet winters on the Pacific Coast.
   (b) Common thread
   (c) Is El Niño the only relevant common factor that has accompanied the wet winters? Did the wet winters result from some independent cause?
   (d) It may be that tidal movements or atmospheric conditions caused the wet winters and possibly El Niño as well. We are not told whether each occurrence of El Niño has been accompanied by a wet winter (only the other way around). If there have been occurrences of El Niño that have not been accompanied by wet Pacific Coast winters, then that makes the argument weaker and increases the likelihood of some other cause.
   (e) None appears.
   (f) This one gets a rating of fair.

7. (a) The question is not, of course, whether the Studebaker or its appearance is responsible for the burglaries, but were the occupants of the Studebaker responsible for the burglaries?
   (b) Common thread
   (c) & (d) Assuming the police decide that the Studebaker is a *relevant* common factor (and does not, for example, belong to the owner of the burglarized building or to some other clearly innocent party) they will still ask if there are other possibly relevant common factors preceding the crimes—other suspicious people, and so on. If there are such factors *and* they turn out to be unrelated to the Studebaker, that fact diminishes the likelihood that the Studebaker's occupants were connected with the crime. The police will also ask if the crimes resulted from independent causes; evidence that they did diminishes the probability that the Studebaker's occupants were involved. Similarly, the possibility of coincidence between the appearance of the Studebaker and the occurrence of the burglaries must be considered by the police; the idea that the appearance of the Studebaker's occupants and the occurrence of the crimes could both be the result of a common cause is possible, but far-fetched.
   (e) None appears.
   (f) The appearances of the Studebaker support the conclusion that the occupants of the Studebaker *may* have been causally connected to the crimes (assuming the presence of the car really is a *relevant* factor. It offers strong support for the contention that the occupants actually were causally connected with the burglaries only if the possibilities discussed above have been ruled out.

*This is probably a somewhat longer account than might have been expected, which shows that apparently simple causal arguments are not always so simple. Dealing with this example in class is further complicated by the fact that some of your students won't be any more familiar with Studebakers than they are with Hupmobiles.*

9. (a) The clickety-clack sound in Egmont's bicycle is caused by the pedal mechanism.
   (b) X is the difference: When the pedals stop going 'round (as he coasts), the sound stops.
   (c) Is the operation of the pedal mechanism the only relevant factor that distinguishes the situation in which the sound is present from situations in which it is not?
   (d) If the claim that the sound has to be due to something that revolves is correct, then the only remaining explanation with any plausibility is that the chain is causing the sound, since the sound stops when the chain stops as well as when the pedals stop.
   (e) None of the fallacies named are present, provided once again it is true that only something that revolves could be causing the sound. There is a chance, of course, that the account provided by the chain is really the correct one.
   (f) A pretty good argument

10. (a) The disinfecting solution is causing Judith's contact lenses to bother her.
    (b) & (c) This looks like a case of *post hoc, ergo propter hoc*, but we can sometimes convert such an argument into another variety that has a better chance at being sound. Such is this example. If we ask the question suggested—"is the earlier event the only thing that could have resulted in the later event?" (see p. 272)—we find that this is a good candidate for the "X is the difference" pattern. What is required is that Judith has considered the possibility of other causes of the irritation and ruled them out.
    (d) If the lenses themselves were new, that would provide an alternative cause, but since no mention is made of it we presume such is not the case. It may also be that Judith has been in an area lately where there is an abnormal amount of dust in the air, and the dust is causing the irritation. Windy days could account for the same phenomenon. If such possibilities have not been considered and determined to be unlikely, then the soundness of the argument becomes much more questionable.
    (e) None
    (f) A fairly good argument, especially if possibilities like those mentioned in (d) have been ruled out.

## Exercise 11-3

1. The claim in question is that cutting coffee out of Malvina's diet caused her post-aerobics pulse rate to drop ten points. The pattern is X is the difference (although a common thread analysis is possible as well). Is the elimination of coffee from her diet the only relevant difference between situations when her pulse rate was higher and situations when it was lower? What if Malvina's exercise has resulted in a more efficient cardiovascular system, and her heart does not have to beat as fast now to recover from the exercise. This is not a very likely account, since the passage indicates the drop in pulse rate happened more or less suddenly; it would have been a gradual drop were this account correct. Another possibility is that Malvina dropped other stimulants from her diet at the same time as she dropped coffee. The elimination of any of these others could be a contributing factor. Provided the considerations raised above are taken into account, this argument is a good one.

2. This is pretty decent common thread reasoning. Unfortunately, though his reasoning is sound, he has overlooked another plausible alternative explanation: that the problem is in

the ignition system, through which current flows whenever the car is running.

5. The claim in question: The Supreme Court's abolition of prayer in the public schools caused metropolitan schools to become homes for criminals, addicts, and so on, where decent students fear for their lives.

   We think this is post hoc. Could any other factor have caused the deterioration in the schools? The answer, clearly, is "yes." The number of other factors that could have played a role is large indeed. There are probably as many alternative accounts as there are educators; we'll leave it to you to choose your favorite.

8. The claim in question: The coffee or the basketball is the cause of his chest pains. The reasoning: X is the difference. He should ask: Are coffee and basketball the only relevant differences? Maybe he took aspirin (or other medication) when he had a cold.

   This one has a chance, but it is not a strong argument. There are other possible relevant differences between the situation with the chest pains and the situation with the cold and no chest pains. Nevertheless, Elroy might test his hypothesis by giving up basketball and coffee while he has no cold, and if the pain abates he should see his physician. Probably he should see his physician anyway.

9. The claim in question: Dipping snuff caused Marsee's death. (Or, more fully, dipping snuff caused Marsee's cancer and the cancer caused his death.) Since the connection between tobacco use and cancer is well known and since *post hoc* reasoning is unsound, it may seem strange to call this *post hoc,* but that's what it is. Our knowledge about the cancer-tobacco correlation comes not from evidence supplied by individual cases like this one but from studies done on large numbers of such cases. There *is* a good argument that Marsee's tobacco use caused his cancer and death, but it's not *this* argument; it's a statistical syllogism of the sort discussed in Chapter 10—that is, "heavy tobacco users who get certain characteristic forms of cancer get it as a result of their use of tobacco; Marsee was a heavy tobacco user who got a characteristic form of cancer; therefore, Marsee got cancer as a result of his use of tobacco." The first premise of this argument is itself the result of studies of the sort covered later in the current chapter.

   Our *post hoc* argument at hand gets its credence from association with the argument just described. If we had no information about cancer-tobacco correlations, the argument at hand would not seem nearly so convincing. Yes, Marsee used a lot of snuff, and yes, Marsee got cancer. Maybe Marsee also drank lots of hot coffee from an early age and bit his tongue a lot. Any of these would make plausible accounts (and do make moderately plausible accounts) but they are less plausible than the tobacco argument because of our abundance of evidence linking tobacco usage to cancer.

10. The claim in question: The Soviet Union is the cause of the terrorist attacks.

    This argument does not fit neatly into any one of our categories, but it would not be a serious distortion to regard it as being of the common thread type of reasoning. We can think of it this way: The attacks on NATO and U.S. military installations in Europe all have something in common: They are well coordinated, well financed, well equipped with sophisticated bombs, and all are directed at the same targets. (That they serve the purposes of the Soviet Union should not be listed as a common factor, since such an item on the list would beg the question—the attacks serve the purposes of all anti-NATO and U.S. organizations, countries, and individuals.) Therefore, the cause of the attacks must be with something that lies within these parameters (that is, the Soviet Union).

    The question, "Could the attacks have resulted from independent causes?" reveals a weakness in the argument, for various well financed anti-U.S. entities could independently have made the attacks. We wouldn't vote for a conviction on the basis of this argument if we were serving on a jury in a trial against the Soviet Union.

## Exercise 11-4

2. (a)
3. (b)
5. (b)
6. (a)
8. (b)
9. (b)
11. (b)
12. (a)
13. (b)
15. (b)
16. (c)
18. (b)
19. (a)

## Exercise 11-6

1. (a) Taking aspirin every other day reduces the risk of heart attack.
   (b) Men
   (c) The use of a placebo indicates that this was a controlled cause-to-effect experiment.
   (d) Experimental and control groups each had about 11,035 members; the first took an aspirin every other day while the second took a sugar pill placebo.
   (e) 104 of the experimental group (.0094 %) and 189 (.0171 %) of the control group had heart attacks, a difference of .0077 %. While this is a tiny percentage difference, it is balanced by the enormous size of the sample: over 22,000 people. (It sounds more impressive when reported, as in the article, as a 47 % reduction in heart attack risk. Results can be misleading when the occurrence of E in one group is reported as a percentage of its occurrence in the other. If there had been two heart attacks in the control group and only one in the experimental group, we'd have a case of a "whopping" 50 % reduction in heart attack risk, but with practically no statistical significance, since *one* more heart attack in one of the groups is certainly attributable to chance.)
   This report does indicate statistical significance: The source (the *New England Journal of Medicine*) is reliable, as is the sponsor ( the National Heart, Lung and Blood Institute), and the fact that the study was cut short so that members of the control group could benefit from aspirin-caused reduced risk says something about the sponsor's confidence in the study.
   (g) None that we can think of
   (h) The report seems to support the claim in (a); but, before we all go reaching for the aspirin bottle, we want to mention that we've heard the aspirin-heart attack connection has been disputed in some medical quarters recently.

3. (a) Cigarette smoking can cause (vascular-associated) impotence; nicotine causes an immediate reduction in sexual arousal.
   (b) Men
   (c) The South African, French, and Canadian studies are nonexperimental effect-to-cause studies. The Southern Illinois-Florida State study is experimental cause-to-effect.
   (d) The South African study mentions no control group. We can only presume that

something less than 93 percent of the South African male population are smokers (but see below). In the U.S. study, we assume that the 42-member sample was divided into three groups of equal size to be administered high-nicotine cigarettes, low nicotine cigarettes, and mints.

(e) The frequency of cause in the South African study is 93 %, which, as noted, is probably higher than the incidence of smokers in the target population. No difference is specified for the U.S. study, although the report leads one to believe that slow arousal was universal among the high-nicotine cigarette smokers.

(f) There is no specific indication of significance in the report, except on the "universal" reading given to the U.S. study.

(g) We're not sure how much confidence we'd have on the results based on this passage. This is especially true given the nonexperimental nature of the South African, French, and Canadian studies. It may be, for instance, that there is a higher than normal percentage of alcohol drinkers among smokers, and that alcohol plays a significant role in some kinds of impotence.

(h) The report gives some support to the claim in (a), but we'd give that claim more credence only after more confirmation.

4. (a) Certain cloned human genes can repair damaged cells (in hamsters; that it would do the same in humans is indicated but still speculative).

(b) Damaged cells in hamsters

(c) Experimental cause-to-effect

(d) Cells in hamsters which had the cloned genes inserted form the experimental group; cells in untreated hamsters are the control group. No figures are given about the sizes of either one.

(e) Two-thirds of the experimental group were repaired, compared to one-tenth of one percent in the control group

(f) There is a huge difference of frequency; even if the sample was relatively small, we'd expect it to be statistically significant.

(g) None that we can spot, except sizes of the groups would have been helpful.

(h) The report supports claim (a). Lawrence Livermore Labs has had its troubles in recent years, but not in areas like this. We're willing to give credence to the report.

6. (a) Circumcision causes pain (and, possibly, "prolonged effects on neurological and social development) in infants.

(b) Male infants

(c) Both studies seem to be experimental cause-to-effect. (Presumably the attending physicians did not select infants to be circumcised at random, but we can probably assume the next best thing, since there's no reason to think that the circumcised infants were more susceptible to pain than the others.)

(d) No sizes are given for either experimental (circumcised) or control (uncircumcised) groups in the first study. The same is true for the second study, although here both groups were composed of circumcised infants, with members of the experimental group given anesthetic before the operation.

(e) & (f) The "almost all" indicates a significantly large difference in frequency of effect in the first study cited; the second study reads as if the effect (less irritability, better motor responses, and so on) was universal among the experimental group.

(g) & (h) No weaknesses that we can think of, although the entire report is pretty vague. It's difficult to assess just what's going on in an infant, of course, but we'd as soon trust the folk at Harvard Medical School as anybody. Frankly, we're surprised (and a little put off) by the fact that physicians knew no more about infant pain than they seem to have known. We wonder what other "medical school myths" may be floating around.

7. (a) & (b) High doses of androgen reduce HDL levels in the blood of adult human males.
   (c) Nonexperimental cause-to-effect study
   (d) The experimental group consisted of sixteen healthy, "well-conditioned" men in their early thirties who took androgens for four weeks as part of their weight training program. The control group consisted of the same men before using androgens, all of whom had normal levels of HDLs.
   (e) The HDL levels were 60 percent decreased in the experimental group.
   (f) We don't know what normal HDL levels are, expressed in numerical terms, so we don't know what a "60 percent drop" amounts to, or whether a drop of 60 percent from a normal level produces a level that's too low. However, the implication of the article is that the drop is medically important.
   (g) It certainly would be nice to know something more about the "self-prescribed and self-administered use" of steroids. Was the overall drop in HDL later due to a very large drop on the part of two very heavy users? Well, probably not, given the source of the study and where it was published.
   (h) The study warrants caution on the part of anyone contemplating taking androgens for medically unnecessary reasons.

12. (a) A medical self-care problem of the sort described reduces visits to the doctor by families that use it.
    (b) American families
    (c) Controlled cause-to-effect experiment
    (d) A group of families of unspecified size randomly chosen from the Rhode Island Group Health Association cared for their medical needs with self-care literature, with back-up telephone counseling available ("in some cases") from a nurse. The control group was of unspecified size; the families in it received no special educational help.
    (e) The frequency of the effect is unstated for both groups.
    (f) There is no reason to believe that these results are statistically significant.
    (g) Details concerning the telephone hot line are much too obscure.
    (h) The first sentence of the item states very nicely the claim that is warranted by the report.

13. (a) Pap smears are effective in reducing the incidence of cancer of the cervix.
    (b) Women
    (c) Nonexperimental cause-to-effect study
    (d) The total of both control and experimental groups is 207,455 Swedish women. How many were in the control group and how many in the experimental group is not stated.
    (e) The frequency of the effect is not given for either group, only that it was "two to four times higher" in the control group. (This way of putting it casts cases of cervical cancer as the effect. Since the study investigates the effects of Pap smears, it may be better to identify the effect as a *failure to contract* cervical cancer, in which case we would say that the frequency of the effect was "two to four times higher" in the *experimental* group.) The "two to four times higher" claim does not tell us anything about the actual frequencies; however, the study is clearly a reputable one, and the co-author's remark implies that the difference in frequency was significant.
    (f) Yes, the report quotes a co-author of the study to this effect.
    (g) None that are obvious
    (h) Same as (a)

15. (a) Vaccine made of living cancer cells from a patient's colorectal cancer can slow or prevent the subsequent appearance of cancer elsewhere.
    (b) Humans
    (c)-(f) This is a modified cause-to-effect experiment, in which there is no control group

*per se.* The experimental group consists of twenty patients with colorectal cancer; four had recurrences in the two to four years they were followed, but none of the group has died. The significance of these findings can only be determined by comparison with recurrence statistics in cancer victims who have not received such a vaccine. Unfortunately, no such statistics are mentioned. This was clearly a reputable scientific experiment, and it is not stated or implied in the report that the study proves that the caccine prevents a recurrence of cancer in victims of colorectal cancer. In fact, the opposite is stated in the last sentence of the report. The experiment does support the claim that further study of the vaccine and its effects should be made.

# Chapter 11 Test Question-Exercise Bank

## Bank 11-1

The following arguments can be evaluated in accordance with the questions listed in the directions for Exercise 11-2 in the text, or they can be discussed more informally. We'll provide only brief comments here.

1. February 2nd is Groundhog Day. If the groundhog sees his shadow there'll be six more weeks of winter. If he doesn't, spring is right around the corner.

   *Groundhog Day claims are not causal: no one thinks the groundhog's seeing or not seeing his shadow* causes *whatever happens to the weather afterward. (A dark February 2 in Pennsylvania, where the official groundhog lives, might be correlated with an exceptionally short winter, for all we know. If it is, look for some sort of meteorological phenomenon as a common cause.)*

2. "Every time I play tennis my wrist hurts for several days afterward. If my doctor can't help me figure what to do about it, I may have to give up the game."

   *X is the common thread. Probably sound, although the likelihood is that tennis is only* part *of the cause; some underlying condition is being exacerbated by playing tennis.*

3. A lottery winner, asked why he thought he had won a major prize, pulled a small rhinestone four-leaf clover out of his pocket and said, "I think this had a lot to do with it."

   *Post hoc:* "I carried my lucky charm and I won."

4. "I had a lot of noise on my car stereo when the engine was running until I read in an old Champion Spark Plug publication that the way to fix the problem is to install a 4 MH choke coil in the hot wire from the battery to the stereo. I did it, and it cured the problem."

   *X is the difference, and in this case sound.*

5. "I'd wash the car but for the fact that we don't need any more rain."

   *This is probably best construed as an unsound case of X is the difference.*

6. "The car usually makes it over the hills between here and the lake without any trouble. The only time it makes any trouble is when we have to pull the boat and trailer; they must make too heavy a load for the car's small engine."

   *X is the common thread, although reading the first part of the second sentence as "The car makes trouble if and only if the boat is pulled" allows an X is the difference interpretation as well. (That isn't what the sentence says, but. . . .)*

7. "Before every voyage, we toss a drink to the old man in the sea."

   *That is, doing so brings good luck; not doing so brings bad luck. The superstition probably originated as a faulty application of X is the difference or X is the common thread, or both. (Before every airplane flight, your authors toss a drink down the hatch, but not from superstition.)*

8. "Of course he was outdoors Wednesday, Watson. That's the only day there has been rain, and he had a good bit of dried mud on the heels of his boots."

   *Wednesday's rain caused the mud to be on the boots: X is the difference. Note: Sherlock Holmes examples are as nice for the first part of this chapter as they are for truth functional inferences.*

9. "I'm over 70 years old and got all of my natural teeth but one. The secret is to eat a dollop of raw veal bone marrow every day."
   —Attributed to Mrs. Keller [a "wise old woman of Ohio"] by Robert L. Tubbesing, *Old Farmer's Almanac* (1986)

   *This item is probably best analyzed as* post hoc, *(I ate veal marrow every day and have all my teeth save one; therefore the former caused the latter). A case for common thread can be made for this one, but not a very good case: too many other possible variables.*

10. "The only packages that suffered damage during the trip were the ones we packed with newspaper instead of that styrofoam packing stuff. I learned a lesson: Make sure you have enough of the proper packing material."

    *Common thread. Our packer might consider, though, whether the materials that were damaged were more fragile than the others—that could be another relevant factor besides packing material. (See remarks at end of #6; they apply here too.)*

11. Raphael is troubled by the fact that when he purchases new guitar strings, they seem always to go dead after just a few weeks of use. A friend suggests that he boil the strings in vinegar when they lose their resonance. Raphael tries it, and the strings sound almost like new again.
    After a few weeks the strings go dead again, and Raphael again boils them in vinegar with the same result. He resigns himself to a session with boiling vinegar every few weeks.

    *X is the difference; the second treatment starts to make common thread look like a possibility, but a far-fetched one. (Does anyone know if this really works? The smell of boiling vinegar wouldn't be worth a failed attempt.)*

12. When Halley's comet hovered over Jerusalem in A.D. 66, the historian Josephus warned it meant the destruction of the city. Jerusalem fell four years later, thus confirming the power of the comet.

    *Post hoc. Somebody applied Josephus' prediction again in 1988, this time to Los Angeles. Didn't work this time.*

13. "A terrible squeaking noise from my tape recorder got so bad I couldn't stand to listen to it any more. I was sure the machine had developed a problem, and just a month after the warranty expired, too. So I cleaned the heads, the capstan, and all the moving parts hoping I could make the noise go away. It remained. Then, just as I had decided I was going to have to take it in for repairs, I played some tapes belonging to a friend of mine and the squeak wasn't there. So the problem is with my tapes, not my machine. I'm not sure I like that any better, since I've got dozens of them."

    *X is the difference. This is a fairly good argument; of course his problem could lie in the combination of the tapes and the machine.*

14. Less than twenty-four hours after seeing the movie, *Glade's Corner*, which depicts the brutal knife-slaying of an elderly man by teenagers, fifteen-year-old Mark Striker attempted to kill his sixty-five-year-old great uncle. His weapon: a knife.

    *Post hoc, but keep in mind the question that should be asked about this type of argument.*

15. Fund raising director for a public radio station: "I know that our music director gets hysterical when we play a lot of tired stuff like the *1812 Overture* and the Grieg piano concerto. But you go back and look at our fund drive programming in the past when we've raised the most money; every big day has been a day heavily loaded with those 'classics.'"

    *Common thread*

## Bank 11-2

The following are for informal analysis or for applying the questions in the directions for Exercise 11-6 as a guide. Once again, we'll provide brief comments.

16. "You don't need to become a complete ascetic in order to lower your cholesterol levels. Scott M. Grundy of the University of Texas Health Science Center at Dallas and his colleagues rotated nine men through two-month stints on each of three diets—the American Health Association diet, in which a maximum of 30 percent of the calories come from fat; a 40 percent fat diet; and a 20 percent fat diet. The subjects' average cholesterol level was 210 mg/dl on entry.

    "In all the men, the blood levels of total cholesterol and of the 'bad' form of cholesterol, LDL-cholesterol, fell to around 175. 'There were no significant differences [in cholesterol levels of the men] on these three diets,' Grundy says."
    —Science News

    *The "control" group consists in effect of the same men before the diets. The article does not make clear what percent of the calories of the men came from fat before going on the diet, a defect in the report. [We've heard that in the standard U.S. diet about 41 percent of calories are fat-derived.)*

17. Do sudden heart attacks increase with vigorous exercise? A community-based study investigated this issue and discovered that persons who habitually exercised vigorously had a *reduced* risk of sudden cardiac death as compared with persons who only occasionally exercised vigorously. One hundred thirty-three married men who experienced out-of-hospital cardiac arrest were chosen for the study. They were classified according to their usual amount of activity and the amount of activity at the time of the cardiac arrest. All appeared healthy prior to the heart attacks. The benefits outweighed the risks for men at the upper levels of habitual high-intensity activity. Their overall risk was 40% of that of sedentary men.
—Adapted from "Stress and Health Report," N.T. Enloe Memorial Hospital Stress and Health Center, Chico, California

*Since we don't know how many of the men qualified as sedentary or habitually high-intensity active, the 40 percent figure tells us little. Since we have no information on who conducted the study, we can make no inferences concerning how reasonable the definitions of the various activity categories are, or whether the 40 percent figure translates into a significant difference. (This is the kind of report you sometimes discover is the summary of a creditable study. However, too many details are missing in this summary to attach great importance to it.)*

18. BOSTON—AP, UPI reports (adapted) The constant bright lights of hospital nurseries, often two to four times as bright as normal office lighting, may contribute to the blinding of hundreds of premature babies each year, a recent study warns. Doctors kept track of the incidence of retinopathy, a disease of the retina, in two groups of premature babies. One group was kept in incubators covered with acetate that reduced the amount of light by 58 percent. The rest stayed in ordinary incubators. Among the smallest babies, the researchers found that 21 of 39 (54 percent) in shielded incubators developed retinopathy, compared with 18 of 21 (86 percent) of those exposed to the bright lights. Dr. Penny Glass, a developmental psychologist at Children's Hospital National Medical Center and Georgetown University Medical Center, who directed the study, recommend that the light levels in hospital nurseries be brought down. "I feel that the increase in light levels has not been demonstrated safe," she said.

*Note the researcher's mild conclusion (last sentence). This controlled cause-to-effect experiment offers strong support for such a cautious conclusion.*

19. Does learning how to program a computer help first graders to think? Douglas H. Clements and Domninic F. Gullo of Kent State University randomly assigned 18 first-graders from a middle-class, midwestern school system into two computer groups. The first group programmed an Apple II computer, using the computer language Logo, during two 40-minute sessions a week for 12 weeks. The other group received computer-based lessons in arithmetic and reading for the same time period. It was found that the children who programmed increased their scores on a creativity test in which they had to devise and draw pictures under time restraints, and became better at identifying when they had not been given enough information to complete a simple task or understand how a magic trick is performed. However, a number of other tests provided no evidence that the programming experience can improve overall thinking abilities.
    The investigation was reported in the *Journal of Educational Psychology*.
—Adapted from *Science News*

*The report of this cause-to-effect experiment leaves it unclear as to how much and what sort of improvement was seen on the tests. Note that the study was published in a respected journal.*

20. Each year in the U.S. a surgical procedure known as extracranial-intracranial arterial (EC/IC) bypass is done on 3,000 to 5,000 people who have had, or are at risk of stroke. The operation, in which an artery on the scalp is attached to an artery on the brain to bypass a partial or total blockage, costs about $15,000. In a new study, researchers from the University Hospital in London, Ontario examined 1,377 people who had recently had strokes or had signs of impending strokes. They randomly assigned 714 to get standard medical care and 663 to get EC/IC bypasses. The group that had the surgery subsequently had a slightly higher rate of stroke and death than the control group, according to the study.
   —Reported in the *New England Journal of Medicine*

   *Remind us not to spend $15,000 on an EC/IC bypass.*

21. In a study designed to test some of the effects of marijuana on the performance of difficult tasks, Jerome A. Yesavage of Stanford University and his colleagues recruited 10 experienced private pilots and trained them on a computerized flight-simulator landing task. All subjects had smoked marijuana at some time in the past, though none was a daily user. None smoked marijuana during the test period, except as required by the test. The test period began with a morning baseline flight, after which each subject smoked a marijuana cigarette containing 19 milligrams of tetrahydrocannabinol, the active agent in marijuana. The pilots repeated the landing task one, four, and twenty-four hours later. The worst performances compared with the baseline occurred one hour after smoking the cigarette. Twenty-four hours later, however, the pilots still experienced significant difficulty in aligning the computerized airplane and landing it in the center of the runway. According to the scientists, there were marked deviations from the proper angle of descent in the last 6,000 feet of approach to the landing.
      The amount of marijuana smoked is comparable to a strong social dose, the researchers said.
   —Adapted from *Science News*

   *The men's baseline performances constitute the control group in this controlled cause-to-effect experiment. One wonders about the pilots' attitudes: Were any out to prove a point?*

22. In a study of telephone operators in North Carolina, Suzanne Haynes of the National Center for Health Statistics in Hyattsville, Maryland, compared 278 women who worked all day at video display terminals (VDTs) with 218 clerical workers in the same companies who did not use VDTs. Twice as many VDT users reported chest pains as clerical workers in the same companies—20 percent compared to 10 percent. Perhaps, Haynes commented, "VDTs can be the ultimate nonsupportive boss."
   —Adapted from *Science News*

   *This is a cause-to-effect study, of course. The report is short on details, but the findings are statistically significant. Nevertheless, we would want to know more about the other duties and responsibilities of the VDT users as compared with the nonusers before indicting VDT use as a cause of chest pain or heart trouble.*

23. Tiffany Field, a psychologist at the University of Miami Medical School, believes that it is good for premature babies to be given short sessions of body stroking and limb movement. She and her co-researchers studied 40 premature babies in a transitional care nursery. Although the infants were stable enough to be released from the intensive care unit, and none needed extra oxygen or intravenous feedings, they had required an average of twenty days of intensive care, and the heaviest among them was under four pounds. Their average age at birth was thirty-one weeks. Half the group was randomly chosen to receive standardized touch and movement stimulation for three fifteen minute periods per day over ten consecutive weekdays. Treated infants averaged a 47 percent greater weight gain per day even though they had the same number of feedings and the same level of calorie intake as control babies. The stimulated group also was awake and physically active a greater percentage of the time. "Since the experimental kids were more active their weight gain was not due to greater energy conservation," Field points out. Infants in the treatment group also outdistanced controls on a number of behavioral measures, and they were hospitalized on the average six days fewer than the controls.
—Adapted from Bruce Bower, *Science News*

*This controlled cause-to-effect experiment provides strong support for the conclusion stated by the researcher.*

24. In 1960, Dutch researchers from the University of Leiden questioned 852 men and their wives about the men's diets, then monitored the men for the next twenty years. They found that the death rate from heart disease was more than fifty percent lower among men who ate at least thirty grams (one ounce) of fish per day compared with men who ate no fish. Just one or two fish dishes a week, the researchers say, "may be of value in the prevention of coronary heart disease."
—Adapted from *Science News*

*Fish in the diet may be of value in the prevention of coronary heart disease, but this study, as reported here, does not show that it is. Unless we know what the death rate actually was, we cannot attach great importance to the "fifty percent lower" claim. Probably the fifty percent figure translates into a difference that is significant, given the scope and likely credibility of the investigators.*

25. A study of 546 men in New Zealand who were identified as leukemia patients between 1979 and 1983 suggests that electrical workers are at increased risk of developing this cancer. Each man was matched with four other men from New Zealand's cancer registry. The study found a significant excess of leukemias among those electrical workers who had been employed as electronic equipment assemblers (four cases where only 0.5 would have been expected) and radio and television repairers (seven cases where only 1.5 would have been expected). The study was conducted by N. E. Pearce and his colleagues at the Department of Community Health, Wellington Clinical School, and National Health Statistics Centre in Wellington, New Zealand.

In a second study, Washington State epidemiologist Samuel Milham Jr., obtained the death certificates for 95 percent of the 296 deceased Washington members of the American Radio Relay League (amateur radio operators) and 86 percent of the 1,642 deceased California members. Twenty-four of the deaths were due to leukemia; sixteen of these were of the myeloid class—nearly triple the 5.7 deaths that would have been expected from this type of leukemia. Milham acknowledges that the difference might be attributable to chance, but points out that three other studies have revealed a tendency toward a relative increase in the acute myelogenous type of leukemia in electrical workers.
—Adapted from *Science News*

*The first investigation, an effect-to-cause study, suggests that something associated with work with electronics is a causal factor for leukemia in humans. The second, a cause-to-effect study, does not support the same thesis. But given the other studies mentioned, we would not think that further investigation of a possible link between leukemia and electrical work would be a waste of money.*

26. "Exercise can temporarily disrupt a woman's menstrual cycle, according to Boston University research published in the May 23 [1985] *New England Journal of Medicine.* The researchers monitored the daily hormone levels in 28 college women who did not exercise regularly and had a history of regular menstrual cycles. The women were then sent to summer camp and participated in a rigorous exercise program—an initial 4-mile daily run, working up to 10 miles a day after five weeks, in addition to three and one-half hours daily of moderate sports such as biking or tennis. Only four, three of whom were on a high-calorie weight maintenance diet, had a normal menstrual cycle during that time. The researchers concluded that, regardless of whether the women lost weight, strenuous exercise disrupted their reproductive function. 'If very active women are having trouble getting pregnant, they probably should slow down intense exercise,' says exercise physiologist Gary Skrinar of BU."
—*Science News*

*This is a cause-to-effect experiment, in which the 'control group' is the same women before the exercise regimen. This is a standard and often sound practice. However, in this instance it is a weakness in the experiment, since menstrual cycles can be affected by nervousness, excitement, going on vacations, and other such things. It would be going out on a limb to conclude, on the basis of this experiment, that women athletes who have menstrual problems owe that fact to their exercise.*

## Bank 11-3

Here are five studies for analysis of whatever sort you'd care to assign.

27. As reported in the *Journal of the American Medical Association,* 26 surgeons-in-training were studied to see whether sleep deprivation impaired their patient-care ability. For 18 to 19 days the residents kept a sleep diary and underwent five tests each morning to measure cognition, visual and auditory alertness and hand-eye coordination. Sleep deprivation was defined as less than 4 hours of continuous sleep in the previous 24 hours, which occurred in 89 percent of the on-duty nights studied. When sleep deprivation occurred, total sleep averaged 3 hours, and the longest uninterrupted sleep averaged 2.2 hours.
Residents did show "trivial" improvement on two tests when they obtained some sleep just before testing, but the researchers said repetitive sleep deprivation did not impair the residents' test performances.
The study "does not support arbitrary recommendations to limit working hours of residents," it was said.
—Adapted from *Science News*

28. A study published in the *New England Journal of Medicine* concludes that the number of handgun deaths in Vancouver, British Columbia, between 1980 and 1986 was less than one-fifth that of Seattle, 120 miles to the south. Seattle's population is approximately 490,000 while Vancouver's is about 43,000.
In Seattle, handguns may legally be purchased for self-defense. After a 30-day waiting period, a permit can be obtained to carry a handgun as a concealed weapon. Recreational

uses are minimally restricted. In Vancouver, self-defense is not a legal reason to purchase a handgun. Concealed weapons are not permitted, and recreational weapons may be fired only at a licensed shooting club.

Dr. Henry Sloan, chief investigator for the study, said 388 homicides occurred in Seattle during the study period, while 204 occurred in Vancouver. The number of gun-related deaths in Seattle was 139, compared with 25 for Vancouver, he said. He stopped short of saying his findings prove Seattle's less strict gun control laws cause more deaths, but said, "It virtually explains it."

Note: New gun control laws went into effect in 1978. Sloan said Vancouver's laws were made stricter in 1978 but didn't change significantly.

—Adapted from Associated Press

29. Twenty-five two-pack-a-day smokers who had tried unsuccessfully to quit smoking were tested at the University of Tennessee in Memphis. For seven weeks 12 took doxepin, and antidepressant, and 13 took placebos. After 56 days nine people on doxepin were no longer smoking, as compared with only one in the other group. The doxepin-takers reported reductions in nervousness, anxiety, and craving for nicotine.

In a second study, Dr. Alexander H. Glassman of Columbia University gave heavy smokers either clonidine, a drug used to treat hypertension, or a placebo. After four weeks, 61 percent of the clonidine group were not smoking, while only 26 percent of the placebo group had stopped.

These studies, reported in *Physician's Weekly*, were given by *Reader's Digest* as grounds for the conclusion that "Two drugs, one for depression, the other for high blood pressure, may help smokers resist cigarettes."

30. We provided evidence that we could prevent myocardial infarction in angina patients, says Pierre Theroux, of the Montreal Heart Institute. As reported in the *New England Journal of Medicine* (October 27, 1988) Theroux and his colleagues placed 479 hospitalized patients who had experienced chest pains into four treatment groups, receiving aspirin, heparin, a combination of the two, or a placebo. Heparin therapy reduced the rate of fatal and nonfatal heart attacks by 89 percent as compared with the placebo. It also reduced chest pain by 63 percent. Previous studies of heparin treatment of chest pain have produced questionable results, Theroux says.

Aspirin therapy also helped: the Montreal team found aspirin reduced the risk of heart attacks by 72 percent as compared with the placebo. But the combination aspirin/heparin treatment showed no particular benefit compared with aspirin alone or heparin alone, and patients getting the two drugs combined had a slightly higher risk of complications, such as bleeding.

The researchers recommend for patients hospitalized with chest pain treatment with heparin upon admission followed by aspirin therapy for long-term management.

—Adapted from *Science News*

31. Barbara Sherwin, director of a research team at McGill University, found that a small quantity of the male hormone testosterone, in addition to estrogen, led to a spicier sex life for some postmenopausal women. Twenty-two of the McGill team's subjects were given 150 milligrams a month of testosterone with estrogen, 11 were given estrogen alone, and 11 took placebos. The testosterone group reported more desire and arousal and more frequent sexual thoughts than did the women in the other two groups. Though 17 percent of the testosterone recipients developed mild facial hair, this side effect receded when the dosage was reduced.

—Elsie Rosner, *Physician's Weekly*, reported in *Reader's Digest*

## Bank 11-4

True/False

32. The claim "fluoridated water prevents tooth decay," if true, implies that fluoridated water would prevent tooth decay in the majority of individuals who use it.

    *False*

33. The claim, "fouled spark plugs kept the car from starting," implies that the car would have started if the spark plugs had not been fouled.

    *True*

34. In a nonexperimental cause-to-effect study the members of the experimental group are exposed to the suspected causal agent by the investigators.

    *False*

35. In a nonexperimental effect-to-cause study *none* of the members of the control group show the effect of the cause being investigated.

    *True.*

36. Arguments that have the *post hoc, ergo propter hoc* pattern can sometimes be converted into a sound version of another pattern.

    *True*

## Bank 11-5

The next five are based on the following paragraph

Lin sends away for a hot-cold serving tray she has seen advertised. The tray is promised to keep hot dishes hot and cold dishes cold without electricity. Lin tries it out by placing a pan of hot beans on it. They stay hot throughout dinner. "It works," she tells her husband.

37. What causal claim (if any) is stated or implied in Lin's conclusion?

    *Placing the pan of beans on the serving tray kept them hot.*

38. What kind of causal claim is this?

    *Causation between specific occurrences*

39. What type of argument or pattern of reasoning is employed?

    *Post hoc, ergo propter hoc*

40. Invent at least one plausible alternative explanation of the effect.

*The beans stayed hot all by themselves—that is, they would have stayed hot had they been placed on a standard trivet.*

41. If you think there could be a better test of the hot plate, explain it in a sentence or two.

    *Compare what happens with two pans of beans of the same temperature, one left on the hot plate and the other on a standard surface.*

    The next five are based on the following paragraph:

    Johnson is hired by a pharmaceutical company to see if a new product, Topocal, will promote hair growth on balding men. He runs an ad in the newspaper inviting men with hair loss to participate and gets fifty respondents who participate in a hair growth experiment. Half the respondents (Group A) rub Topocal on a preselected one-inch-square bald patch on their scalps. The other half (Group B) apply a liquid that is a mixture of lemon juice and water in a similar manner. At the end of one month, Johnson compares the appropriate patches of each man's scalp and notes the results.

42. What is the causal claim at issue?

    *Topocal causes hair growth on bald men.*

43. What type of argument or pattern of reasoning is employed?

    *Controlled cause-to-effect experiment*

44. Which group is the experimental group?

    *Group A*

45. Suppose that the result were significant at the .05 level. That means we could say with a __95__ percent degree of confidence that Topocal produces hair growth in balding men.

46. Briefly criticize Johnson's experiment. Are there things you do not know that you would need to know in order to have confidence that the experiment were sound?

    *It is essential that the men from each group be alike save for the fact that Group A men are treated with Topocal. Were they? Could their hair losses have resulted from different causes? Age and medical condition of the subjects could also affect the findings. Also, how were the before-and-after scalp areas compared? By hair-count? The comparison should not be subjective or impressionistic on the part of the observer.*

## Bank 11-6

Essay questions

47. It is widely believed that chocolate causes acne, since people susceptible to acne frequently assert that eating chocolate is invariably followed by an outbreak of the skin condition. However, Donald G. Bruns, in a letter to *Science News*, wondered if those who have the belief that chocolate causes acne might not have things backwards. Some studies indicate that hormonal changes associated with stress may cause acne, he notes. Other studies

indicate that people fond of chocolate may tend to eat more chocolate when under stress. Given these studies, Bruns comments, it may be easy to confuse which is the cause and which is the effect, the chocolate or the acne.

In a brief essay, explain what pattern of reasoning seems to underlie the belief that chocolate causes acne *(probably X is the difference—the only relevant difference between this situation, in which there was an outbreak of acne, and situations in which there was none, is that in this situation I ate chocolate)*, and then answer this question: Brun complains that those who believe that chocolate causes acne may be guilty of the fallacy of reversed causation. Given the studies he cites, has Brun correctly identified the fallacy? *No. The fallacy is that of ignoring a common cause.*

48. "An FBI study of 35 serial-killers [killers of several people, not all at once] revealed that 29 were attracted to pornography and incorporated it into their sexual activity, which included serial-rape-murder." This assertion, taken from an anti-pornography ad [which is excerpted in an earlier chapter], seems to have been intended to show that pornography is a causal factor of serial-rape-murder. Does it show that?

*An essay on this question should demonstrate sensitivity to the following points: The assertion about the FBI study would support the causal claim in question only if the frequency of attraction to pornography in the "experimental group" cited above were known to exceed significantly the frequency in a "control group" of people who had not committed serial-rape-murder. Further, that condition, while necessary for the FBI study to support the causal claim in question, would not be sufficient. Were the subjects in the "experimental group" different from the control group and the rest of us in some relevant way other than that they were murderers? Almost certainly. Were these biasing differences controlled? The essay should perhaps consider directly the question of whether the attraction to pornography and the propensity for sexual violence were both the result of some other factor or factors. It might also indicate the vagueness of the phrase "attracted to pornography."*

# Chapter 12
# Moral Reasoning

Our opinion is this: When people disagree on the general moral principles that underlie a moral discussion, it's not part of the task of critical thinking (and, more to the point, not part of the task of this text) to resolve which principle, if either, is correct. However, it emphatically *is* a part of the task of critical thinking (1) to become clear on what those principles are and how they function in the discussion, (2) to detect inconsistencies in their application, and (3) to see the consequences of adhering to them.

Thus we do not intend that this chapter substitute for a course in moral philosophy. Our intent is only to set forth a few of the basic concepts and ingredients of moral reasoning, those that seem to us crucial in accomplishing the above three tasks. Our objective is not that students should emerge as moralists or moral philosophers, but merely that they become better prepared to deal intelligently and critically with moral argumentation and clearer in their own reasoning about moral issues.

## Exercises Unanswered in the Text

### Exercise 12-1

2. Prescriptive
3. Prescriptive
5. Descriptive
6. Prescriptive
8. Prescriptive
9. Descriptive

### Exercise 12-2

2. Moral value
3. No value (Even though being well informed is something that we often do attach a (nonmoral) value to, it isn't done in this claim.)
5. Nonmoral value
6. No value
8. Nonmoral value
9. Nonmoral value

### Exercise 12-3

1. A borrower should pay for any damages that occur to the borrowed item while the item is in possession of the borrower.

3. A person should abide by the terms of contracts he agrees to.

5. A person should take care of his (or her) parent when the latter cannot take care of herself or afford to pay for someone else to do so.

6. A person who feeds his pets too little ought to treat them better.

8. A child with a new possession should treat neighbor children equitably when allowing them to use it.

9. A parent should not push his children into dangerous sports or activities.

## Exercise 12-4

1. A physician should not set his fee schedule based solely upon the law of supply and demand.

3. Morally responsible parents do what they can in order to ensure that their children grow up to be morally responsible adults.

5. In circumstances where others may desperately need help, one ought to make oneself available to give such help.

## Exercise 12-5

2. Should downtown parking spaces for bicycles be removed so that more spaces can be made available to automobiles?

   (a) Relevant. Theoretically, the two cases would be treated fairly if your chances of finding a parking place were about the same whether you went downtown in your car or on your bicycle. It is sometimes a matter of social policy to encourage some kinds of behavior and discourage others, however.
   (b) Irrelevant, except insofar as there is a policy to decrease the amount of pollution downtown. That it ought to be reduced would require further argument.
   (c) Relevant, since several bicyclists must lose spaces in order for one driver to have one
   (d) Relevant. This requires the consideration that people who cannot afford automobiles deserve equal treatment with regard to parking downtown.
   (e) This is relevant only if there is reason to believe that a substantial number of cars that need parking downtown actually do carry more than one or two people.

3. Should the hockey player be criminally liable for offenses committed in the course of a hockey game (just as he would be liable for those offenses if they were committed under other circumstances)?

   (a) Irrelevant. It may be dangerous to drive an automobile, but it doesn't follow that anybody who recklessly hits you is excused.
   (b) Irrelevant. For the same reason as the preceding item.
   (c) This may be relevant to the *nature* of the assault, since it rules out (or at least lessens the force of) the claim that the defendant was acting from emotion resulting from extreme provocation.
   (d) Irrelevant. Seeing this factor as relevant amounts to appealing to common practice (see that topic in Chapter 6, Pseudoreasoning).

(e) Relevant. If fighting were such a part of the game, the defendant would probably be the team's owner rather than the player. Alternatively, fights among hockey players would be treated like prizefights.

5. If handguns should be outlawed because they result in the deaths of people, shouldn't automobiles also be outlawed since they also result in the deaths of people?

(a) Relevant, but not so obviously so as it may at first appear. If the social purpose behind outlawing an object were simply decreasing the number of deaths, then outlawing the automobile would accomplish that purpose. Presumably the purpose is best put in terms of eliminating *purposeful* killings—that is, intentional crimes. And the automobile is probably involved in fewer of those than the handgun (although we're speculating about this).
(b) Irrelevant
(c) Irrelevant, except insofar as the harmless uses serve a much more important function in one case than in the other (see next item).
(d) Relevant. The harmless function of the automobile is, for better or worse, crucial to the ordinary activities of most people. Outlawing it would create enormous hardships, and this must be weighed in considering the issue. The same cannot be said for handguns (despite the fact that they are a source of interest for a number of people).
(e) Relevant, but not on the order of importance of (d).

### Exercise 12-6

1. Issue: Whether Marina ought to treat other people and her pets with the same compassion.

Both pets and people are sentient creatures, a relevant similarity, and that alone supplies a reason for treating both with at least a minimal level of sympathy. But one could still argue that Marina is not inconsistent in lavishing *extra* kindness on her pets. Pets, Marina might say, are unable to fend for themselves, but people can. She'd be right in thinking this relevant, provided it were true. But of course it isn't true about all people nor about all animals.

On the other side, society would hardly be possible if we always treated other people coldly and with indifference. This strikes us as the most important consideration we can think of. It makes for a relevant difference between people and pets (and favors people, of course).

Frankly, we expect that folks with Marina's attitudes have them for underlying psychological reasons and not because of some belief about any particular species.

2. Issue: Whether Hopper is as morally guilty as Jenkins.

Jenkins left the store with one fewer item to sell; Hopper returned the record in almost as new condition as that in which he found it. This fact might convince some that Hopper's offense is of a lesser sort than Jenkins's. We find this relevant, but it hardly excuses Hopper.

Jenkins and Hopper both made off with something for nothing at the store's expense, and the value of what they made off with is roughly equal. This fact supports treating the two cases equally. If everybody followed Hopper's example, record stores would go out of business just as surely as if they followed Jenkins's example. This too supports equal treatment of the two.

5. Issue: Whether it is fair to Professor Stein's freshman and sophomore classes to grade

them more harshly than his upper-division students.

One might think that one relevant difference that would support Stein's practice is the fact that freshman and sophomore classes are sometimes used to "winnow" students from programs. We think this is irrelevant. The same winnowing would be possible if grades were awarded the same in upper-division courses as in lower-division courses.

It's probably true that, as a rule, juniors and seniors tend to do better work than freshmen and sophomores. Even if it's true, however, it's relevant only to the issue of whether juniors and seniors should actually receive better grades, not to the manner in which Stein grades (setting one class level's average at B and the other at C). If Stein were to get an especially good freshman class, they would still receive lower grades by his method.

Pretty clearly, we disapprove.

6. Issue: Whether a newspaper is inconsistent if it censors sexually explicit advertising and does not censor tobacco advertising.

Whatever their respective harmfulness, tobacco advertising is socially acceptable by custom but sexually explicit advertising is not. This fact is relevant in an interesting way: It shows that the newspaper is being consistent with general social standards, but it points up the fact that those very standards may be inconsistent.

Sexually explicit advertising is no more likely to cause harm than tobacco advertising. We think this is relevant, and that it supports equal treatment. Whether that treatment is to publish both kinds of advertising or to *ban* both kinds is another question, of course.

7. Issue: Whether it is fair to denounce the Nicaraguan government and support guerrillas who oppose it and support the El Salvadoran government against the guerrillas who oppose it.

The most obvious thing to say here is that the government of Nicaragua is Marxist and the government of El Salvador is not. This is a relevant consideration, of course, but only if the relevance of a government's being Marxist is adequately supported. Sometimes people take the fact that a government is Marxist as reason enough to believe that it should be opposed, even when those same people cannot state two true claims abut Marxism.

Nicaragua is exporting revolution and civil war to other Latin American countries, it is said by some, while El Salvador is not. If this is true, then it's relevant, but we don't know the extent to which it is actually true.

The fact that Nicaragua is closer to the United States strikes us as irrelevant, even if it were true: The difference in distance is in fact negligible.

A sometimes overlooked point is that several other Latin American countries oppose U.S. aid to Nicaraguan rebels. We think this is relevant in the long run, since relations with those other countries are important to the long run stability of the area.

Obviously, this is a big issue, and we should not expect a student essay to better job of clearing it up than the U.S. State Department. We'd be delighted to get an essay that covered the above points.

8. Issue: Whether Joseph is inconsistent in protesting American intervention in Grenada but not protesting Soviet intervention in Afghanistan. (Notice that, if we make the issue one of whether Joseph's protest of American intervention is proper, we might have nothing more than a case of ad hominem of the pseudorefutation variety. Whether Joseph's actions are inconsistent is another matter.)

In a nutshell: A protest in the U.S. against U.S. intervention may have some effect; a protest in the U.S. against Soviet intervention is unlikely to have any effect. We think this is probably the most important factor in such an issue, on the reasonable assumption that it is true. It may be that protests at the Soviet embassy in the U.S. would have an effect, but we aren't sure about this. Closely related is the fact that Joseph may feel more obliged to protest the actions of *his own* government than that of another country. (It's much like the greater obligation we feel to ensure good behavior of our own children compared to the children of others.)

One might also consider such factors as the claim that Joseph knows quite a lot about American foreign policy and much less about Soviet policy. Hence he is simply not speaking about an issue about which he knows little. This doesn't seem to cut much ice. Any observer would know enough to have *some* sort of opinion.

Finally, and importantly, nobody has the inclination or energy to deal with every matter in cases like this. If Joseph finds the two interventions without real relevant differences, then indeed he should treat them similarly, but we can hardly require him to stage protests about those he feels less strongly about than others.

9. Issue: Whether it is morally justifiable for Derreaux, a lawyer, to defend a guilty defendant with as much enthusiasm and skill as a guilty defendant.

In our legal system, one is not considered guilty until proven so. However much it may seem related, this fact is irrelevant to the issue. The dictum means only that one is not to be convicted of a crime unless he or she has been proven to have committed it.

The only truly relevant issue here is that every person is entitled to a defense, whether innocent or guilty. To presume otherwise is to turn the judgment of the court over to defense attorneys, who would provide effective defenses only for those they believed innocent.

### Exercise 12-7

We provide the required premises.

1. (a) The government has the responsibility for ensuring care of any infant whose parents do not ensure such care.
   (b) No person or agency should intervene to ensure the life of any child that will lead a less than satisfactory life. (Supports the denial of the principal claim)
   (c) The decision to intervene on behalf of an infant with serious medical problems is a family matter. (Supports the denial of the principal claim)
   (d) The government should intervene in any medical matter in which physicians' expertise does not qualify them to advise patients or those responsible for patients.
   (e) If the government intervenes and requires medical treatment of a newborn with serious medical problems, it will cause the family of the newborn to suffer because of an unhappy genetic accident. (Supports the denial of the principal claim)

3. (a) Blowing the whistle is disloyal. (Supports the denial of the principal claim) (Notice that consideration (a) in the text means, or implies, that employees should be loyal to their firms.)
   (b) Accomplices to wrongful acts have the duty to speak up.
   (c) What is immoral should not be done. (Supports the denial of the principal claim) This premise is analytic, and hence not logically necessary to the argument.
   (d) A person should overlook wrongful deeds on the part of his company if not doing so can ruin his employability or endanger the well-being of his family. (Supports the denial of the principal claim)

(e) Everyone is duty bound to speak up about bad business.
(f) This one is more complicated. We'll unpack the entire argument:
   Living with injustice and unfairness eventually causes people to lose their own senses of justice and fairness. (Stated premise)
   One should not lose her own sense of justice and fairness. (Unstated premise number 1)
   Therefore, one should not live with injustice and unfairness. (Unstated conclusion)
   One who lives with illegal or unscrupulous tactics on the part of their companies without blowing the whistle lives with injustice and unfairness. (Unstated premise number 2)
   Therefore, one should blow the whistle.

4. (a) We should do away with all forms of murder.
   (b) It is acceptable to impose the death penalty on those who have given up their own right to live. (Supports the denial of the principal claim)
   (c) Society must impose *some* solution to the problem of violent criminal offenders. (Supports the denial of the principal claim)
   (d) Any person who owes a life should receive the death penalty. (Supports the denial of the principal claim)
   (e) We should do away with (i.e., change) anything that is an admission that we don't care enough to rehabilitate offenders. In effect, this says that we should care enough to rehabilitate offenders.
   (f) Any penalty that cannot be administered fairly should be done away with.

5. (a) Anyone should be free to make any choice that is one's own business.
   (b) Not everyone who chooses euthanasia is of sound mind. (Supports the denial of the principal claim)
   (c) One ought not be able to choose what one has no right to choose. (Supports the denial of the principal claim)
   (d) Not all cases where the question of euthanasia is an issue are cases where the subject is "vegetating"—i.e., no longer capable of consciousness. (Supports the denial of the principal claim)

# Chapter 12 Test Question-Exercise Bank

## Bank 12-1

For identification as descriptive or prescriptive

1. "Morgan is old enough to have known what would happen if he didn't pay the fine on time."

*Descriptive*

2. "Morgan should have paid the fine on time."

   *Prescriptive*

3. "Twenty past ten. We should go home."

   *Prescriptive*

4. "Jake will pay Mr. Sly the money he owes if he knows what's good for him."

   *Prescriptive*

5. "Hazel owes Bert $100 and was supposed to pay him back last month."

   *Descriptive*

6. "The program Sam wrote for finding repeating decimals works wonderfully, and it's only thirty-five lines long—that's real elegance."

   *Prescriptive (at a minimum, it prescribes approval)*

7. "The dog was clearly in pain but nobody was doing anything about it."

   *Descriptive*

8. "It is wrong for the United States to supply Nicaraguan rebels with military aid."

   *Prescriptive*

9. "It is not in the best interests of the United States to supply Nicaraguan rebels with military aid."

   *Descriptive*

10. "It is hard to think of any nostrum that has less to recommend it than rent control."

    *Prescriptive*

11. "There ought to be a law against doing what Selena has done to her hair."

    *Prescriptive (even if it isn't literally prescribing a statute)*

12. "If you don't get rid of your dog's fleas, it's going to be miserable."

    *Descriptive*

13. "You should get rid of your dog's fleas so that it won't be miserable."

    *Prescriptive*

14. "You ought to get to know Samuel."

    *Prescriptive*

15. "Brooke and Richard are pleasant enough fellows once you get to know them."

   *Descriptive*


   **Bank 12-2**

   These should be sorted into those that express moral values, those that express nonmoral values, and those that do not express values at all.

16. "The paint job on Linda's car is awful—looks as though somebody did it with a brush."

   *Nonmoral value*

17. "Alicia has not been entirely honest with her husband; that much is clear."

   *No value*

18. "Kelly did the right thing when he turned in the wallet he found."

   *Moral value*

19. "The Pittsburgh Steelers were the best football team of the 1970s, but the Bears will turn out to be the best of the '80s."

   *Nonmoral value*

20. "Everybody should be as fair as Mario tries to be."

   *Moral value*

21. "All cigarette advertising should be strictly regulated."

   *Moral value, under most circumstances*

22. "The advertising for that "miracle" cleaner is fraudulent."

   *Moral value*

23. "It is bothersome to be telephoned after 9 p.m."

   *No value*

24. "She was really hurt by the way he treated her."

   *No value (in most contexts)*

25. The Marxist regime in Poland is harshly repressive.

   *Moral value*

26. "Everybody has a right to an education."

    *Moral value*

27. "I like Beethoven's Third Symphony better than his Ninth."

    *Nonmoral value*

28. "His whole lecture was boring."

    *Nonmoral value*

29. "It is too my turn to deal!"

    *No value*

30. "It's no surprise that they've stopped seeing each other."

    *No value*


### Bank 12-3

In order for the conclusion to follow from the premise in each of the following passages that contain arguments, a moral principle is necessary as an extra premise. Such a principle should be supplied.

31. "Knowing how to think critically may help save someone's life some day, so you ought to develop your ability to do so."

    *A person should develop whatever abilities that might help save someone's life someday.*

32. "You have no right to complain about Stephenson's performance; after all, you voted for him."

    *Voting for (or otherwise supporting, presumably) a person eliminates one's right to complain about what he or she does later.*

33. "It's time to restore diplomatic relations with Cuba. Doing so will make the hemisphere a safer place."

    *Steps that will make the hemisphere a safer place ought to be taken.*

34. "You shouldn't have criticized David so harshly; his mistake was a trivial one."

    *Nobody should be criticized harshly for trivial mistakes.*

35. "In 1965 there were 47,000 road fatalities in the U.S. By 1984 there were only 44,250 fatalities, but that is still far too many. The reductions between 1965 and 1984 were due primarily to federal motor vehicle safety requirements. So even stricter federal safety controls should be required."

*Unstated nonmoral premise: Regulations that have reduced road fatalities in the past will, if strengthened, reduce the present number of fatalities. Unstated moral principle: Steps to reduce the number of fatalities should be taken.*

36. "Galileo's hypothesis should be suppressed. The Biblical account in Ecclesiastes clearly states that the sun rises and sets and hastens to the place where it will rise again."

    *Unstated nonmoral premise: Galileo's hypothesis contradicts a Biblical account. Unstated moral principle: Any claim that contradicts a Biblical account should be suppressed.*

37. "We ought not to leave the showroom model's accessories off the price tag, since that will really mislead customers."

    *One ought not to mislead customers.*

38. "Smoke from wood-burning stoves has become a serious health-hazard. They ought to be banned."

    *Health hazards, or what produce them, ought to be banned.*

39. "You shouldn't have included that material on the exam. It was never mentioned in class."

    *One ought not examine on material that has not been mentioned in class.*

40. "The dog has been out so long she's probably freezing. You ought to let her in."

    *One should not allow animals to suffer unnecessarily.*

41. "We shouldn't have meddled in the affairs of Chile because our meddling was done covertly."

    *Covert operations should not be undertaken in other countries.*

42. "The vandals who destroyed the landing lights at the airport should be imprisoned without parole."

    *Not an argument as it stands*

43. "He shouldn't have been punished for what he did, since nobody got hurt."

    *One should be punished for one's actions only when they result in somebody's getting hurt.*

44. "He shouldn't have been punished for what he did, since there was no risk of anybody getting hurt as a result."

    *One should be punished for one's actions only when they result in a risk of somebody's getting hurt.*

45. "The state legislature takes a break each January. In spite of the press of business, the capitol remains silent. The waste of time is appalling—this year alone the legislature recessed while 153 bills were pending."

*Unstated conclusion: Congress should not recess in January. Unstated nonmoral premise: Every January there is a press of business in January; many bills remain unsigned. Unstated moral principle: The legislature should not recess when there is press of business.*

46. "The utility companies should have been made to rebate payments to their customers because of the way they conspired to keep energy-saving fluorescent lighting from becoming known."

    *Unstated nonmoral premise: The utility companies' conspiracy to keep energy-saving lighting from becoming known was a case of taking advantage of their customers and costing them money. Unstated moral principle: Any company that takes advantage of its customers and costs them money ought to have to make rebate payments to those customers.*

47. "The zoo now has 14 acres; the master plan calls for an additional five acres. This expansion will not be enough to meet the needs of the whole community. The average acreage in cities our size is 67."

    *Unstated conclusion: The zoo should be expanded beyond what the masterplan calls for. Unstated moral principle: City zoos should be large enough to meet the needs of the whole community. Unstated nonmoral premise: The zoo-acreage needs of a city are determined by the average zoo-acreage in cities of similar size.*

48. "This weekend marks the start of the first national celebration of Dr. Martin Luther King Jr.'s birthday. It's a sad commentary that the official commission set up to honor the man who did so much for black equality is itself a financial orphan. . . . Congress did not appropriate any funds, specifying that the commission's work must be funded by private donations."
—Jack Anderson

    *Unstated conclusion: The commission should receive federal funding. Unstated moral principle: Commissions set up to honor people whose deeds have earned recognition by a national holiday should receive federal funding.*

**Bank 12-4**

Determine which of the following five items are relevant to the following issue:

Should motorcyclists be forced by law to wear helmets?

49. "Society bears part of the cost of motorcycle injuries."

    *Relevant*

50. "The more serious motorcycle injuries are, the higher motorcycle insurance rates are."

    *Relevant*

51. "Motorcycle helmets are expensive; good ones cost well over a hundred dollars."

    *Irrelevant, or very little relevance*

52. "Making people do something simply for their own good is an infringement of their right to self-determination."

*Relevant*

53. "Some motorcyclists claim that helmets reduce visibility."

*Relevant*


## Bank 12-5

Each passage below poses a moral question. Students should decide which factors are relevant to the issue and which are not, and explain why. (We'll offer an opinion without comment—you may not agree.) These can evoke, or provoke, some lively class discussions. You'll probably find that a good bit of such discussion is about whether some of the claims that state allegedly relevant considerations ("factors") are in fact true. We've included a few here and there that are arguably false.

54. An advertisement in a medical journal shows an attractive, but worried-looking young woman with an armful of books. The ad indicates some of the problems that face new college students: "Exposure to new friends and other influences may force her to reevaluate herself and her goals. . . Her newly stimulated intellectual curiosity may make her more sensitive to and apprehensive about national and world conditions." The headline above the ad reads: "TO HELP FREE HER OF EXCESSIVE ANXIETY . . . LIBRIUM."
   Some people find this kind of advertisement (and physicians who are susceptible to such advertising) at least unprofessional and probably immoral.
   Is it? Are they?

   Suggested factors:

   (a) The kinds of problems described in the ad are not extraordinary; they are the sort of circumstances nearly everyone finds herself in at one time or another, and they do not produce extraordinary anxiety in most people. (*Some* anxiety from time to time is normal, we assume.) (Relevant)
   (b) A substantial number of people find it easy to become addicted to psychoactive drugs. (Relevant)
   (c) Drug therapy can relieve symptoms of stress and anxiety and prevent a person from seeking other kinds of therapy. (Relevant)
   (d) Physicians are intelligent and conscientious enough to know when a drug is really called for and when it's not. (Relevant)
   (e) Drug companies should be allowed to advertise in whatever nonfraudulent way they wish; the First Amendment guarantees them that right. (Relevant)

55. In some states high schools receive state funds if students at the school perform exceptionally well on batteries of standardized tests. The funds are used for improvement-of-instruction programs. Some students believe that the funds should be given to the students to do with what they like. Should they?

   (a) The students are the ones responsible for their school's receiving the funds. (Relevant)
   (b) Students would spend the funds frivolously. (Relevant, if true)

(c) All schools could use funds for improvement-of-instruction programs. (Relevant)

(d) Return of funds to students would motivate them to do better on the tests. (Relevant, if true)

(e) Students in some years do well on the tests; those in other years don't. (Irrelevant)

56. The death penalty has been in force in many states for much of the past 200 years, and it has been found unconstitutional on a few occasions, at least in the forms in which certain states implemented it. But it has always been a source of controversy and moral debate. Is it ever morally justified to take the life of a human being because of some action he has performed?

(a) According to many experts on the subject, the death penalty does not deter others from committing capital crimes. (Relevant)

(b) A person who commits murder has indicated that he has no respect for life. (Relevant? True?)

(c) Another life is the only price that is large enough to adequately pay for having taken a life. (Relevant? This claim is metaphorical. Is its literal meaning clear?)

(d) Capital punishment is just a way of disguising society's insistence on revenge. (Irrelevant, we think)

(e) Society sets a bad example by sanctioning the taking of lives, even those of people who have taken others' lives. (Relevant, if true)

(f) The death penalty has been inflicted more often on the poor than on the wealthy, more often on members of minorities than on whites, and more often on men than on women. (Irrelevant to the question posed, although relevant to similar questions )

(g) The death penalty can result in an innocent person being executed. (Irrelevant to the question posed, although relevant to similar questions)

57. Harold, 48, and his fiancée, Sharon, 43, will be visiting Harold's parents, who are wondering whether they should object if Harold wants to share a bedroom with Sharon during their stay. Should they object?

(a) Harold and Sharon have both been married before. (Relevant?)

(b) Harold has made it clear that he wishes to share a bedroom with Sharon. (Relevant)

(c) Harold's parents would never allow their 18-year-old grandson to share a room with his fiancée, were they ever to visit. (Relevant)

(d) What if Sharon were not Harold's fiancée but his (one and only) ladyfriend of long standing? (Irrelevant)

(e) Harold's parents are friends with Sharon's parents. (Relevant?)

**Bank 12-6**

Discuss whether Marina is treating relevantly similar cases in sufficiently similar fashions. There are some instances below when it is not a matter of treating different cases at all; students should have to spot these. You may adjust the circumstances of each case as you see fit. (Note: It may be a good idea to emphasize the independence of each item; Marina could not possibly do everything we have her doing in this bank!) We offer our comments without much elaboration.

58. Marina's will stipulates that her son by birth will receive substantially more of her estate than will her adopted son, even though both sons love her equally, have treated her with similar regard, and have lived with her for about the same amount of time.

*Our view is that she is treating relevantly similar cases differently.*

59. Marina is the principal source of financial support for one of her sons at college; the other son won a large scholarship, and Marina sends him a much smaller amount.

   *From what's said here, we'd count this as sufficiently similar treatment, given the dissimilarities of the cases.*

60. She calls it to the clerk's attention when she is overcharged, but not if she is undercharged.

   *Here she is inconsistent; the cases are relevantly similar but are treated differently.*

61. She leaves large tips at a posh restaurant where meals are quite expensive, but she leaves much smaller tips at another, much plainer and less expensive restaurant, even though the service is as good and the waiters work just as hard at the second establishment.

   *We think this is treating like cases differently, but we're afraid Marina has a lot of company.*

62. She criticizes her brother for expressing racist views but does not criticize Mr. Durban, a business associate, who holds similar views.

   *Like cases are treated differently.*

63. Marina's automobile is a large, gas-guzzling, luxury car, but in some circumstances (such as cocktail parties when she is among strangers) she will make it a point to criticize people who drive such cars.

   *This is not a case of treating like cases differently; there's another name for this kind of inconsistency: hypocrisy.*

64. She instructs her children to always be truthful but lies to her young daughter when the daughter asks if her (the daughter's) illness is running up large medical bills.

   *The cases are not relevantly similar.*

65. Marina tells her children to tell the truth but she claims deductions on her income tax return to which she knows she is not legally entitled.

   *This is hypocrisy again: There is an inconsistency between what she says and what she does, but it is not one of treating similar cases differently. She would be treating such cases in dissimilar ways if, for example, she told her children to tell the truth and also told them to lie on their income tax forms.*

66. Marina offers her daughter's fiancé a job in the company she owns, but it never occurs to her to do the same for her son's fiancée.

   *Different treatment of relevantly similar cases*

67. She tells her children not to smoke but smokes herself.

   *Here once again we find her not practicing what she preaches. But this is an inconsistency*

234

*between word and deed, not between deed and deed or between word and word. She would be guilty of treating relevantly similar cases in a dissimilar way if, for instance, she told her children not to smoke cigarettes but to smoke cigars, if that can be imagined. Note: The issue here is her treatment of the cases; if her children were to reject her advice, they commit an ad hominem, as per Chapter 7.*

68. At election time, Marina votes for the candidate she thinks will do the best job in every election except one. In that race she votes for her second choice, because she is certain that the best person for the job has no chance of winning and she believes her second choice is still better than any of the rest of the candidates.

    *The cases are different enough to justify the different actions.*

69. Marina opposes tyrannical despots in several countries in the world. But even though the government of Almería is equally tyrannical, she is not inclined to oppose it because she has a friend who works in the Almerían foreign ministry.

    *Treating like cases differently*

70. She criticizes the Japanese for killing and eating whales, but she eats beef.

    *That is, she approves beef killing but not whale killing. The cases are arguably dissimilar.*

71. The company that Marina owns allows the secretarial staff to accumulate one vacation day per month, but managers at the company accumulate one and one-half days per month.

    *We expect it may be controversial in some quarters, but we think this is treating relevantly similar cases dissimilarly.*

72. She says she believes in equality but she tells lots of ethnic and racial jokes.

    *Whether it is unlikely, it is not impossible that a person could tell such jokes and believe in equality.*

73. Marina is usually a careful shopper, looking for bargains and buying generic products when she's at the market. But she has a weakness for gloves and handbags, and she owns a closet full of elegant and expensive examples.

    *The opposite of this kind of inconsistency is not injustice, it's tedium.*

74. She watches a viewer-supported public television station, but she does not make contributions to it.

    *She is taking selfish advantage of the public station, but this is not a case of treating relevantly similar cases differently. Perhaps she is perfectly consistent and takes selfish advantage of others every time she gets the chance.*

75. Marina's twins, Mary and Myron, have different aspirations. Mary wants to be an engineer. She's good at mathematics and has a good chance of winning a scholarship to a good college. Myron is both inept and uninterested in such matters. He shows signs of artistic talent and wants to study painting. For their seventeenth birthdays, Marina got them a computer.

*Unless Myron gets interested in computer graphics, Marina has been somewhat unfair to him in treating his relevantly different case as if it were just like his sister's. This is the other side of the coin.*

76. Marina votes against a tax increase for maintenance of her city park even though she uses the park and plans to continue using it whether or not the measure passes.

    *The comments on this item should parallel those on item 74.*

77. Although she doesn't believe in stealing, Marina uses the office copy machine for personal business and makes person-to-person long-distance calls to fictitious persons as a code to avoid paying for the calls.

    *These activities are relevantly similar to stealing.*

**Bank  12-7**

For each of the items in the preceding bank that seems to be an instance of Marina's treating relevantly similar cases with an insufficient similarity, imagine a set of "extenuating circumstances" that would serve to exonerate her from a charge of moral inconsistency. Here's an example: She calls it to the clerk's attention when she is overcharged but not if she is undercharged. Extenuating circumstance: She is purchasing a life-saving drug for her sister and discovers that she doesn't have quite enough money to pay for the drug. She also knows the clerk and knows that he doesn't believe she has a sister and would not give her the medication if she informed him that he undercharged. She mentions the overcharge by reflex and immediately regrets having done so, since the overcharge and undercharges cancel each other out.

**Bank  12-8**

To the student: Below are five moral claims, each followed by a list of considerations, some in support of the claim, some against it, and possibly some irrelevant. For each relevant consideration construct an argument that has the claim (or its denial) as a conclusion and the consideration as a premise. When you're finished, weigh the arguments pro and con and determine whether or not you agree with the claim, given those arguments. Your instructor may call on you in class to explain and defend your views.

78. Boys who question the existence of God should not be permitted to join the Boy Scouts.

    (a)  Part of the Boy Scout oath is to do one's duty to God and country.
    (b)  The Boy Scouts are supposed to be open to anyone regardless of race, religion, or creed.
    (c)  Some saints questioned the existence of God when they were the age of Boy Scouts.
    (d)  Boy Scouts of America can limit membership as it chooses.
    (e)  Probably many scouts come to question God's existence shortly after they leave or even while they are in the Boy Scouts.
    (f)  A boy barely in his teens cannot be sure what he believes and what he doesn't believe about God.

79. When a person buys a car, either new or used, he should receive full descriptions in writing of the physical condition of the car, the warranty, and so on; in short, he should get a written version of everything he might need to know about that automobile.

   (a) A car is at least the second largest purchase most people ever make, second only to a house.
   (b) A person depends on a car to get him where he needs to go.
   (c) A person's life hangs on the safety of the car he drives or rides in.
   (d) It would be expensive to produce the documentation described above for every car sold.
   (e) Most people do not read the directions for the things they buy beyond learning how to turn them on.

80. Rock music that promotes drug use, sexual activity, or violent behavior should be banned.

   (a) Banning such music would place restrictions on rock artists' creativity.
   (b) Banning the music would restrict the freedom of people who want to listen to it.
   (c) Such music can be purchased by anyone—even very young children and people who are emotionally unstable.
   (d) Books that praise similar activities are not banned unless they are overtly pornographic.
   (e) What counts as promoting drug use, sexual activity, or violent behavior is subjective.
   (f) Some operatic masterpieces are suggestive and violent.

81. The government ought to insure people against harm or loss due to crime.

   (a) More attention is currently paid to the rights of a criminal than to those of his victim.
   (b) Many people cannot afford a serious robbery or burglary loss, never mind a serious injury and the associated medical costs.
   (c) Such insurance would cost an enormous amount of money.
   (d) It is not the government's job to see that nothing bad ever happens to anybody without compensation.
   (e) Such a program would invite fraudulent claims.

82. In championship prizefights, in the event of a tie the current champion retains his title. This is not proper. The title should be shared or remain undecided until a rematch takes place.

   (a) If the fight is a tie, then the challenger is at least as good as the champion.
   (b) In certain other sports championship honors are shared; for example, two or more individuals can share an Olympic gold medal.
   (c) Championship honors have never been shared in professional boxing.
   (d) If a title is shared, then a person could become a boxing champion without actually defeating the champion—which is absurd.
   (e) There is a certain amount of subjectivity in boxing scoring, so it is never absolutely certain who won a close fight.

**Bank 12-9**

Each of the following describes a situation in which someone is debating which of two courses of action to take. Construct an argumentative essay on the issue of which course of action should be taken. Take into account as many relevant features of the situation as you can.

83. An employer who is considering hiring Eva has asked Donna, Eva's former supervisor, for a report on Eva. In truth, Eva's work for Donna has been only average. However, (a) Eva is Donna's friend and Donna knows that Eva probably will not get the job if she says anything negative about Eva, and Donna knows that Eva desperately needs the job. Further (b) Donna knows that if the situation were reversed she would not want Eva to mention her deficiencies. But on the other hand (c) it has been Donna's policy to reveal the deficiencies of employees when she has been asked for references by employers, and she knows that some of Eva's faults may be bothersome to this particular employer. Finally, (d) this employer has leveled with Donna in the past when Donna has asked for a report on people who have worked for him. Should Donna reveal deficiencies in Eva's past performance?

84. The water pump in Michelle's Toyota isn't working and her friend Felipe replaces it for her as a favor. Michelle decides to repay Felipe's kindness by promising to buy him a six-pack of beer. Unfortunately, Michelle isn't quite old enough to buy beer legally, so she asks her friend Carol, who is, to buy the beer for her, and explains why. Felipe too is slightly under the legal age, but Carol knows Felipe and regards him as a responsible and mature individual. Further (a) Carol knows that Michelle will be embarrassed if she has to tell Felipe she cannot get beer for him after all, and (b) Michelle has recently done something nice for Carol, and Carol owes her a favor. However, (c) Michelle is aware that if Felipe drinks the beer all at once and goes driving—an unlikely event in Carol's opinion—he could be injured or injure others. Carol could be held liable in that event. But (d) Carol knows Michelle's other friends and doubts that any of them are old enough to buy beer for Michelle. If Carol turns Michelle down, Carol will have to live without getting Felipe the beer she promised to give him. Should Carol get the beer for Michelle, everything considered?

85. Lisa's algebra class has a quiz every other Friday. This is the third time she's been so worried about *other* matters that she hasn't done quite as well on the quiz she might have otherwise. What has her upset is the fact that the instructor leaves the room while the students take the quiz, and over half the class is taking the opportunity to cheat. She knows and likes several of the other students in the class, and some of the ones she likes are among those who are cheating. Lisa knows that (a) a failure to speak to the teacher about the cheating will result in her own grade being lower, since the teacher grades in part on the curve. But (b) she will be doing her friends and the others a great harm, since cheating is taken very seriously at the school. If she doesn't "turn in" her classmates, (c) the only other alternative to getting a worse grade than she deserves is to begin cheating herself, something she's never done. What should she do?

86. Jan witnessed a certain Mr. Gaines commit a crime several months ago, but despite his certain knowledge of Gaines's guilt, becaue of an error in the investigation the charges against him were dismissed. Jan is especially upset about the nature of the crime—(a) Gaines was defrauding a charitable organization that Jan happens to think accomplishes a lot of good. Jan also knows that the crime was committed out of greed, since (b) Gaines owns a large jewelry store and is already well off. Gaines has spoken to his friends about how he got away without having to stand trial, and (c) he is gloating about it.

One day Jan is walking up the alley that runs behind Gaines's store, and he notices that the back door has been left unlocked and, from the look of things, it appears that the burglar alarm has not been turned on. One of several vaults in the back room has a half-open door. He realizes that he could make off very easily with a large amount of expensive jewelry. (d) The likelihood of his being caught is very small. It occurs to him that it wouldn't be quite the same as stealing, certainly not as bad as what he saw Gaines do, if (e) he did not keep the loot for himself but gave it away. It occurs to him that (f) if he takes what doesn't belong to him he may not be any better than Gaines, and on the small chance he did get caught, nobody would believe him and (g) the penalties would be stiff. But (h) this is his chance to see justice done with regard to Gaines and he can make some people who deserve it very happy with the proceeds of the burglary. Should Jan grab the jewels?

87. Kevin's mother and father are divorced. Kevin is eight and he lives with his father, John, for three months every summer. The rest of the time, except for occasional weekends, he lives 200 miles away with his mother. John is the one with the problem: He and Kevin talked a lot last summer about getting a dog. The house John lives in is the first one that has had a back yard big enough to keep a dog and a fence around it as well. John had always used the "no place to keep it" line to avoid making promises, but that no longer applies. John finally promised to get Kevin a dog at the beginning of the next summer, and he knows Kevin is hoping to get one. In fact, John knows that Kevin is expecting a dog with enough confidence that (a) he'll be very disappointed if he doesn't get one, even though he may not say much about it. Furthermore, (b) not getting a dog will deprive both Kevin and John of considerable pleasure, since John knows how happy it would make his son to get one. But the danger of having a dog around is that John lives alone during most of the year, and having a dog means being responsible for another creature. (c) When John travels, as his job requires from time to time, who will look after the dog? He can't leave it with a friend for a week or two at a time. And he has no neighbors close by who could look after it. It looks like a difficult trade-off: Three months a year of pleasure for John, Kevin, and a dog, balanced against what might be nine months a year of frequent unpleasantness for both John and the dog. What should he do?

## Supplementary Essay Question

88. Shelley and Maurita are both disturbed by their C+ final grades in Mr. Carlton's geography class, and they request that he recheck his grade book. He does so and finds that, indeed, he had made mistakes. Maurita was supposed to get a B- and Shelley was supposed to get a C-. He gives Maurita the B- and allows Shelley to keep the C+.

Should he have lowered Shelley's grade to a C-? Construct one argument the conclusion of which is that he should, and construct one argument the conclusion of which is that he should not. Be sure to spell out clearly any moral principles in the arguments.

# Appendices

The first time around, partly because of the pressures of time and partly because we didn't realize there would be such a call for it, we didn't include sections in this manual for the appendices. But we've heard from quite a few of you who've requested additional exercises for both appendices. We hope you'll find the ones that follow helpful.

These appendices can replace Chapter 9 of the text, if a more thorough treatment of traditional logic is desired. There are some advantages to replacing at least the part of Chapter 9 that deals with categorical inferences with Appendix 1. If students learn the syllogistic argument patterns found in Chapter 9, they will still not be in a position to evaluate perfectly good syllogistic arguments that do not fit those patterns—for example, those with I or O type claims in them. With a general technique for evaluating syllogisms—by means of either diagrams or rules—every such argument can be adequately tested. It will take more time to do either one or both appendices, however.

Some students find the "logic" section of our courses much more to their liking than the rest. We presume that's because many of the answers are pretty cut and dried: If you know the material, you get most of the answers right. This contrasts with much of the "critical thinking" part of the course where the material can be a good bit slipperier. Lots of other students, however, especially the mathophobes, find any kind of technical work a real chore to learn. The best solution is practice and more practice—preferably practice that's guided by an experienced tutor. Watching an instructor work a problem on the chalkboard does only a little more to teach a student logic than listening to Itzhak Perlman play the violin teaches the listener to fiddle.

## Appendix 1
## Categorical Logic

It often comes as a surprise to students that so much can be said using nothing but the four standard form categorical types of claims. Much of what can be said must be said awkwardly, of course—in "logician's English"—but said nonetheless.

If we were being especially careful (and a little less worried about confusing students unnecessarily), we would make a bigger deal than we do about the distinction between a categorical claim and a categorical claim *form*. "All Xs are Ys" is not a claim at all, but a claim *form* (or an open sentence, or a propositional function), since it contains variables for the subject and predicate terms. Such expressions can't be true or false; only their instantiations can have truth values. We've discovered that, technically correct or not, the distinction between claims and forms can be ridden over in a pretty roughshod manner most of the time. It keeps you and your students from having to be so careful when you're talking about the material, and we've found that, by and large, students don't miss the distinction. If a student *does* remark that a form can't be a claim because it can't be true or false, we simply identify the distinction and point out that we're ignoring it most of the time in the interest of economy. You, of course, are welcome to be more careful than we if you like.

An understanding of the usual categorical inferences, both immediate and syllogistic, is valuable to a student. But we believe that learning to translate from informal English claims to standard form claims serves an equally valuable purpose. We can hardly help but wonder how deeply a student is thinking about the claims he hears and makes himself when he has great difficulty deciding whether a claim should be translated as "All Xs are Ys" or All Ys are Xs." The requirement of such translations must, at a minimum, get students to thinking a little harder than usual about the kind of sentences they use all the time.

Regarding the square of opposition, sharp students will notice that contraries *could* both be true if the subject class were empty, and subcontraries could both be false under the same condition. True enough, we have to tell them. Contradiction is the only inference on the square that does not require the assumption of at least one member of the subject class. So every other inference tacitly begins, as it were, with, "On the assumption that there is at least one S. . . ." Since we rarely reason about the empty set outside a math or symbolic logic course, this shouldn't offend the sensibilities of the rigorous.

Another square of opposition note: We don't discuss subalternation (the relationship between an A claim and it's corresponding I and between an E and it's corresponding O). It just provides one more piece of terminology to learn, and students find that going from an A to an E and then to an I, that is, going across the top of the square and then diagonally, is just as fast and intuitive as learning a new relationship up and down the sides of the square. Things are complicated enough without throwing in everything that's been tacked onto categorical logic since the time of Aristotle. (The same holds true for the names of syllogisms, although some students are amused to learn that they have names like "Barbara." Those are probably students whom *anything* would amuse.)

When we get to the operation of obversion and have to explain the notion of a class complement, we find it helpful to begin with a little discussion of a "universe of discourse." We thought that, rather than burden the text with it, we'd mention it here: One of the assumptions underlying most any claim is that there is a universe in which the claim is asserted to hold. Different universes are assumed by different claims, of course. If you tell your students, "Everybody passed the last exam," you don't mean to imply that George Bush passed the exam nor that your mother passed the exam, etc. The assumed universe includes just the people who took the exam. Then, a class's complementary term can be seen as everything *in the assumed universe of discourse* that isn't in the original class. This means that "persimmons left out to dry" ordinarily has the complementary term, "persimmons not left out to dry," which does not apply to George Bush nor to your mother.

## Exercises Unanswered in the Text

*But first: some notes on translation.* Despite the fact that it is not one of the four standard forms, students will sometimes suggest claims of the type "All Xs are not Ys" as translations. It's a good idea to point out that such claims are ambiguous. They are usually intended as equivalent to "Some Xs are not Ys." But, now and then, such a claim will be intended as equivalent to "No Xs are Ys." The ambiguity is more obvious in some examples than in others: "All juniors are not eligible to take the LSAT" is a good case in point.

Our way of treating claims about individuals is to turn them into classes with just one member. Numbers 14 and 15 in the first exercise are done that way. Socrates gets turned into the class of people who are identical to Socrates, (which we'll express, "{people = Socrates}". Since this is about as awkward as things get, we can avoid it by leaving the claim alone ("Socrates is a Greek," for number 14 in A1-1, for example) but making sure students realize that such claims must be treated as A or E type claims. *Some* (and *only* some) of Socrates can't be Greek, except metaphorically.

## Exercise A1-1

When we ask student to turn exercises like these in, we make them put parentheses or brackets around the subject and predicate terms—it helps them keep things straight and it helps us read them.

1. All salamanders are lizards.
3. Some lizards are not salamanders.
5. All semiaquatic reptiles are snakes.
7. All places there are snakes are places where there are frogs.
9. All times the frog population decreases are times the snake population decreases.
11. All frogs are reptiles.
13. All people who arrived are cheerleaders.
15. All {people = the guy who held up the bank} are {people = my next-door neighbor}.

## Exercise A1-2

1. A: All mice are short-tailed animals. (Undetermined)
   E: No mice are short-tailed animals. (False)
   O: Some mice are not short-tailed animals. (Undetermined)

3. I: Some evergreens are softwoods. (True)
   A: All evergreens are softwoods. (True)
   E: No evergreens are softwoods. (False)

5. O: Some Muslims are not Methodists. (Undetermined)
   I: Some Muslims are Methodists. (True)
   A: All Muslims are Methodists. (Undetermined)

## Exercise A1-3

1. Some percussion instruments are clarinets.
3. Some non-Celts are not non-Englishmen.
5. All freshwater fish are nonsharks.

## Exercise A1-4

Some students find this among the most difficult types of exercise in this Appendix. For those with no teaching experience with this material, here's how we do it: Work on such problems needs to be divided into two parts: Make the claims correspond, if possible, then use the square of opposition. We do them by putting the first claim high on the chalkboard and the second one near the bottom, then working toward the middle (using only equivalent-producing operations of conversion, obversion, and contraposition) until they correspond, if they can be made to correspond. If they can, the square of opposition produces the answer; if they can't, the second claim remains undetermined. In hopes of making this clear, we've laid number 2 out this way.

2.           (a) Some students are not ineligible candidates. (T)

obverts to     ($a_1$) Some students are eligible candidates. (T)

converts to     ($a_2$) Some eligible candidates are students. (T)

by sq. of opp.     (b) No eligible candidates are students. (F)

Begin by writing (a) and (b) with space between, then ask students what needs doing. One term needs changing into its complement, and the terms are in the wrong places. So we obvert (a) to get ($a_1$), then convert ($a_1$) to get ($a_2$). Since ($a_2$) corresponds to (b), the square of opposition gives us the answer: Since ($a_2$) is true, (b) must be false. We expect this is overkill and will just give answers and a note or two for the remainder.

4. False. Obvert (a), convert (b), and use sq. of opp.
6. Undetermined. From a true I claim, nothing follows about the O claim.
7. True. Translate (a) as "Some of Gary Brodnax's novels are novels in which the hero gets killed." The square of opposition tells us the corresponding O claim must be true.
8. Undetermined. These cannot be made to correspond without converting an A or an O claim. So there isn't enough information to tell what (b)'s truth value is.
10. True. Translate (a) as "All persimmons that have not been left to dry are astringent persimmons," then contrapose this claim. Obvert, then convert (b). It's now an I that corresponds to (a)'s contrapositive.
    *This one is a killer. Notice, though, that there's nothing unusual about the original claims—they're the sort students use all the time. Most students can't stare at them and tell you what follows about (b), and this justifies the technique they're learning: They need some way of determining just exactly what they're talking about if they're ever going to do things like sign contracts.*

### Exercise A1-5

2.

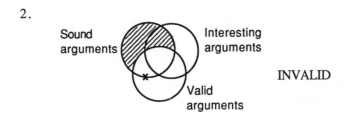

INVALID

3.

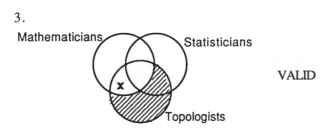

VALID

5.

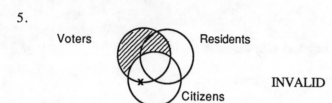

Voters        Residents

                   INVALID

Citizens

6.

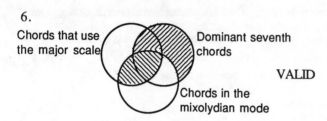

Chords that use the major scale    Dominant seventh chords

                   VALID

Chords in the mixolydian mode

8.

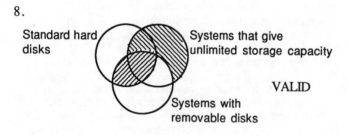

Standard hard disks      Systems that give unlimited storage capacity

                   VALID

Systems with removable disks

9.

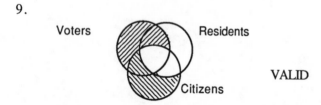

Voters        Residents

                   VALID

Citizens

*Before diagramming this argument, the term "citizens" must be turned into "noncitizens" or vice versa. The easiest way to do this is to change the second premise, "No noncitizens are voters." If we convert it, then obvert the result, we get "All voters are citizens."*

### Exercise A1-6

Some of these exercises can be done more than one way. You may prefer to use obversion, etc., on different claims from the ones we've worked on.

2.  No ears w/ white tassels are ripe ears.
    <u>Some ripe ears are not ears w/ full-sized kernals.</u>

    Some ears w/ full-sized kernals are not ears w/ white tassels.

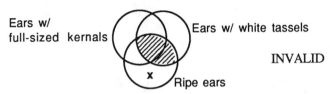

3.  No prescription drugs are drugs that can be taken w/o a doctor's order.
    <u>All OTC drugs are drugs that can be taken w/o a doctor's order.</u>

    No OTC drugs are prescription drugs.

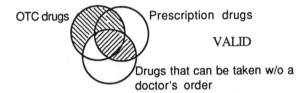

5.  Some compact disk players are players that use 4x sampling.
    <u>No players that use 4x sampling are players that cost under $100.</u>

    Some compact disk players are not players that cost under $100.

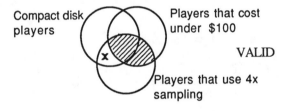

6.  All things that Bob won are things that Pete won.
    <u>All things that Bob won are junk.</u>

    All things that Pete won are junk.

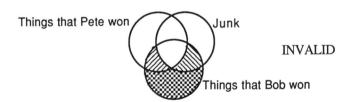

8.

No off-road vehicles are vehicles allowed in the...park.
Some off-road vehicles are not four-wheel-drive vehicles.
Some four-wheel-drive vehicles are vehicles allowed in the...park.

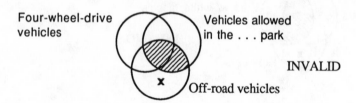

9.

Some people affected by the drainage tax are residents of the county.
Some residents of the county are people paying the sewer tax.
Some people paying the sewer tax are people affected by the drainage tax.

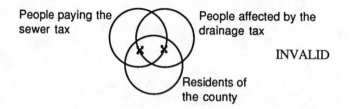

## Exercise A1-7

Whether the answers below fit the questions will depend on the shape of the argument after the appropriate obversions, and so on, were carried out. If you modified different claims, an invalid syllogism may break a different rule. Still, if a syllogism breaks a rule in one version, it'll break *some* rule in any other version. We have presumed the versions of the syllogisms found above and in the answer section of the text.

1. Valid; breaks no rule
3. Valid; breaks no rule
4. Valid; breaks no rule
6. Invalid; breaks rule 3
9. Invalid; breaks rule 2
10. Valid; breaks no rule

## Exercise A1-8

Refer to Exercise 9-7.

1. Invalid; breaks rule 2

3.  Valid; breaks no rule
5.  Valid; breaks no rule
7.  Invalid; breaks rule 3
9.  Valid; breaks no rule

# Test Question/Exercise Banks

## Bank A1-1

Translate the following into standard form categorical claims.

1.  Not every product that's organic is actually a chemical-free product.

    *Some organic products are not chemical-free products.*

2.  The only organic products are chemical-free products.

    *All organic products are chemical-free products.*

3.  Chemical-free products are the only organic products.

    *All organic products are chemical-free products.*

4.  Only organic products are chemical-free products.

    *All chemical-free products are organic products.*

5.  Chemical-free products are not the only organic products.

    *Some organic products are not chemical-free products.*

6.  It's not only chemical-free products that are organic.

    *Some organic products are not chemical-free products.*

7.  Not all savings institutions are banks.

    *Some savings institutions are not banks.*

8.  Banks are the only savings institutions.

    *All savings institutions are banks.*

9.  Banks are not the only savings institutions.

    *Some savings institutions are not banks.*

10. Only banks can be savings institutions.

    *All savings institutions are banks.*

11. People always leave when Tony plays the accordion.

    *All times Tony plays the accordion are times people leave.*

12. People always duck when Richard picks up a golf club.

    *All times Richard picks up a golf club are times people duck.*

13. Whenever Tony plays the accordion, people leave.

    *All times Tony plays the accordion are times people leave.*

14. People duck whenever Richard picks up a golf club.

    *All times Richard picks up a golf club are times people duck.*

15. Tricia's dog goes wherever she goes.

    *All places Tricia goes are places her dog goes.*

16. Except for members of the Lucero family, there's nobody in the park.

    *All people in the park are members of the Lucero family.*

17. There's nobody in the park except members of the Lucero family.

    *All people in the park are members of the Lucero family.*

18. Lydia is the only person in our group who sold stock before the crash.

    *All people in our group who sold stock before the crash are {people = Lydia}. (That is, people identical to Lydia)*

19. The morning star is actually the evening star.

    *All {things = the morning star} are {things = the evening star}.*

20. Mr. Ashcroft isn't at home.

    *No {people = Mr. Ashcroft} are people at home.*

### Bank A1-2

Using the square of opposition and the truth value of the first claim, determine what, if anything, follows about the truth values of the other claims.

21. (a) True: All surprises are unpleasant events.
    (b) No surprises are unpleasant events. *False*
    (c) Some surprises are unpleasant events. *True*
    (d) Some surprises are not unpleasant events. *False*

22. (a) True: Some winters are dry seasons.
    (b) No winters are dry seasons. *False*
    (c) All winters are dry seasons. *Undetermined*
    (d) Some winters are dry seasons. *Undetermined*

23. (a) False: No guppies are egg-layers.
    (b) All guppies are egg-layers. *Undetermined*
    (c) Some guppies are egg-layers. *True*
    (d) Some guppies are not egg-layers. *Undetermined*

24. (a) False: Some frozen dinners are nutritious meals.
    (b) All frozen dinners are nutritious meals. *False*
    (c) No frozen dinners are nutritious meals. *True*
    (d) Some frozen dinners are not nutritious meals. *True*


## Bank  A1-3

Assume that the original claim is true, and follow the directions given. What follows about the truth value of the claim you wind up with?

25. Some uninsured investments are risky deals.
    Convert this claim, then obvert the result.

    *Some risky deals are not insured investments. True*

26. All people who win lotteries are people who get lots of mail.
    Find the contrapositive, then convert.

    *All people who do not win lotteries are people who do not get lots of mail. Undetermined: requires converting an A-claim*

27. No medical books are inexpensive books.
    Convert, then find the contradictory.

    *Some inexpensive books are medical books. False*

28. Some plutonium-contaminated soil storage areas in New Mexico are not areas that are isolated from drinking water supplies.
    Find the obverse, convert that, then find the subcontrary.

    *Some areas that are not isolated from drinking water supplies are plutonium-contaminated soil storage areas in New Mexico. Undetermined*

29. All nonisolated computer systems are systems that are at risk from computer viruses.
    Find the contrapositive, then find the contrary of the result.

*No systems that are not at risk from computer viruses are isolated computer systems.*
*False*

30. No public television stations are stations that broadcast commercials.
Obvert, then convert, then find the contradictory.

    *Some stations that do not broadcast commercials are not public television stations.*
    *Undetermined: cannot convert an A-claim*

## Bank A1-4

These items should be treated like those in Exercise A1-4, on p. 358 of the text: Determine the truth value of the second claim based on that given for the first. The first few are given as forms, which makes the relationships between terms easier to see. Translation into standard form will be required for most of the remainder. (Many student find this type of problem pretty tough.)

31. (a) No Xs are nonYs. (True)
    (b) Some Xs are Ys. *True*

32. (a) All Xs are nonYs. (True)
    (b) Some Ys are Xs. *False*

33. (a) Some nonXs are not Ys. (False)
    (b) No Xs are nonYs. *False*

34. (a) Optical disks never wear out. (False)
    (b) Some disks other than optical disks do sometimes wear out. *Undetermined*

35. (a) Some fish from the river have been found to contain toxic levels of trace minerals. (True)
    (b) No fish in which toxic levels of trace minerals have not been found have come from the river. *Undetermined*

36. (a) Every editorial that Smathers has written has been one in which he attacks the City Council. (True)
    (b) At least one of the editorials that has not attacked the City Council was not written by Smathers. *True*

37. (a) British comedies are always more sophisticated than American comedies. (False)
    (b) Some comedies that are no more sophisticated than American comedies come from Britain. *True*

38. (a) None of the clothes that were bought at Severn's lasted very long. (True)
    (b) Some of the clothes that lasted a long time are clothes that were were not bought at Severn's. *True*

39. (a) Not everybody who was indicted by the grand jury went to trial. (False)
    (b) Some of the people who did not go to trial are people who were not indicted by the grand jury. *True*

40. (a) Not everybody who was indicted by the grand jury went to trial. (True)
    (b) Some of the people who did not go to trial are people who were not indicted by the grand jury. *False*


## Bank A1-5

Determine whether the following arguments (or, in the case of the first few, forms of arguments) are valid by using either the diagram method or the rules of the syllogism.

41.    No Xs are Ys.
       Some Ys are not Zs.
   So, some Xs are not Zs.                *Invalid*

42.    All Xs are Ys.
       No Ys are Zs.
   So, no Xs are Zs.                *Valid*

43.    Some Xs are Ys.
       No Zs are Ys.
   So, some Xs are not Zs.                *Valid*

44.    No coinsurance policies are policies that cover the full value of the property.
       Some policies that cover the full value of the property are discounted policies.
   So, some discounted policies are not coinsurance policies.
                *Valid*

45.    Some early Christians were rationalists.
       All early Gnostics were rationalists.
   So, some early Gnostics were Christians.        *Invalid*

46. Everybody who exhibits hubris is an arrogant person, and some arrogant people are not sympathetic people. So some people who exhibit hubris are not sympathetic people.

                *Invalid*

47. All the networks devoted considerable attention to reporting poll results during the last election, but many of those poll results were not especially newsworthy. So the networks have to admit that some unnewsworthy items received quite a bit of their attention.

                *Valid*

48. Only people who have lost a job can appreciate the difficulties it can cause. Some of the people in this room have lost jobs in the past, so there are people in this room who can appreciate the resulting troubles.

                *Invalid*

49. If a person doesn't understand that the Earth goes around the sun once a year, then he can't understand what causes winter and summer. Strange as it may seem, then, there are many American adults who don't know what causes winter and summer, because a survey a year or so ago showed that many such adults don't know that the Earth goes around the sun once a year.

                *Valid*

251

50.     All legislatures are more influenced by the legal profession than by any other, but it is legislatures that make the rules by which the legal profession operates. So the result is that the bodies that make the rules for the lawyers' profession are bodies most influenced by that very profession.

    *All legislatures are bodies influenced most . . .*
    *All bodies that make rules . . . are legislatures.*
  *So, all bodies that make rules . . . are bodies influenced most . . . .*

*Valid*

# Appendix 2
# Truth Functional Logic

When students first confront Appendix 2, many recoil from the symbolizations they see in those pages. They get the idea that there will be a lot to memorize, and this can cause trouble if they're not disabused of it right away. In fact, the basic truth tables for the truth functional symbols are very easy to learn. Without learning them immediately, of course, a student is going to get absolutely nowhere. We like to give a brief quiz on the basic truth tables as soon as possible, to keep our students from getting behind.

We said at the beginning of the previous appendix section that we believe the translation of informal claims into standard form categorical claims gets students to do some hard thinking about their language. And, when they get things wrong, it demonstrates that things are not so obvious as they thought. The same holds true for the display of claims' truth functional forms, the result of the type of symbolization we do in this appendix. We try to make this point early by calling students' attention to items like those found in Bank A2-3, below. This is unpleasant news (amounting, as it were, to telling them that they're ignorant), but it's quickly compensated for by their first successful symbolizations. Most of the early ones in Exercise A2-1 in the text are not difficult, and students learn quickly that, if they're careful, they can learn this stuff.

For those of you who do spend time doing truth functional proofs (derivations), there's an additional rule of Conditional Proof given at the end of the section. It can be reproduced and turned into a handout if desired. This can be augmented by showing how an Indirect Proof strategy can be based on it. (Students can be referred to the discussion of indirect proof in Chapter 9 (pp. 252ff. of the text) for an idea of what's going on with this strategy.)

## Exercises Unanswered in the Text

### Exercise A2-2

Note: We've given the most obvious symbolizations, but we feel obliged to take anything that's truth functionally equivalent as correct.

2. $P \rightarrow (Q \mathbin{\&} R)$
3. $(P \mathbin{\&} Q) \rightarrow R$

5.  P v (Q → R)
6.  (P v Q) → R
8.  P → ~(Q v R)   or   P → (~Q & ~R)
9.  ~P → Q
11.  P → Q
12.  Q → P
14.  R v Q   or   ~Q → R
15.  Q → P

## Exercise A2-3

To save space and the tedium of repeating the reference columns, we've laid these items out horizontally.

|  | | #2 | #3 | #5 | #6 |
|---|---|---|---|---|---|
| P Q R | | P → (Q & R) | (P & Q) → R | P v (Q → R) | (P v Q) → R |
| 1. T T T | | T | T | T | T |
| 2. T T F | | F | F | T | F |
| 3. T F T | | F | T | T | T |
| 4. T F F | | F | T | T | F |
| 5. F T T | | T | T | T | T |
| 6. F T F | | T | T | F | F |
| 7. F F T | | T | T | T | T |
| 8. F F F | | T | T | T | T |

|  | #7 | #8 | #9 | #11 | #12 | #14 |
|---|---|---|---|---|---|---|
|  | P → (Q v R) | P → ~(Q v R) | ~P → Q | P → Q | Q → P | R v Q |
| 1. | T | F | T | T | T | T |
| 2. | T | F | T | T | T | T |
| 3. | T | F | T | F | T | T |
| 4. | F | T | T | F | T | F |
| 5. | T | T | T | T | F | T |
| 6. | T | T | T | T | F | T |
| 7. | T | T | F | T | T | T |
| 8. | T | T | F | T | T | F |

Note:  Numbers 13 and 15 have the same table as number 12.

## Exercise A2-4

For items that are invalid, we've produced only as many rows as are necessary to demonstrate invalidity. That is, when we come across one row in which the premises are true and the conclusion false, we stop. If the item is valid, we just say so, since no row will produce true premises and a false conclusion.

2.  Valid

3. Invalid: The first row of the table shows this:

| | F Q P | F v (Q→P) | Q v ~P | ~F |
|---|---|---|---|---|
| 1. | T T T | T | T | F |

5. Invalid: The second row shows it:

| | P Q R | P v (Q→R) | Q & ~R | ~P |
|---|---|---|---|---|
| 1. | T T T | T | F | F |
| 2. | T T F | T | T | F |

6. Invalid: The fourth row shows it:

| | P Q R | (P→Q) v (R→Q) | ~P → ~R | Q |
|---|---|---|---|---|
| 1. | T T T | T | T | T |
| 2. | T T F | T | T | T |
| 3. | T F T | F | T | F |
| 4. | T F F | T | T | F |

8. Valid: The premises are both true in only the second row, and the conclusion is true in that row as well.

9. Invalid: The second row shows it:

| | L J R | L v ~J | R → J | J → R |
|---|---|---|---|---|
| 1. | T T T | T | T | T |
| 2. | T T F | T | T | F |

10. Valid: The table for this one, which is 16 rows long, demonstrates the virtues of the short truth table method.

## Exercise A2-6

2. 4. . . . . . . 1, 3, DA
   5. . . . . . . 2, SIM
   6. . . . . . . 4, 5, MP

3. 4. . . . . . . 1, CONTR
   5. . . . . . . 3,4, CA
   6. . . . . . . 2,5, CA
   7. . . . . . . 6, IMPL
   8. . . . . . . 7, EXPORT

5. 4. . . . . . . 1, DeM
   5. . . . . . . 4, SIM
   6. . . . . . . 2,5, MT
   7. . . . . . . 4, SIM
   8. . . . . . . 6,7, CONJ
   9. . . . . . . 8, DeM
   10. . . . . . . 3,9, MT

## Exercise A2-7

Note: What level of formality you hold your students to is of course up to you. We allow combining Double Negation steps with others (CONTR, IMPL, etc.). In the items that follow, we've indicated such combinations in the annotation. We probably don't need to indicate that there is often—usually—a different, and equally correct, way of constructing a derivation.

2. 
| | | |
|---|---|---|
| 1. | ~P v S | Premise |
| 2. | ~T → ~S | Premise  / P → T |
| 3. | P → S | 1, IMPL |
| 4. | S → T | 2, CONTR |
| 5. | P → T | 3,4, CA |

3. 
| | | |
|---|---|---|
| 1. | F → R | Premise |
| 2. | L → S | Premise |
| 3. | ~C | Premise |
| 4. | (R & S) → C | Premise  / ~F v ~L |
| 5. | ~(R & S) | 3,4, MT |
| 6. | ~R v ~S | 5, DEM |
| 7. | ~F v ~L | 1,2,6, DD |

5. 
| | | |
|---|---|---|
| 1. | (S & R) → P | Premise |
| 2. | (R → P) → W | Premise |
| 3. | S | Premise  / W |
| 4. | S → (R → P) | 1, EXPORT |
| 5. | R → P | 3,4, MP |
| 6. | W | 2,5, MP |

6. 
| | | |
|---|---|---|
| 1. | ~L → (~P → M) | Premise |
| 2. | ~(P v L) | Premise  / M |
| 3. | ~P & ~L | 2, DEM |
| 4. | ~L | 3, SIM |
| 5. | ~P → M | 1,4, MP |
| 6. | ~P | 3, SIM |
| 7. | M | 5,6, MP |

Note: Students usually hit on such things themselves, but we'll mention it anyhow: When it isn't clear how to proceed, the best strategy sometimes is to work backwards—"I could get *this* if I had *that,* and I could get *that,* if I had such-and-such."

8. 
| | | |
|---|---|---|
| 1. | Q → L | Premise |
| 2. | P → M | Premise |
| 3. | R v P | Premise |
| 4. | R → (Q & S) | Premise  / ~M → L |
| 5. | P v R | 3, COM |

6.  ~P → R                  5, DN/IMPL
7.  ~P → (Q & S)     4,6, CA
8.  P v (Q & S)          7, DN/IMPL
9.  (P v Q) & (P v S)   8, DIST
10. P v Q                  9, SIM
11. M v L                 1,2,10, CD
12. ~M → L               11, DN/IMPL

9.  1.  Q → S                 Premise
    2.  P → (S & L)          Premise
    3.  ~P → Q               Premise
    4.  S → R                 Premise    / R & S
    5.  P v Q                 3, DN/IMPL
    6.  (S & L) v S         1,2,5, CD
    7.  S v (S & L)         6, COM
    8.  (S v S) & (S v L)  7, DIST
    9.  S v S                8, SIM
    10. S                    9, TAUT
    11. R                    4,10, MP
    12. R & S               10,11 CONJ


**Exercise A2-8**

2.  U → (Q v D)
    J → ~D          / ~J v Q

Invalid:  The following assignment of truth values (which would occur in the next-to-last row of the truth table for the argument) makes both premises true and the conclusion false:

$$\underline{U\ Q\ D\ J}$$
$$F\ \ F\ F\ T$$

3.  Valid, as per the following derivation:

    1.  ~R v A               Premise
    2.  A → E                Premise
    3.  M → ~E               Premise   / ~R v ~M
    4.  E → ~M               3, DN/CONTR
    5.  A → ~M               2,4, CA
    6.  R → A                1, IMPL
    7.  R → ~M               5,6, CA
    8.  ~R v ~M              7, IMPL

256

5. $V \rightarrow O$

  $T \rightarrow O \quad / V \rightarrow T$


Invalid, as per the following:

$$\frac{V \; O \; T}{T \; T \; F}$$


# Test Question-Exercise Banks


## Bank A2-1

Symbolize the following claims using the letters indicated.

A = Action is taken to reduce the deficit.
B = The balance of payments gets worse.
C = There is (or will be) a financial crisis.

1. The balance of payments will not get worse if action is taken to reduce the deficit.

   $A \rightarrow \sim B$

2. There will be no financial crisis unless the balance of payments gets worse.

   $\sim C \; v \; B$

3. The only thing that can prevent a financial crisis is action taken to reduce the deficit.

   $\sim A \rightarrow C$

4. The balance of payments will get worse only if no action is taken to reduce the deficit.

   $B \rightarrow \sim A$

5. In order for there to be a financial crisis, the balance of payments will have to get worse and there will have to be no action taken to reduce the deficit.

   $C \rightarrow (B \; \& \; \sim A) \quad or \quad \sim(B \; \& \; \sim A) \rightarrow \sim C \quad or \quad (\sim B \; v \; A) \rightarrow \sim C$

6. With regard to action to reduce the deficit and the worsening of the balance of payments: Neither one will happen.

   $\sim(A \; v \; B) \quad or \quad \sim A \; \& \; \sim B$

257

7. Action cannot be taken on the deficit if there's a financial crisis.

   $C \rightarrow \sim A$

8. We can avoid a financial crisis only by taking action on the deficit and keeping the balance of payments from getting worse.

   $\sim C \rightarrow (A\ \&\ \sim B)$

9. Either the balance of payments will get worse or, if no action is taken on the deficit, there will be a financial crisis.

   $B \lor (\sim A \rightarrow C)$

10. If either the balance of payments gets worse or no action is taken on the deficit, there will be a financial crisis.

    $(B \lor \sim A) \rightarrow C$

## Bank A2-2

Same directions as the preceding bank.

W = Wildlife are (or will be) threatened.
A = Agricultural production is increased.
P = The use of pesticides is continued.

11. The only way we can avoid threatening wildlife is to avoid increasing agricultural production.

    $\sim W \rightarrow \sim A$

12. We cannot both increase agricultural production and avoid threatening wildlife.

    $\sim (A\ \&\ W)$

13. If we are to increase agricultural production we'll have to continue the use of pesticides, but if we do that wildlife will be threatened.

    $(A \rightarrow P)\ \&\ (P \rightarrow W)$

14. Wildlife will not be threatened provided we do not continue the use of pesticides.

    $\sim P \rightarrow \sim W$

15. Wildlife will be threatened if either agricultural production is increased or pesticide use is continued.

$(A \lor P) \rightarrow W$

16. The continuation of pesticide use will be sufficient to ensure that wildlife will be threatened.

    $P \rightarrow W$

17. The continued use of pesticides is necessary for increased agricultural production.

    $A \rightarrow P$

18. Together, the continued use of pesticide and the increase in agricultural production will guarantee that wildlife will be threatened.

    $(P \& A) \rightarrow W$

19. Agricultural production will not increase even though the use of pesticides will continue.

    $\sim A \& P$

20. While pesticide use will continue, agricultural production will not increase.

    $P \& \sim A$

**Bank A2-3**

Determine which of the lettered claims is equivalent to the numbered ones. You will have to use one letter twice. (These are easy to do if students symbolize the claims first and have some familiarity either with truth tables or with the Group 2 Rules for derivations—the truth functional equivalences.)

A. If Steve can give blood then he has been tested.
B. If Steve has been tested then he can give blood.
C. Steve cannot give blood and he has not been tested.
D. Steve has not been tested but he can give blood.

21. Steve can give blood if he has been tested.

    *Equivalent to B*

22. Steve cannot give blood unless he has been tested.

    *Equivalent to A*

23. Although Steve can give blood, he has not been tested.

    *Equivalent to D*

24. It's necessary for Steve to be tested in order for him to give blood.

    *Equivalent to A*

25. Steve can neither be tested nor give blood.

*Equivalent to C*

## Bank A2-4

For each of the following argument symbolizations, assign truth values to the letters to show the argument's invalidity. (There is only one such assignment for each—one counterexample—which makes these easy to grade.)

26. Q v P
    ~Q → ~R          / R → P

    $P = F$
    $Q = T$
    $R = T$

27. ~Q → P
    R v S
    Q → ~S           / R

    $P = T$
    $Q = F$
    $R = F$
    $S = T$

28. P v Q
    P → R            / R → Q

    $P = T$
    $Q = F$
    $R = T$

29. ~R → ~Q
    ~P → (R v Q)     / P

    $R = T$
    $Q = F$
    $P = F$

30. (Q & P) → R
    S → ~R           / S → ~Q

    $Q = T$
    $P = F$
    $R = F$
    $S = T$

31. $S \rightarrow (P \vee R)$
    $Q \rightarrow S$        $/ Q \rightarrow P$

    $S = T$
    $P = F$
    $R = T$
    $Q = T$

32. $T \rightarrow \sim S$
    $S \vee \sim Q$
    $\sim T \rightarrow (Q \vee R)$     $/ \sim Q \rightarrow R$

    $T = T$
    $S = F$
    $Q = F$
    $R = F$

33. $(Q \& S) \rightarrow (P \vee R)$
    $T \rightarrow Q$
    $\sim T \vee S$        $/ T \rightarrow R$

    $Q = T$
    $S = T$
    $P = T$
    $R = F$
    $T = T$

34. $P \rightarrow (Q \rightarrow S)$
    $Q \vee R$        $/ (P \& R) \rightarrow S$

    $P = T$
    $Q = F$
    $S = F$
    $R = T$

35. $P \rightarrow (Q \vee R)$
    $\sim (Q \rightarrow R)$
    $S \rightarrow P$        $/ \sim S$

    $P = T$
    $Q = T$
    $R = F$
    $S = T$

36. $P \vee Q$
    $(Q \& R) \rightarrow S$
    $\sim P \rightarrow \sim R$     $/ R \rightarrow S$

$P = T$
$Q = F$
$R = T$
$S = F$

37. P v (Q → R)

    S → ~(P v R)          / S → Q

    $P = F$
    $Q = F$
    $R = F$
    $S = T$

38. ~L & ~S

    (P v Q) → L          / Q v S

    $L = F$
    $S = F$
    $P = F$
    $Q = F$

39. P → (T & R)

    (R → S) v T

    ~(S & Q)          / Q → ~P

    $P = T$
    $T = T$
    $R = T$
    $S = F$
    $Q = T$

40. ~P v (Q → R)

    Q → (R v S)          / Q → (~P v S)

    $P = T$
    $Q = T$
    $R = T$
    $S = F$

## Bank A2-5

Using only rules from Group 1, construct deductions to prove the following symbolized arguments valid. (These are pretty simple, but they're good for getting students used to formatting deductions, seeing complicated cases of simple symbolizations ("substitution instances"), and realizing that Group 1 rules can be used only on *parts* of lines—three of the main problems encountered early in this kind of work.)

41. 1. P → (Q & R)        Premise
    2. (Q & R) → S        Premise  / P → S

    3. *P → S*            *1,2, CA*

42. 1. P → Q             Premise
    2. P v R             Premise
    3. R → (S & T)       Premise  / Q v (S & T)

    4. *Q v (S & T)*      *1,2,3, CD*

43. 1. (P & Q) → (R v S)  Premise
    2. (R v S) → T        Premise
    3. P & Q              Premise  / T

    4. *R v S*            *1,3, MP*
    5. *T*                *2,4, MP*

44. 1. (R v Q) & S        Premise
    2. (R v Q) → ~P       Premise
    3. P v T              Premise  / T

    4. *R v Q*            *1, SIM*
    5. *~P*               *2,4, MP*
    6. *T*                *4,5, DA*

45. 1. P → (S v T)        Premise
    2. S → Q              Premise
    3. P                  Premise
    4. T → R              Premise  / Q v R

    5. *S v T*            *1,3, MP*
    6. *Q v R*            *2,4,5, CD*

46. 1. ~P & Q             Premise
    2. R → P              Premise  / Q & ~R

    3. *~P*               *1, SIM*
    4. *~R*               *2,3, MT*
    5. *Q*                *1, SIM*
    6. *Q & ~R*           *4,5, CONJ*

47. 1. P → M             Premise
    2. ~M v ~Q            Premise
    3. S → Q             Premise
    4. (~P v ~S) → R     Premise  / R

5. ~P v ~S             1,2,3, DD
6. R                      4,5, MP

48. 1. Q → (P → R)       Premise
    2. ~R & Q           Premise   / ~P

    3. Q                  2, SIM
    4. P → R            1,3, MP
    5. ~R                2, SIM
    6. ~P                4,5, MT

49. 1. (P v Q) → (X & Z)     Premise
    2. (X → W) & (Z → Y)   Premise
    3. P                  Premise   / W & Y

    4. P v Q            3, ADD
    5. X & Z            1,4, MP
    6. X                  5, SIM
    7. X → W           2, SIM
    8. W                  6,7, MP
    9. Z                  5, SIM
    10. Z → Y          2, SIM
    11. Y                9,10, MP
    12. W & Y          8,11, CONJ

50. 1. (P v Q) → M       Premise
    2. S v ~M          Premise
    3. L                  Premise
    4. L → ~S         Premise   / ~(P v Q)

    5. ~S                3,4, MP
    6. ~M               2,5, DA
    7. ~(P v Q)        1,6, MT

## Bank A2-6

Using rules from both Group 1 and Group 2, construct deductions to prove that the following are valid.

51. 1. P & Q           Premise
    2. R v ~(P & Q)     Premise   / R

    3. ~~(P & Q)       1, DN
    4. C                 2,3, DA

52. 1.  ~(P v Q)                    Premise   /~Q

    2.  ~P & ~Q              1, DEM
    3.  ~Q                   2, SIM

53. 1.  (P v Q) & (P v R)           Premise
    2.  ~P                          Premise   /Q & R

    3.  P v (Q & R)         1, DIST
    4.  Q & R               2,3 DA

54. 1.  P v Q                       Premise
    2.  Q → R                       Premise   /~P → R

    3.  ~P → Q              1, IMPL
    4.  ~P → R              2,3, CA

55. 1.  P → Q                       Premise
    2.  R → Q                       Premise
    3.  P v R                       Premise   /Q

    4.  Q v Q               1,2,3 CD
    5.  Q                   4, TAUT

56. 1.  P v ~Q                      Premise
    2.  R → Q                       Premise   /R → P

    3.  ~Q v P              1, COM
    4.  Q → P               3, IMPL
    5.  R → P               2,4, CA

57. 1.  P v (Q & R)                 Premise
    2.  Q → ~R                      Premise   /P

    3.  ~Q v ~R             2, IMPL
    4.  ~(Q & R)            3, DEM
    5.  P                   1,4, DA

58. 1.  (M v P) → Q                 Premise
    2.  Q → (~L v R)                Premise
    3.  (L → R) → S                 Premise   /(M v P) → S

    4.  (M v P) → (~L v R)    1,2, CA
    5.  (M v P) → (L → R)     4, IMPL
    6.  (M v P) → S           3,5, CA

*This item shows the advantage of the deductive method for proving validity over even the*

265

*short truth table method: Only a modest familiarity with CA and IMPL is required to do this problem in one's head.*

59. 1. P → ~(M & R)                Premise
    2. ~P → Q                      Premise   / ~Q → (~M v ~R)

    *3. ~Q → P*                    *2, DN/CONTR*
    *4. ~Q → ~(M & R)*            *3,1, CA*
    *5. ~Q → (~M v ~R)*          *4, DEM*

60. 1. P v (Q & P)                 Premise
    2. P → R                       Premise   /R

    *3. (P v Q) & (P v P)*        *1, DIST*
    *4. P v P*                     *3, SIM*
    *5. P*                         *4, TAUT*
    *6. R*                         *2,5, MP*

61. 1. P → (Q → R)                 Premise   /Q → (P → R)

    *2. (P & Q) → R*              *1, EXPORT*
    *3. (Q & P) → R*              *2, COM*
    *4. Q → (P → R)*              *3, EXPORT*

62. 1. (P → Q) & (R → S)           Premise
    2. Q → ~S                      Premise
    3. ~T → (P & R)                Premise   /T

    *4. P → Q*                     *1, SIM*
    *5. R → S*                     *1, SIM*
    *6. ~Q v ~S*                   *2, IMPL*
    *7. ~P v ~R*                   *4,5,6, DD*
    *8. ~(P & R)*                  *7, DEM*
    *9. T*                         *3,8, MT/DN*

63. 1. P → (Q & R)                 Premise
    2. ~S → ~(Q v R)               Premise   /P → S

    *3. ~P v (Q & R)*             *1, IMPL*
    *4. (~P v Q) & (~P v R)*      *3, DIST*
    *5. ~P v Q*                    *4, SIMP*
    *6. (~P v Q) v R*             *5, ADD*
    *7. ~P v (Q v R)*             *6, ASSOC*
    *8. P → (Q v R)*              *7, IMPL*

9. $(Q \lor R) \rightarrow S$      2, CONTR
10. $P \rightarrow S$      8,9, CA

*Examples like this one are not designed to show off the deductive method, obviously; but you can't have a rule for everything, can you?*

64.
1. $P \rightarrow (Q \& R)$      Premise
2. $R \rightarrow (S \lor T)$      Premise   / $\sim(\sim P \lor S) \rightarrow T$

3. $\sim P \lor (Q \& R)$      1, IMPL
4. $\sim P \lor (R \& Q)$      3, COM
5. $(\sim P \lor R) \& (\sim P \lor Q)$      4, DIST
6. $\sim P \lor R$      5, SIM
7. $P \rightarrow R$      6, IMPL
8. $P \rightarrow (S \lor T)$      2,7, CA
9. $P \rightarrow (\sim S \rightarrow T)$      8, DN/IMPL
10. $(P \& \sim S) \rightarrow T$      9, EXPORT
11. $(\sim\sim P \& \sim S) \rightarrow T$      10, DN
12. $\sim(\sim P \lor S) \rightarrow T$      11, DEM

65.
1. $P \rightarrow (Q \& R)$      Premise
2. $\sim(S \& Q)$      Premise
3. $(R \rightarrow S) \& Q$      Premise   / $\sim P$

4. $\sim S \lor \sim Q$      2, DEM
5. $\sim Q \lor \sim S$      4, COM
6. $Q \rightarrow \sim S$      5, IMPL
7. $Q$      3, SIM
8. $\sim S$      6,7, MP
9. $R \rightarrow S$      3, SIM
10. $\sim R$      8,9, MT
11. $\sim R \lor \sim Q$      10, ADD
12. $\sim(R \& Q)$      11, DEM
13. $\sim(Q \& R)$      12, COM
14. $\sim P$      1,14, MT

## Bank A2-7

*The following examples can be used for symbolization practice, for determining invalidity, or for constructing deductions. We've indicated which ones are valid and which invalid, and we've produced counterexamples or deductions for some, including the first five and a couple of others which have a quirk we thought was interesting.*
*Sample directions:*

Symbolize the following arguments and test them for validity. For those that are valid, construct a deduction; for those that are invalid, assign truth values that show that the premises can be true while the conclusion is false. Numbers 66-70 use the following letters:

D = The drought will continue.
S = We get an early storm.
M = Managers of the ski areas will be happy.
F = There will be great fire danger next year.

66. The drought will continue if we don't get a storm. If we do get a storm, the managers of the ski areas will be happy. Since we'll either get a storm or we won't, it follows that either the drought will continue or the ski area managers will be happy.

*Valid*

| | | |
|---|---|---|
| *1.* | $\sim S \rightarrow D$ | *Premise* |
| *2.* | $S \rightarrow M$ | *Premise* |
| *3.* | $S \lor \sim S$ | *Premise  / D $\lor$ M* |
| *4.* | $D \lor M$ | *1,2,3 CD* |

67. Unless an early storm moves in, the drought will continue and there will be great danger of fire next year. But the drought is not going to continue. Therefore there will not be a great danger of fire next year.

*Invalid*

$\sim S \rightarrow (D \,\& \,F)$
$\sim D$       */ $\sim F$*

$S = T; D = F; F = T$

68. If there's no early storm, the drought will continue. And if the drought continues, there will be a great danger of fire next year. So, if there is to be no great danger of fire next year, there must be an early storm.

*Valid*

| | | |
|---|---|---|
| *1.* | $\sim S \rightarrow D$ | *Premise* |
| *2.* | $D \rightarrow F$ | *Premise  / $\sim F \rightarrow S$* |
| *3.* | $\sim S \rightarrow F$ | *1,2, CA* |
| *4.* | $\sim F \rightarrow S$ | *3, CONTR/DN* |

69. There will be a great danger of fire next year only if the drought continues, and it will continue unless we get an early storm. On the other hand, if we do get an early storm, the ski area managers will be happy. So, if the ski area managers are not happy, it'll mean that there's going to be a great danger of fire next year.

*Invalid*

$(F \rightarrow D) \,\& \,(\sim S \rightarrow D)$
$S \rightarrow M$       */ $\sim M \rightarrow F$*

$F = F; D = T; S = F; M = F$

268

70. Either there will be an early storm or the drought will continue. If there's no continuation of the drought, then the managers of the ski areas will be happy and there will be no great danger of fire next year. So, if we're to both avoid any great danger of fire next year and make the ski area managers happy, it will be necessary for there to be an early storm.

*Invalid*
$E \vee D$
$\sim D \rightarrow (M \text{ \& } \sim F)$ $\qquad$ $/ (F \text{ \& } M) \rightarrow S$

$E = T \text{ or } F; D = T; M = T; F = T; S = F$

71. Either John will go to class or he'll miss the review session. If John misses the review session, he'll foul up the exam. If he goes to class, however, he'll miss his ride home for the weekend. So John's either going to miss his ride home or foul up the exam.

*Valid*

72. If you had gone to class, taken good notes, and studied the text, you'd have done well on the exam. And, if you'd done well on the exam, you'd have passed the course. Since you didn't pass the course and you did go to class, you must have not taken good notes and not studied the text.

*Invalid*

73. In a class like this, it's necessary to work a lot of problems on your own in order to be familiar with the material, and such familiarity is necessary to do well on the exams. So, if you work a lot of problems on your own, you'll do well on the exams.

*Invalid*

74. If there was no murder committed, then the victim must have been killed by the horse. But the victim could have been killed by the horse only if he, the victim, was trying to injure the horse before the race, and, in that case, there certainly was a crime committed. So, if there was no murder, there was still a crime committed.

*Valid*

75. Holmes cannot catch the train unless he gets to Charing Cross Station by noon, and if he misses the train Watson will be in danger. Because Moriarty has thugs watching the station, Holmes can get there by noon only if he goes in disguise. So, unless Holmes goes in disguise, Watson will be in danger.

*Valid*

76. It's not fair to smoke around nonsmokers if secondary cigarette smoke really is harmful. If secondary smoke were not harmful, the Lung Association would not be telling us that it is. But they are telling us that it's harmful. That's enough to conclude that it's not fair to smoke around nonsmokers.

*Valid*

77. The creation story in Genesis is compatible with the theory of evolution, but only if the creation story is not taken literally. If, as most scientists think, there is plenty of evidence for the theory of evolution, the Genesis story cannot be true if it is not compatible with the theory. Therefore, if the Genesis story is taken literally, it cannot be true.

*Invalid*

78. The creation story in Genesis is compatible with the theory of evolution, but only if the creation story is not taken literally. If there is plenty of evidence for the theory of evolution, which there is, the Genesis story cannot be true if it is not compatible with the theory. Therefore, if the Genesis story is taken literally, it cannot be true.

*Valid*

79. The number of business majors increased markedly during the 1980s, and if you see that happening, you know that younger people have developed a greater interest in money. Such an interest, unfortunately, means that greed has become a significant motivating force in our society, and, when greed becomes significant, charity becomes insignificant. We can predict that charity will not be seen as a significant feature of this decade.

*Valid*

80. If Jane does any of the following, she's got an eating disorder: If she goes on eating binges for no apparent reason; if she looks forward to times when she can eat alone; or if she eats sensibly in front of others and makes up for it when she's alone. Jane does in fact go on eating binges for no apparent reason. So it's clear that she has an eating disorder.

*Valid*
1. $[(B \lor A) \lor (S \& M)] \rightarrow D$
2. $B$                 $/D$
3. $B \lor A$         1, ADD
4. $[(B \lor A) \lor (S \& M)]$     3, ADD
5. $D$

## Addendum:  Conditional Proof

Conditional proof (CP) is based on the following idea: Let's say we want to produce a deduction for a conditional claim, $P \rightarrow Q$. If we produce such a deduction, what have we proved? We've proved the equivalent of "If P were true, then Q would be true." So, one way to do this is simply to *assume* that P is true (that is, add it as an additional premise) and then prove that, on that assumption, Q has to be true. If we can do that—that is, prove Q after assuming P—then we'll have proved that if P then Q, or $P \rightarrow Q$.

Here is the way we'll use CP as a new rule: Simply write down the antecedent of whatever conditional we want to prove; in the annotation list "Premise (CP)" for that line. Then, circle the line number of the line, like so:

1. $P \lor (Q \rightarrow R)$     Premise
2. $Q$              Premise $/\sim P \rightarrow R$
③. $\sim P$          Premise (CP)

Then, after we've proved what we want—the consequent of the conditional—on the next (or any later) line, we write the full conditional. In the annotation, list *all the lines from the one with the circled number to the one with the conditional's consequent,* give CP as the rule, and go back up and cross off the extra premise we assumed by putting a slash through the circled line number. (This indicates that we've stopped making the assumption that the antecedent of our conditional is true—that we've "discharged the premise," as they say.) Here's how it looks:

1. P v (Q→R)　　　Premise
2. Q　　　　　　　Premise / ~P→R
Ø. ~P　　　　　　Premise (CP)
4. Q→R　　　1,3, DA
5. R　　　　2,4, MP
6. ~P→R　　3-5, CP

Here are some restrictions on the CP rule:

1. Obviously, CP can be used only to produce a conditional claim.
2. If more than one use is made of CP at a time, that is, if more than one additional premise is assumed, they must be crossed off in exactly the reverse order from that in which they were assumed.
3. All premises assumed must be crossed off.

Here's an example of CP where two additional premises are assumed and crossed off in reverse order.

1. P→ (Q v (R & S))　　　Premise
2. (~Q→S)→T　　　　　Premise　/ P→T
Ø. P　　　　　　　　　Premise (CP)
4. Q v (R & S)　　1,3, MP
Ø. ~Q　　　　　　　　Premise (CP)
6. R & S　　　4,5, DA
7. S　　　　　6, SIM
8. ~Q→S　　5-7, CP
9. T　　　　2,8, MP
10. P→T　　3-9, CP

Notice that the additional premise that was added on line 5 gets crossed off when line 8 is completed, and the premise on line 3 gets crossed off when line 10 is completed.
Whenever you're crossing off a premise, it will be when you've just made that premise the antecedent of a new line in your deduction. (You might try this problem without using CP; it helps one appreciate having it around. Many deductions are either shorter, easier, or both using CP.)

# Pre- and Post-Test

## About The Test

We offer the following test with numerous caveats.

The test has not been subjected to statistical analysis. We can provide no information at this time about its reliability or validity. We can supply no normative information. Those who have need of a researched test should consider using one of the standard instruments, for example, the Cornell Critical Thinking Test, Level Z, or the Watson-Glaser Critical Thinking Appraisal. The test we provide here can give you a sense of a student's or a class's abilities on some selected critical thinking skills, but we make no stronger claims for it.

We do not think this test is suitable for a final examination because it is not sufficiently comprehensive of the material covered in the text. To make it sufficiently comprehensive would make it too long to be a useful pre-test (we give two-hour final exams) and would require the use of certain terms that would not be familiar to all pre-test students. It would perhaps be possible to introduce such concepts as "interdependent premises," "induction," "statistical significance," "prescriptive claim," and so on, on the pre-test itself by use of examples, but the test would then take too long to read.

Incidentally, we do not think any of the usual critical thinking test instruments, including those mentioned above, adequately test all the skill areas we regard as falling within the scope of critical thinking either. So they too are unsuitable as final examinations. It's likely, of course, that subjects who score well in the areas sampled on these tests would score well in other areas as well. But a final exam should not assume that this is the case, and it should be comprehensive of all the skill areas attended to in the course. (We think this last point is more important in critical thinking courses than in certain other kinds of courses.)

As you will see, you are required to use your judgment in scoring certain items in the test. One could adapt the test to a multiple choice format to save the time that judgment-grading requires, but we have found it beyond our abilities to devise decent multiple-choice questions and answers on many of the topics covered. We should say, though, that as judgment-graded exams go, this one grades very quickly.

We would like to call your attention to Part III of the test, in which subjects are asked to explain what, if anything, is wrong with each claim in a set of claims. If your pre-test students are anything like ours, some of them will find so few of these claims defective in any way that they will tell you they don't understand what they are supposed to do. You *might* give them an example of a defective claim of some sort, but doing so is likely to result in tunnel vision for the specific type of defect you illustrate. It is better, we think, to elaborate on the instructions a bit (although post-test takers should receive the same instructions).

Finally, whatever the deficiencies of the test, it's not a bad way to begin a critical thinking course. Students like taking it. Some have commented that, if *that's* what this course is going to be about, they're glad they signed up. Despite our general interest in the truth, we have not checked to see if they still feel this way at the end of the term.

## General Directions

This test can be taken in forty-five minutes or less. (Most students take far less time than this.) You might tell your students something like the following:

"The test has four parts. Each part is preceded by instructions. When you finish one part, go on to the next. Do not spend too much time on any one question. To help you budget your time, in ten minutes I'll tell you to begin the second part, and then when to begin the third and fourth parts. If you finish a part early, go right on to the next part. If you have not finished a part, you may have time at the end to return to it."

After ten minutes, tell the class to begin working on the second part if they have not already done so. Be sure to tell them that they may go back and finish the first part later if they have time at the end. Remind students of the instructions at the end of each part. Allow the following times:

Part I: ten minutes
Part II: five minutes
Part III: fifteen minutes
Part IV: fifteen minutes

# Logic and Critical Thinking Assessment

**Part I** (10 minutes) Each of these items consists of one or more assertions together with a conclusion that may or may not follow from the assertions. You are to assume the assertions are true, and then determine whether the conclusion necessarily follows from them. Base your answers only on the information contained in the assertions.

EXAMPLE:

*ASSERTION:* If Charles was late in paying his rent then he was evicted.
*ASSERTION:* Charles was late in paying his rent.
*CONCLUSION:* Charles was evicted.

Answer: Yes, the conclusion necessarily follows from the information contained in the assertions.

1. *ASSERTION:* If the students from the Ivy League schools perform better, on the average, on the Graduate Record Exam than do students enrolled at Big Ten Universities, then it is reasonable to assume that Ivy League students are in general academically more talented than their Big Ten counterparts.
   *ASSERTION:* But we know that Big Ten students are in general at least as talented academically as Ivy League students.
   *CONCLUSION:* The students from the Ivy League schools do not perform better, on the average, on the Graduate Record Exam than do Big Ten students.

   Circle one:   **YES**   (The conclusion necessarily follows from the information contained in the assertions.)
                   **NO**    (The conclusion does not necessarily follow from the information contained in the assertions.)

2. *ASSERTION:* The people who voted for Theodore Roosevelt in the 1896 election of the Mayor of New York City were Republicans.
   *ASSERTION:* In 1896 all conservatives were Republicans.
   *CONCLUSION:* The people who voted for Theodore Roosevelt in the 1896 mayoral election for New York City were all conservatives.

   Circle one:   **YES**   (The conclusion necessarily follows from the information contained in the assertions.)
                   **NO**    (The conclusion does not necessarily follow from the information contained in the assertions.)

3. *ASSERTION:* If Charles was evicted than he was late in paying his rent.
   *ASSERTION:* Charles was late paying his rent.
   *CONCLUSION:* Charles was evicted.

   Circle one:   **YES**   (The conclusion necessarily follows from the information contained in the assertions.)
                   **NO**    (The conclusion does not necessarily follow from the information contained in the assertions.)

4. *ASSERTION:* If people trust an individual, then that person will have many friends.
   *ASSERTION:* If a person has many friends, then he strikes others as sincere.
   *CONCLUSION:* If a person strikes others as sincere, than people will trust him.

   Circle one:   YES   (The conclusion necessarily follows from the information
   contained in the assertions.)

                   NO   (The conclusion does not necessarily follow from the information
   contained in the assertions.)

5. *ASSERTION:* The manned space program will be discontinued if American scientists
   become convinced that unmanned probes would provide a cheaper, safer, and more
   efficient means of space research.
   *ASSERTION:* American scientists will not become convinced that unmanned probes
   would provide a cheaper, safer, and more efficient means of space research.
   *CONCLUSION:* The manned space program will not be discontinued.

   Circle one:   YES   (The conclusion necessarily follows from the information
   contained in the assertions.)

                   NO   (The conclusion does not necessarily follow from the information
   contained in the assertions.)

6. *ASSERTION:* People who lived prior to any civilization all lived in caves.
   *ASSERTION:* No cave-dwellers had musical instruments.
   *CONCLUSION:* No people who lived prior to any civilization had musical instruments.

   Circle one:   YES   (The conclusion necessarily follows from the information
   contained in the assertions.)

                   NO   (The conclusion does not necessarily follow from the information
   contained in the assertions.)

7. *ASSERTION:* People who lived prior to any civilization all lived in caves.
   *ASSERTION:* None of the people who lived prior to any civilization had musical
   instruments.
   *CONCLUSION:* No cave-dwellers had musical instruments.

   Circle one:   YES   (The conclusion necessarily follows from the information
   contained in the assertions.)

                   NO   (The conclusion does not necessarily follow from the information
   contained in the assertions.)

## Part II (five minutes)

1. What claim or principle, if any, is the author of the following passage taking for
   granted?

   "The United States should not halt the testing and development of nuclear weapons.
   This is because the Soviets will wage nuclear war against the United States unless they
   believe our weapons are as modern and sophisticated as theirs—and we must continue
   testing and developing nuclear weapons if the Soviets are to believe this."

2. What claim or principle, if any, is the author of the following passage attempting to establish?

"I am writing in response to the recent letters about giving the governor a free hand in keeping killers and rapists behind bars. Killers and rapists are undesirable in society, to be sure. However, I would suggest that perhaps we should take a lesson from history. Power corrupts, and absolute power corrupts absolutely."

**Part III** (fifteen minutes) Explain in a sentence or two what, if anything, is wrong with each of the following remarks.

1. "People who work hard frequently sleep poorly."

2. "The reason she finds it impossible to make a presentation to an audience is that she has stage fright."

3. "Women are more tolerant than men."

4. "Ninety-seven percent of Chicago's heroin addicts say they smoked marijuana at least once before ever trying heroin."

5. "What's wrong with that book? Why, it's trash, that's what."

6. "Building a new school will increase my taxes, so I guess it would not benefit the community as much as the school board says."

7. "The liberal's answer to every problem is 'tax, tax, tax, and spend, spend, spend.'"

8. "How much more time are you going to waste watching that program, anyway?"

9. "It's true that, just to read them, you would think that Johnson's exam was as good as Carter's; but I've had Carter in several classes before so I gave him the benefit of the doubt on a few items here and there."

10. "Dr. Spaulding was once a physicist for the space program, so I believe him when he says that acid rain has become the most serious environmental problem of the decade."

11. "That even normal individuals eventually become immune to the degrading aspects of pornography is demonstrated by countless statistics."

12. Said over the telephone by a physician to a patient: "Do you still have some of those capsules I prescribed for you last year? If you do, take some of them every time you feel uncomfortable."

**Part IV** (fifteen minutes) Explain in what way, if any, the thinking in each of the following paragraphs is wrong, defective, or otherwise erroneous. Although the selection is about the effects of smoking, you do not need to know anything about smoking to complete this part of the test.

*Paragraph 1*

The American Medical Association now wants to extend the ban on television advertising of cigarettes and cigars to the print media. The AMA's current view is that smoking is killing people at an alarming rate even though advertising these tobacco products on television has been prohibited for years. But the AMA is not much of an authority on the subject, as it turns out, and it's position ought to be rejected. In the late 1960s, according to a report in the *New York Times*, the AMA promised the tobacco makers that it would *oppose* requiring health warnings on cigarette packages if in return the tobacco lobby would help the AMA fight Medicare.

*Paragraph 2*

Furthermore, I am not altogether convinced that smoking is the health menace it is commonly believed to be. The economic well-being of millions of people in hundreds of communities is dependent upon tobacco, including growers, sellers, industry workers, and the multitudes who receive indirect benefit from the tax monies collected from tobacco.

*Paragraph 3*

In addition, I've been a smoker all my life, and I have suffered no ill effects. My father was a life-long smoker too. He died when he was in his mid-eighties, from causes unrelated to smoking. The statistics that purport to show that cigarette smoking is dangerous, therefore, are not as convincing as they appear.

*Paragraph 4*

One tobacco company has reported on an interesting study. Sixty-one percent of the respondents in a survey of more than one hundred health-care professionals do not believe that smoking increases the risk of a heart attack. You know that there is something wrong with the position taken by the AMA when sixty-one percent of their own physicians disagree with it.

*Paragraph 5*

That same report mentions an experiment that shows that, contrary to popular opinion, smoking actually has health *benefits*. A group of smokers was compared with a similarly sized control group of nonsmokers with respect to the number of days of work the members of each group missed during the past month due to illness. It was found that nonsmokers reported missing twenty percent more days than smokers.

For all these reasons, I think it is reasonable to dispute the assertions made by the AMA. If smoking is unsafe, that fact has not yet been proved to my satisfaction.

**ANSWER KEY** (With suggested values for correct answers)

**Part I**  Give one point for each correct answer.

1. The correct answer is YES.
2. NO
3. NO
4. NO
5. NO
6. YES
7. NO

**Part II**  Your judgment is required in evaluating these and the remaining items. Give either one or two points for correct answers.

1. The claim taken for granted is that any step necessary for preventing a Soviet nuclear attack on the United States should be taken. This can be phrased in various ways, of course.

2. The author is attempting to establish the claim that the governor should not be given a free hand in keeping killers and rapists behind bars.

**Part III**  Give either one or two points for correct answers. The subject need not display mastery of the technical vocabulary used here. Give credit for any unforeseen insights.

1. This is a structurally ambiguous claim.
2. Circular explanation
3. Vague comparison
4. Unknowable statistic
5. Begs the question
6. Rationalizing
7. Stereotyping
8. Loaded question
9. Inconsistency; the speaker's words show that he or she does not treat relevantly similar cases in adequately similar ways.
10. Appeal to illegitimate authority
11. Proof surrogate; vague  (As vague as this claim is, it can also be said to be unknowable.)
12. All the following are much too vague for the context in which they appear: "those capsules I prescribed for you last year," "some of them," and "every time you feel uncomfortable."

**Part IV**  Give either one, two, or three points for correct answers. Once again, credit should be given for unanticipated insights.

*Paragraph 1:*  That the AMA struck a bargain with the tobacco makers in the 1960s has no bearing on its ability to recognize health hazards. However, the fact that the AMA once had an ulterior motive behind its pronouncements is a relevant inductive reason for thinking that it might have an ulterior motive behind its pronouncements now. But the paragraph does more than urge caution or suspension of judgment on the AMA's position; it calls for outright rejection of it. Thus it is an *ad hominem.*

*Paragraph 2:* This is what we call "pseudoreasoning": an irrelevancy disguised to look like a reason.

*Paragraph 3:* This is an example of what we call the fallacy of anecdotal evidence. (Please see Chapter 10.)

*Paragraph 4:* Health-care professionals include more than physicians. That sixty-one percent of the sample of health-care professionals say such-and-such does not warrant the conclusion that exactly sixty-one percent of all health-care professionals (let alone sixty-one percent of all physicians) would say such-and-such. No details of the survey are provided, and without them, or a credible authority to vouch for them, no credence can be given to the conclusion drawn from the survey.

*Paragraph 5:* The twenty percent figure is meaningless without information about the experiment. Further, even if this difference were significant, it would not offer much support for the conclusion. Nonsmokers may miss more days not because they are sicker but because they are more health conscious and take care of themselves better. (Other plausible accounts are also possible.)